IMAGES
of America

BRIDGEPORT

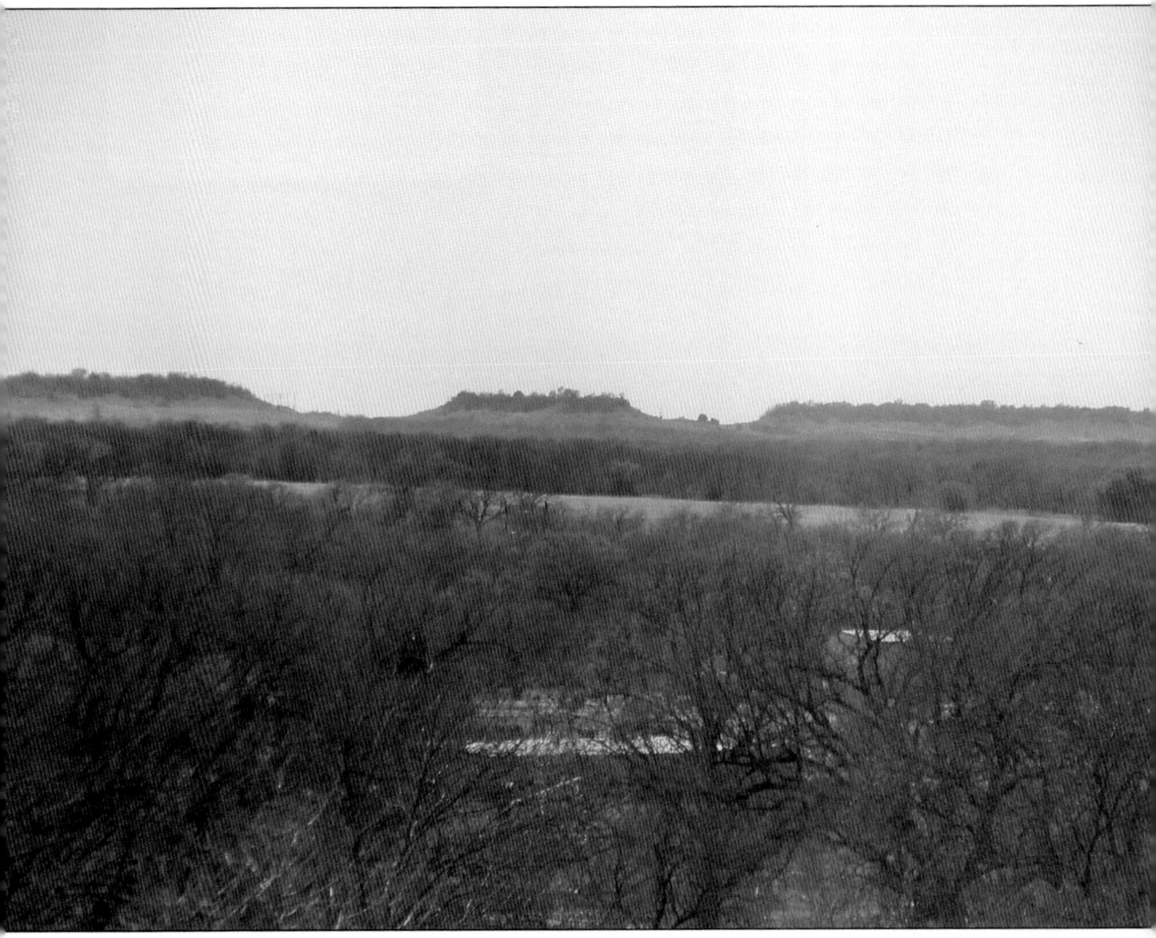

These familiar geological formations, referred to as mounds or mesas, have silently gazed down on the earliest prehistoric traveler and today remain as sentinels to what is known as western Wise County. (Courtesy author.)

On the Cover: In 1903, J. W. Cage, his wife Dovie, and their children moved to Bridgeport from nearby Alvord to enter the hotel business. This hotel was one of the first structures in the newly relocated Bridgeport and was situated in the 1100 block of Cates Street below Methodist Hill. (Courtesy Frank G. Bordner.)

IMAGES
of America

BRIDGEPORT

Ken Sprecher and the
Bridgeport Historical Society

ARCADIA
PUBLISHING

ISBN 978-0-7385-8461-4

Published by Arcadia Publishing
Charleston SC, Chicago IL, Portsmouth NH, San Francisco CA

Printed in the United States of America

Library of Congress Control Number: 2010926994

For all general information contact Arcadia Publishing at:
Telephone 843-853-2070
Fax 843-853-0044
E-mail sales@arcadiapublishing.com
For customer service and orders:
Toll-Free 1-888-313-2665

Visit us on the Internet at www.arcadiapublishing.com

To Cheryle, for your love, patience, and understanding

Contents

Acknowledgments

I want to thank the Bridgeport Historical Society for supporting me in pursuing this venture. This book would not have been possible without the access afforded me by the society to its collection of vintage photographs. Thanks go to president Virginia Wood for allowing me a great deal of latitude with this project as well as the museum. Members Myrle Duncan, Letha Tebbetts, Bill Paschall, Joann Pritchard, and Ann Nimmo also provided helpful information.

Two individuals with a lifetime of stories and experiences gave a colorful perspective of what life was like in Bridgeport many years ago. Thank you to Reba Boase and Frank "Petie" Bordner.

Two other works provided useful background material. *History of Wise County*, edited by Rosalie Gregg, and *From Wagon Wheels to Rocket Ships*, authored by the late Dr. D. C. Sipes, are wonderful accounts of early Bridgeport. Appreciation is also expressed to Bridgeport mayor Don Majka for his unwavering support of Bridgeport and heritage preservation.

Special thanks are in order for Royce Raven. Your technical expertise, historical knowledge, and encouragement made the difference. I could not have done it without your help.

I must also acknowledge my great uncle Gene Hembree. His curiosity and love of local history must have rubbed off on me.

Dr. Robert Marlett's interpretive work on the Butterfield Overland Mail Company in Bridgeport and Wise County is invaluable and will benefit the town for many years to come.

And finally, a note of thanks to acquisitions editor Luke Cunningham of Arcadia Publishing, who knows his stuff and was able to convey a small portion to me. And last but not least is my wife, Cheryle, who has been there every step of the way.

Any errors or omissions are entirely my fault. I know there are additional photographs out there, and I hope this effort will encourage someone else to collect and tell those stories as well.

Unless otherwise noted, all images appear courtesy of the Bridgeport Historical Society. Some photographs appear courtesy of the Tarrant Regional Water District (TRWD).

INTRODUCTION

According to prominent American West author Willa Cather, "We come and go, but the land is always here. And the people who love it and understand it are the people who own it—for a little while." The story of Bridgeport is about the land and how the people used their hands, minds, and machines to create a life for themselves that, in the process, helped shape a growing country.

The origins of Bridgeport can be traced back to the western expansion of the country during the middle part of the 19th century. Wise County, Texas, was carved out of a Comanche-dominated, sparsely populated portion of north central Texas. There was no shortage of colorful, strong pioneers, which later on led to entrepreneurs who managed to put their mark on the town that became known as Bridgeport.

Looking for adventure, 21-year-old New York native William Hunt had made his way to Texas by the end of the Texas Revolution in 1836. Eventually obtaining the rank of lieutenant colonel in the Republic of Texas Army, Hunt demonstrated proficiency for surveying land. He later was named as the official surveyor of school lands and proposed roads. Hunt also served as a member of the council responsible for locating the site of the state capitol building in Austin. During the ill-fated Santa Fe Expedition, Colonel Hunt was captured and forced to march 2,000 miles to Mexico City, where he was imprisoned for a year.

In 1855, Hunt settled in what would become Wise County and amassed thousands of acres of land that he took in lieu of payment for his state surveying work. He operated a large sheep and cattle ranch on his property and called it Cactus Hill, which was located under what is now Lake Bridgeport. He was instrumental in organizing the county, and his beloved Cactus Hill home was always bustling with activity. Hunt maintained an excellent library, collected expensive china, and music was available on an imported melodeon. In addition to bringing a love of culture to the wilds of the frontier, he also established a post office in 1858 and helped organize one of the first churches in the county.

Colonel Hunt was a shrewd businessman who recognized the benefit of using the land to his advantage. When he convinced John Butterfield to change the course of the Overland Mail line, it provided the impetus for the creation of Bridgeport. However, Hunt was not alone in seeing the value of land and the riches it held.

Soon after the toll bridge was erected, coal was discovered nearby while a water well was being dug. Several years later, in 1882, the Wise County Coal Company was chartered and thus launched a search for valuable resources below the surface that continues to this day. The opening of the coal mines brought a wave of immigrants, mainly from Mexico, to Bridgeport. Their valuable contributions to this and succeeding industries is an important cultural story that deserves recognition.

Much like Colonel Hunt before him, William Howell John relocated to Bridgeport in 1900 for a business opportunity. John was an engineer by training and a coal miner at heart. When the Bridgeport Coal Company bought out the Wise County Coal Company, John was brought in as the superintendent. "Super John," as he was generally referred to, was a champion of the immigrant miner but also a demanding boss.

He and his wife, Julia, were prominent citizens in the community and very protective of the Mexican workers. John donated a building to be used as a school for the children of the Mexican miners and also helped organize a church for his workers. Unfortunately W. H. John died from black lung disease in 1935 at the age of 67.

Due to the availability of coal, the Rock Island Railroad Company laid tracks nearby, which connected Fort Worth and Chicago. The old town of Bridgeport, located near the river and bridge, decided its future was better suited close to the railroad, so in 1893 the town picked up and moved a couple of miles east of its original location. From this new beginning, modern-day Bridgeport commenced on its journey through the next century.

The brick plants and then the quarry industry, which still prospers today, followed the coal industry. The products and material that have been retrieved from the land has had a vast influence on many generations of Texans. But the granddaddy of all these buried treasures is the natural gas that has been recovered thousands of feet below the surface.

In true Texas tradition, Houston wildcatter George Mitchell spent nearly half a century punching holes in the land around Bridgeport in an effort to solve the puzzle of getting natural gas out of the ground and into homes while making a profit. Finally Mitchell's tenacity was rewarded when his company developed drilling techniques that broke into the famous Barnett Shale gas play, which all started in Bridgeport's backyard. The impact of George Mitchell's efforts has affected millions of people and will continue to do so for years to come. While he had critics and credit problems, George Mitchell became a billionaire because of his vision, patience, and knowledge about a special prize the earth held.

The rampant West Fork of the Trinity River that caused Butterfield to reroute his Overland Stage also plagued the citizens of Bridgeport and other nearby settlements, including the growing city of Fort Worth. Bridgeport was severely flooded in 1908, and business and mail service came to a halt for a week until the water receded, leaving a layer of mud throughout the town. A few years later, in 1922, Fort Worth suffered massive property damage and 10 deaths due to severe flooding. It was at this time that planning was begun to tame the sometimes-violent waterway.

This large construction project came as the country and Wise County were slipping into the Great Depression. Building the dam and clearing the land provided enough work for many local people who were desperate for a job. Once again, the land was put to use and the river harnessed behind a dam that provided flood control, fresh drinking water, and exciting recreational opportunities.

Throughout the history of Bridgeport, there have also been determined, rugged individuals who have struggled to make a living off the land through farming and ranching. Some made it, and some did not. The legacy of these proud families persists today as fields are plowed and livestock graze much as they have for decades.

Not to be overlooked in the life of a community is the support systems that must provide for the people. Throughout the life of the town, retail business, churches, and schools have been the lifeblood that has sustained it. The lives these people have led and the accounts that have been told are important in the annals of Bridgeport and should be included alongside those of more recognized or famous individuals.

The people of Bridgeport love the land here and have rich stories to share—at least for a little while.

One

The Butterfield Stage Got Bridgeport Rolling

The United States was still a young country in the 1850s, and settlement was relatively thin and scattered west of the Mississippi River. In an effort to accommodate pioneer movement toward the Pacific, Congress authorized the postmaster general to contract for mail service from Missouri to California. The mail would be delivered via stagecoach and would run twice a week and not exceed 25 days in duration.

A route was selected that passed through the southern portion of the country that included Texas and Wise County. The contract was awarded to New York native John Butterfield in 1857, and the Butterfield Overland Mail Company started service the next year.

The original route the stage followed through this region was from Gainesville to Jacksboro that included three stops between the two towns. The line crossed the West Fork of the Trinity River east of Jacksboro, but the stage often encountered a flooded river that made crossing more difficult and time consuming.

About that time, Col. William Hunt and several colleagues from Decatur received a charter from the state to build a toll bridge across the Trinity River near Hunt's ranch. The group also built bridges across other creeks in the county and improved the existing trail. Butterfield was persuaded to reroute his stagecoach across the toll bridge and dropped the previous stations in favor of the toll bridge route. The new path traveled north of where Wizard Wells is located and included a stop in Decatur.

The Butterfield Overland Mail Company operated in Texas from 1858 until 1861, when the route was moved farther north due to financial problems and the Civil War. In the meantime, a community sprang up at the location of the toll bridge and was called Bridgeport. The new town soon boasted of having many fine homes, a hotel, post office, cotton gin, sawmill, school, general store, saloon, and Masonic lodge.

The decision to send the mail over the southern route changed Texas history. Towns such as Bridgeport helped establish the frontier, and the "impossible" stagecoach ride through what is now the town helped create a legend symbolizing the Old West. The Butterfield Trail became the longest stagecoach line in the world and completed the first transcontinental path across the North American continent.

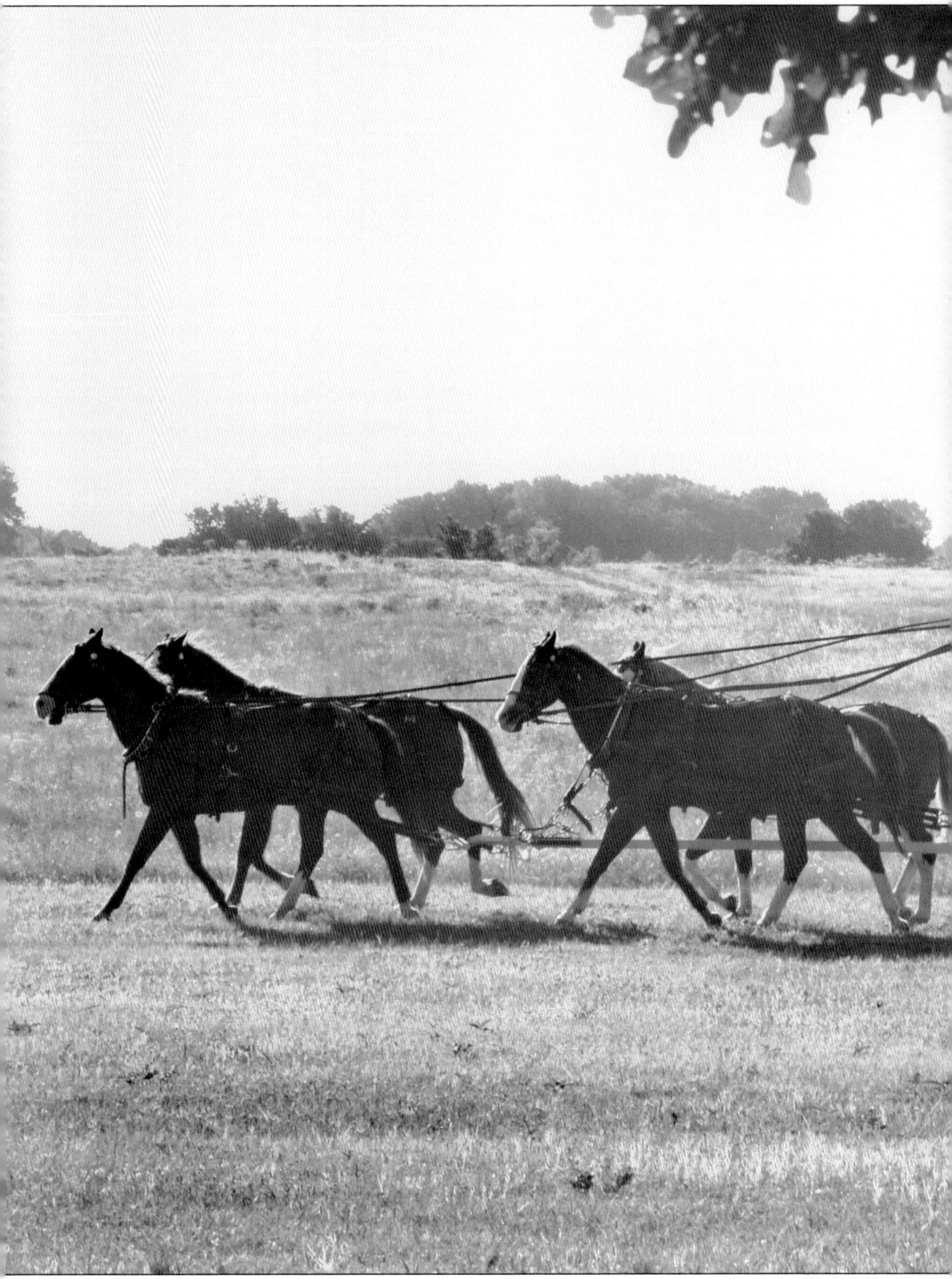

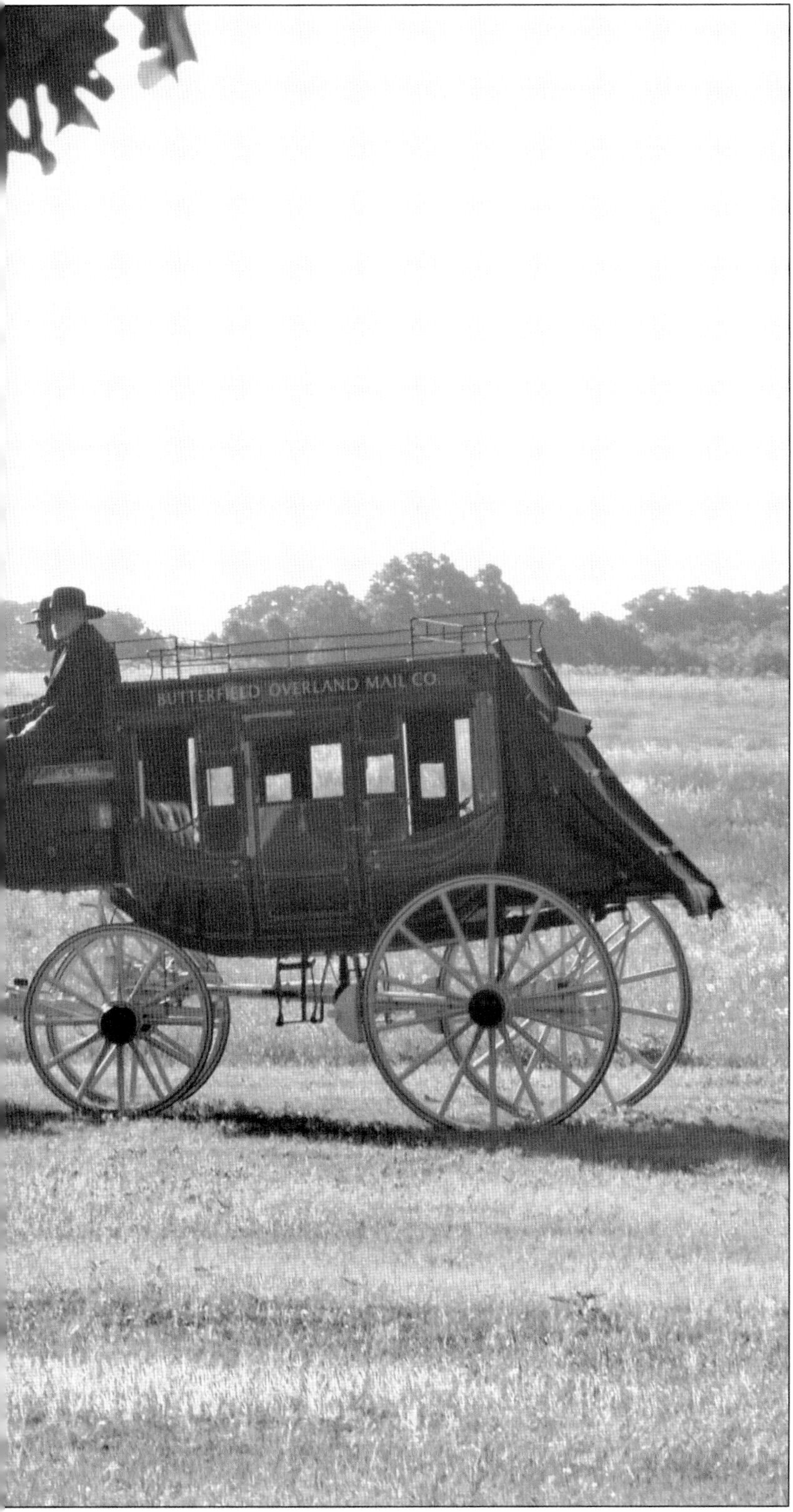

As the Overland Mail Company (more commonly referred to as the Butterfield Stage) approached a relay station, the conductor would alert the station to have the new team of horses ready by using a coach horn. The passengers had only a few minutes to grab something to eat, stretch their legs, and use the minimal toilet facilities. At the call of "all aboard," the stage was off again and heading down the trail. The stagecoach operated 24 hours a day and took a little over three weeks to complete the trip from Missouri to California. Pictured here is the authentic replica of a Concord stagecoach acquired by the Bridgeport Chamber of Commerce in 2008. (Courtesy Keith Bridwell, the *Bridgeport Index*.)

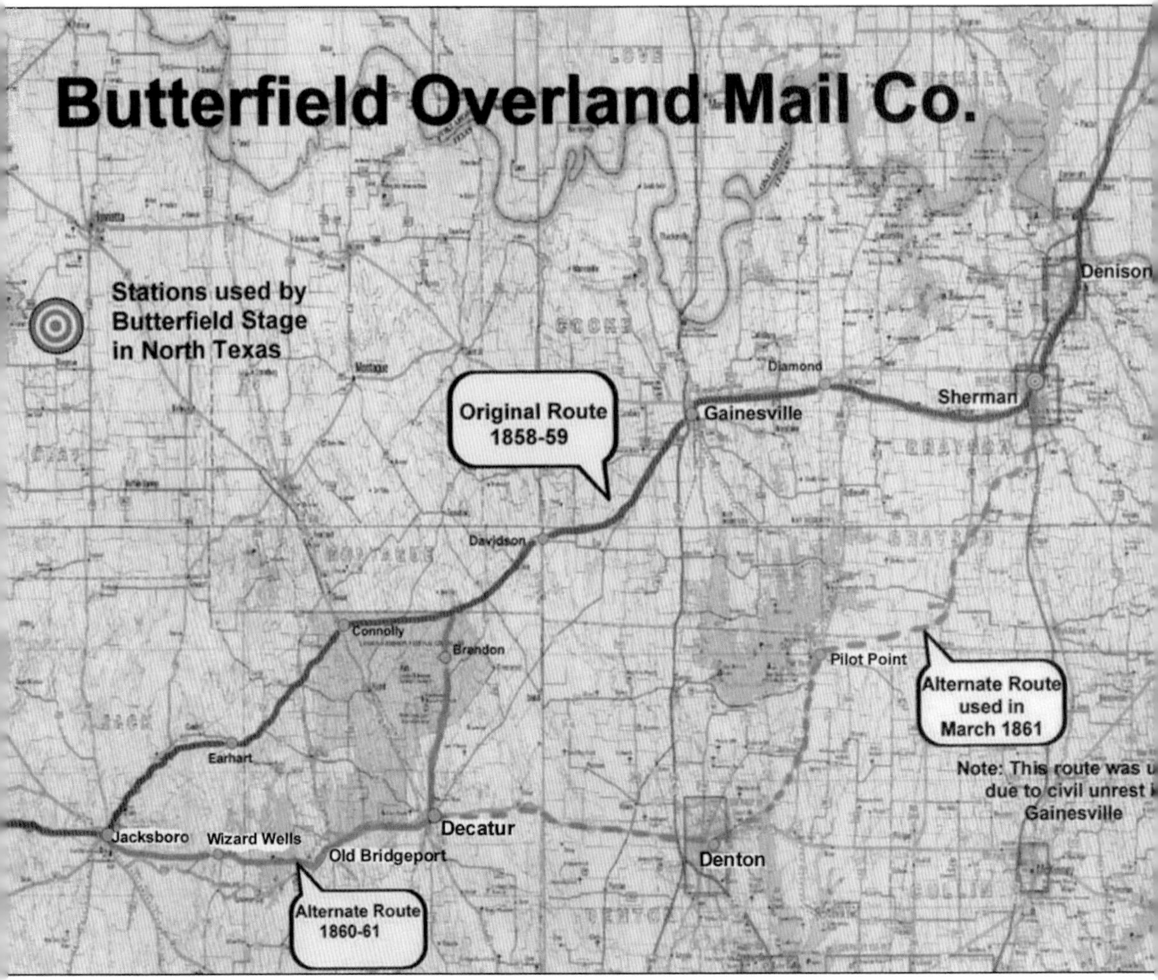

The Butterfield Stage crossed the Red River from the Oklahoma Territory at Colbert's Ferry and proceeded south to Sherman. From there, it headed west toward Gainesville. Jacksboro was the next town on the route with three relay stations in between. When John Butterfield changed the course of the stage through this area in 1860, he eliminated the Davidson, Connolly, and Earhart relay stations and added Decatur and Brandon to the route. This is when the route first traveled over the toll bridge of the West Fork of the Trinity River. In Decatur, the stage stopped at Absalom Bishop's store on the northwest corner of the square. With the start of the Civil War looming, vigilantes in Gainesville gathered numerous citizens believed to be Northern sympathizers and held trials that resulted in 40 men being hung for treason. In an attempt to avoid the civil unrest in Gainesville, Butterfield dropped this stop and routed the line through Denton, Pilot Point, and on to Sherman. The final eastbound stage rolled through Denton on March 14, 1861. (Author's collection.)

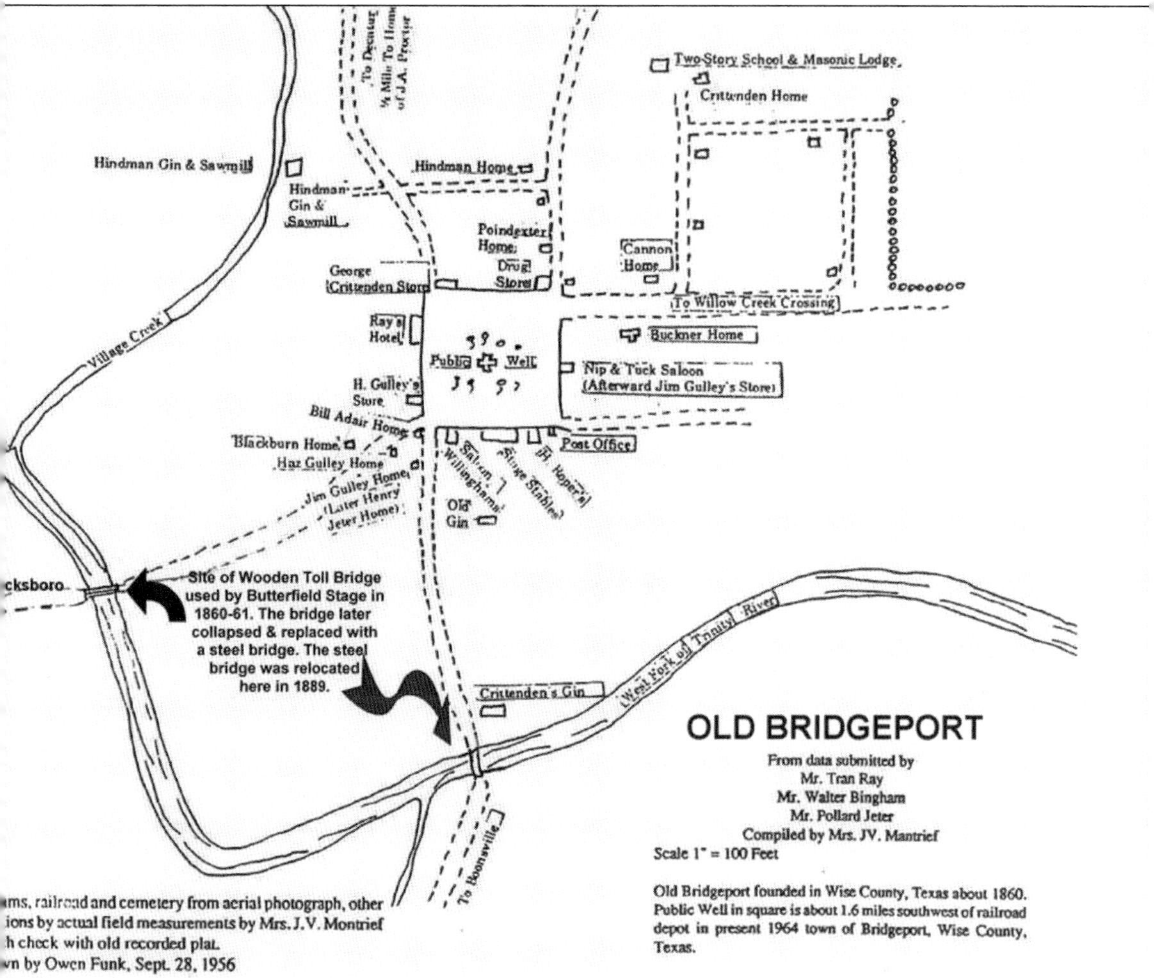

A railroad trestle that connects the Devon Energy Corporation's gas processing plant to the Union Pacific tracks in Bridgeport now occupies the site of the wooden toll bridge that served the Butterfield stage. All that remains of the old Bridgeport town is the Westside Cemetery, a state historical marker that recognizes the location, and an abandoned water well believed to be the public well depicted on the map. (Courtesy Owen Funk.)

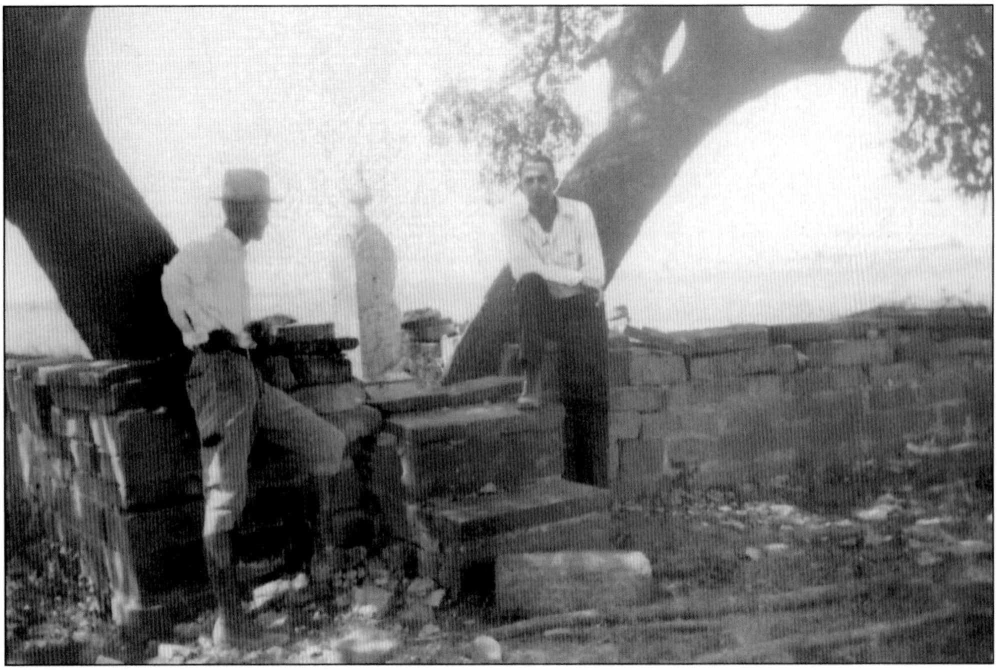

Colonel Hunt's ranch headquarters now lies at the bottom of Lake Bridgeport. Standing under two huge live oak trees next to the Hunt family cemetery are Gene Hembree (left) and Jim Hudson in 1929. Buried at the site were Colonel Hunt and his family. After Lake Bridgeport was completed, the graves were moved to the Eastside Cemetery in Bridgeport, where the site is marked with a state historical marker.

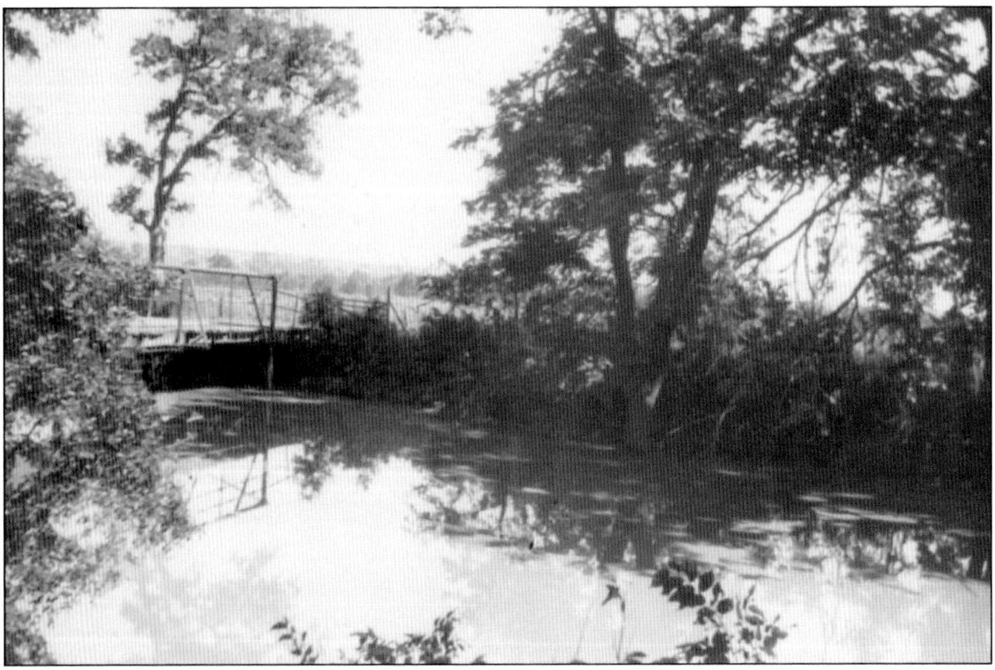

This is the bridge over Hunt's Creek that was close to Colonel Hunt's Cactus Hill ranch. It was probably the site where the Butterfield stage crossed Hunt's Creek.

Two

Time to Move

The transcontinental railroad was completed in 1869 and helped stitch the country together. This growing mode of transportation also had a tremendous impact on the nation as a whole. Markets were created, people traveled more, and the United States became an industrial power. The cities grew because raw materials and finished goods could be moved easier around the different regions; however, the small communities that dotted the landscape from coast to coast often thrived or died due to the location selected by the railroad.

Meanwhile, Bridgeport continued to put down roots as a small farming village nestled on the banks of the river. Things began to change in the 1890s as railroads began crisscrossing Texas. Dallas and Fort Worth evolved into major cities, and the railroads gravitated to them. In 1893, the Rock Island Railroad finished laying tracks between Fort Worth and the Oklahoma border, which then connected Chicago with Texas.

It was during this time that railroads used coal as a fuel for the locomotives. Fortunately it was also during this time that coal was being mined locally and provided an incentive for the Rock Island to choose a path that was close to this vital resource. However, for the small town of Bridgeport, these 2 miles were a significant distance. The decision was made that being close to the railroad was more important than staying by the river. A new town of Bridgeport was laid out, and the Rock Island began selling lots for those people who wanted to move.

It did not take long before the "Old Bridgeport" started taking on the shape of the Bridgeport known today. The streets, stores, and homes of the little town by the toll bridge soon vanished. Growth was initially on the west side of the tracks, but a few years later it had spilled over to the east side where downtown is currently located.

Bridgeport enjoyed a steady growth for many years due to the fact that the town had moved closer to the railroad. Retail businesses flourished, fine homes were built, and hard-working individuals greeted visitors passing through much as they had during an earlier time.

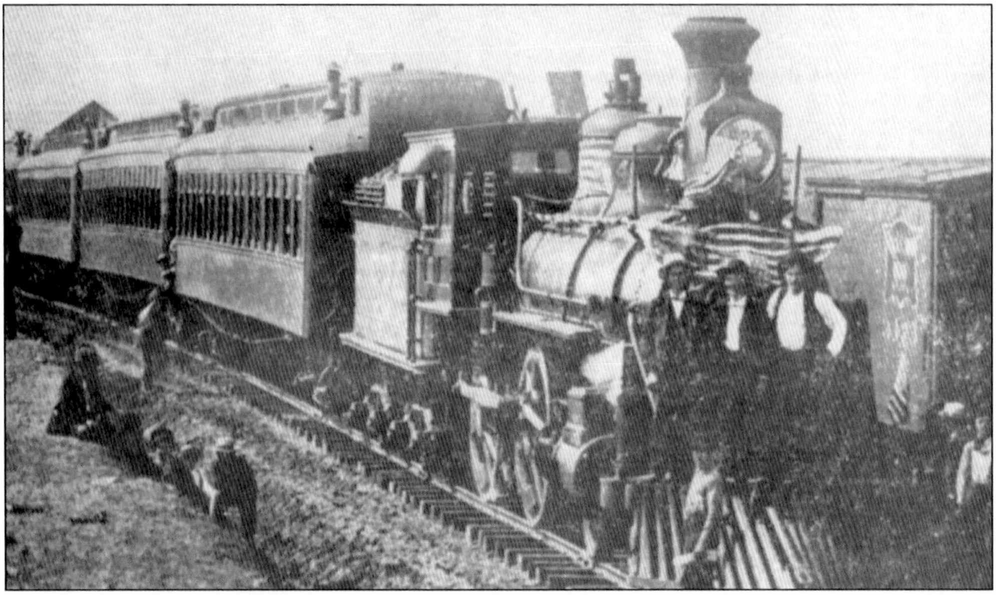

In 1898, the Rock Island Railroad began laying tracks between Bridgeport and Graham, 55 miles away. This photograph depicts the celebration commemorating the event.

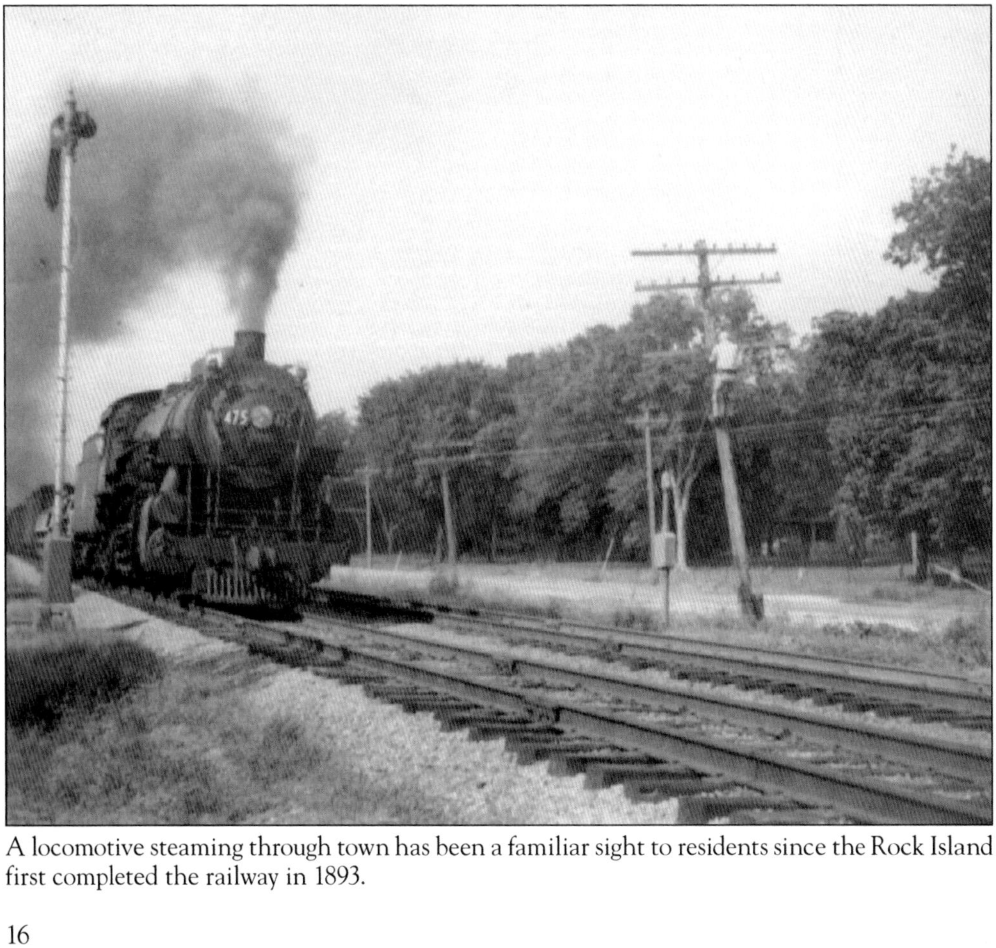

A locomotive steaming through town has been a familiar sight to residents since the Rock Island first completed the railway in 1893.

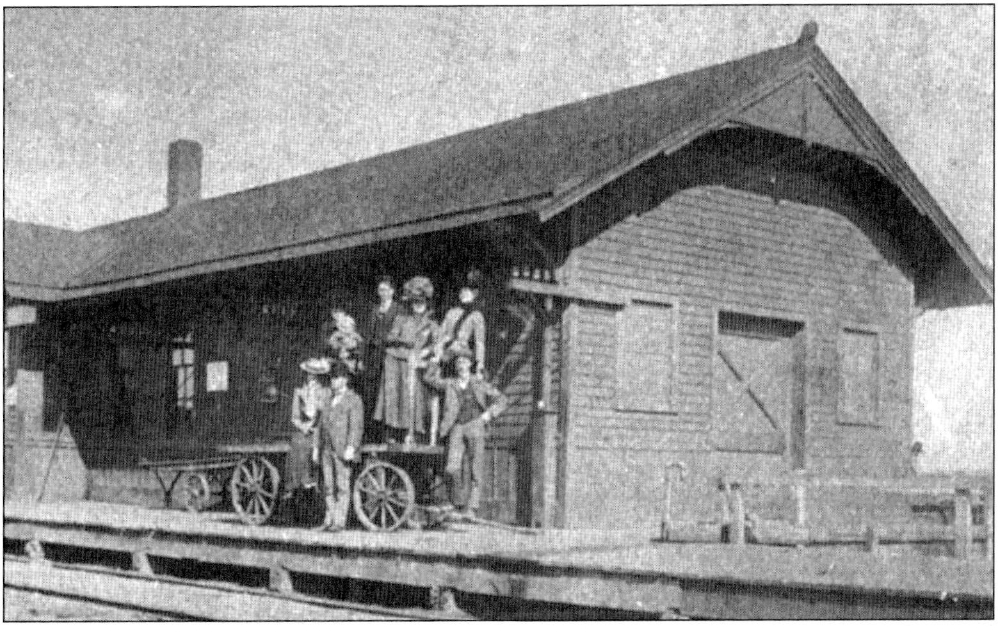

The railroad depot was a flurry of activity when a train arrived, and it was also a center for social activity at other times. It was a place where young people often gathered to meet friends, discuss current events, and catch the south local to the big city of Fort Worth.

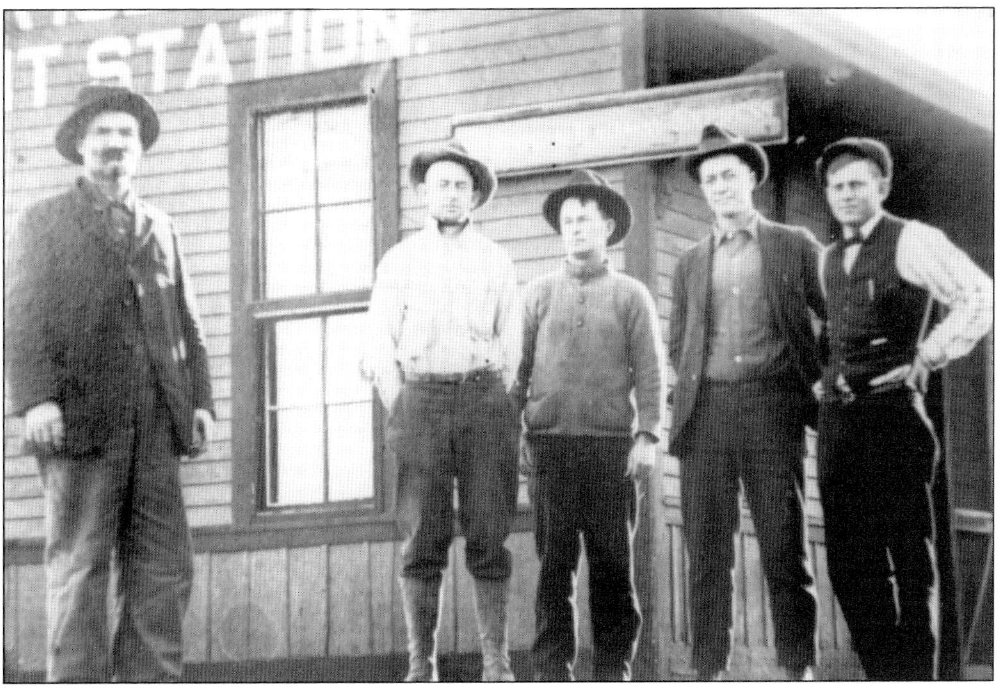

Depending on the importance of the town, a railroad company placed either a combination passenger and freight station or one of each. Bridgeport had both a passenger depot and freight house. In this photograph from the turn of the 20th century, local residents are seen outside the freight station.

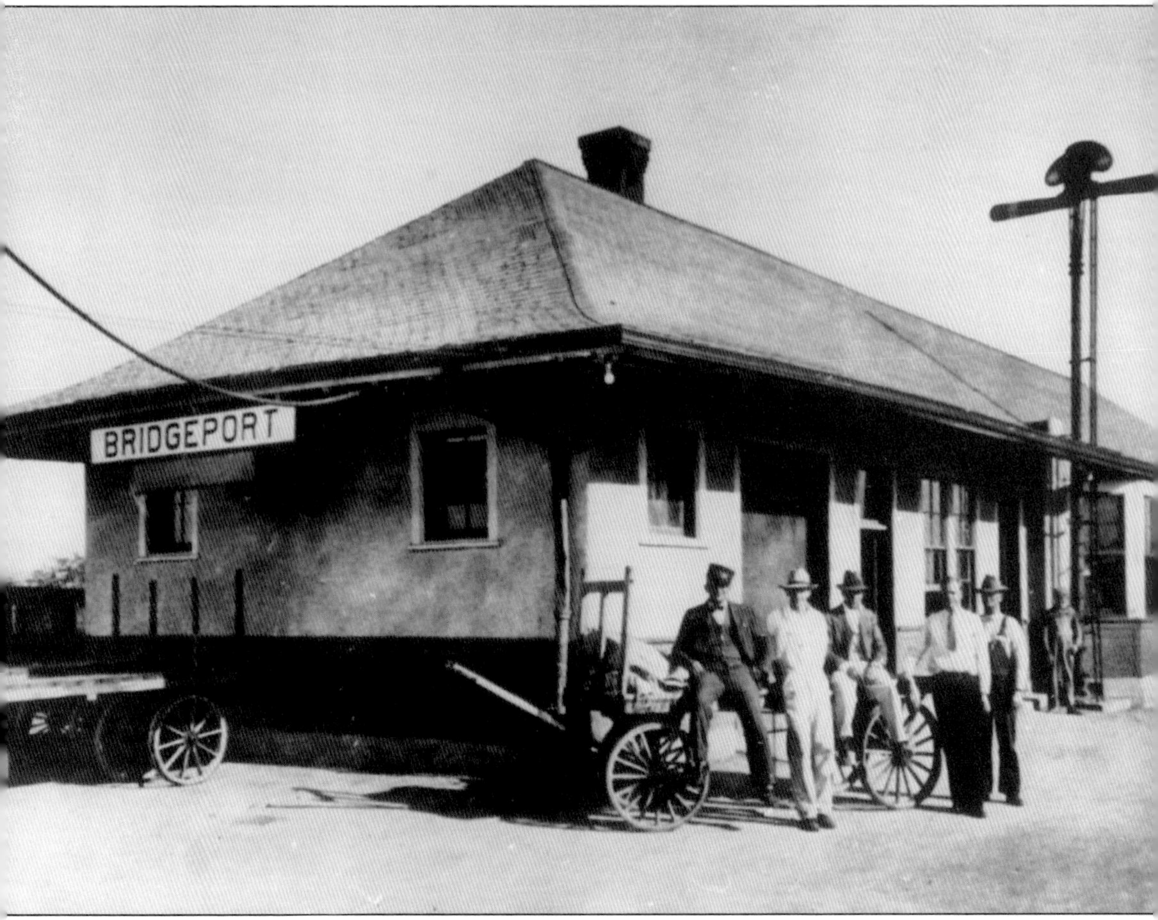

The train depot was manned 24 hours a day, seven days a week. Freight and passenger trains came and went on a regularly scheduled basis. Railroad agents logged freight in and out and sold tickets to departing passengers. Information on railroad operations was constantly being updated via telegraph, and workers always could find a cup of hot coffee inside. The engine switchyard constantly moved cars around, and the night watchmen kept thieves away and the locomotives engines hot and ready to go. Railroad agents at the time were Jack Waters, Ben Read, and John Curley. Acting as an independent contractor, Bob Taylor ferried the mail to the post office and packages to local stores.

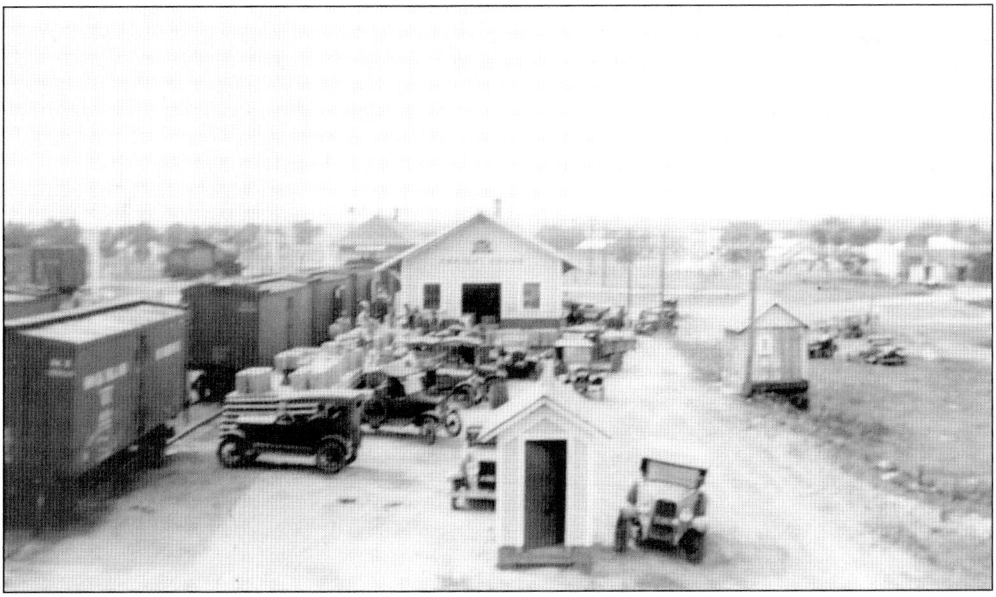

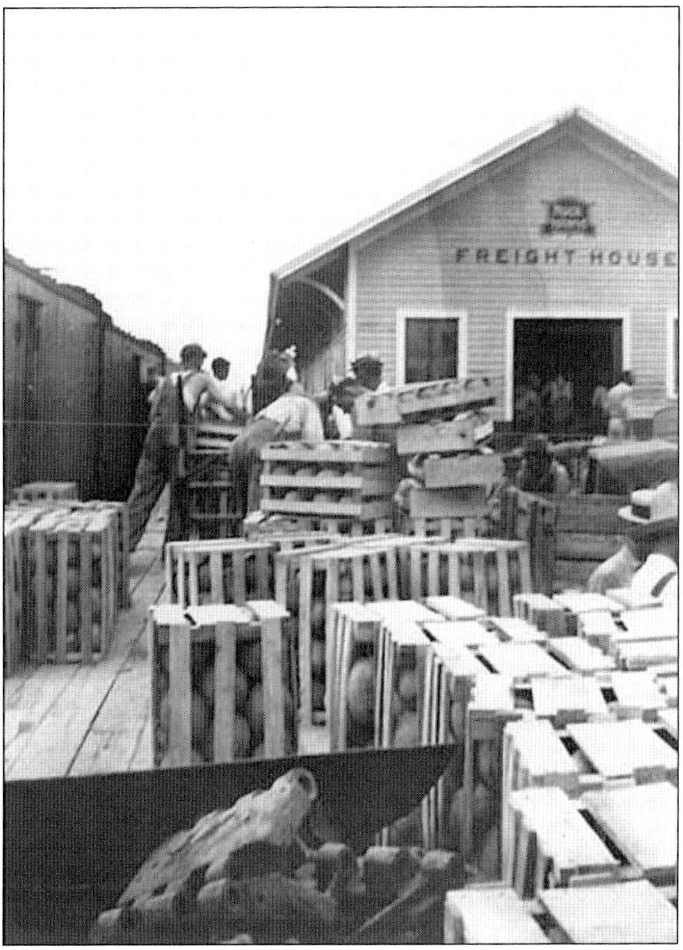

The railroad opened markets for the local farmers that were unavailable to them prior to the railroad coming through the area. In these 1930s photographs, watermelons are being shipped to urban areas. (Both courtesy Betty Carlton.)

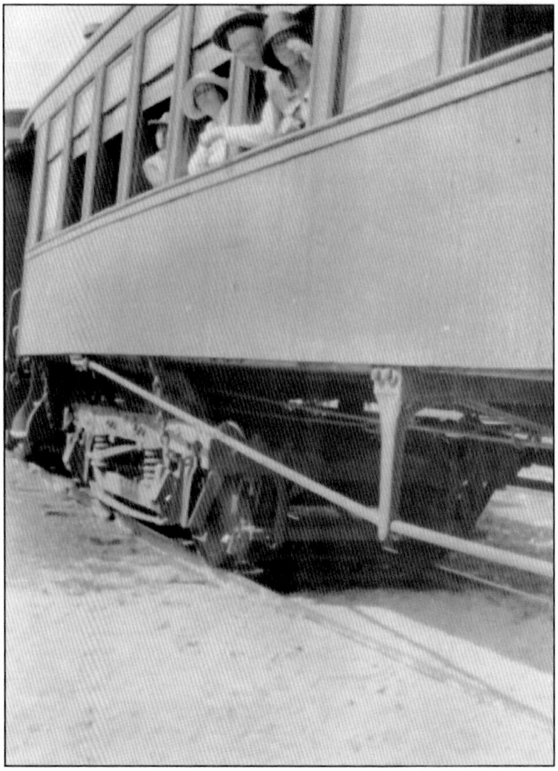

With new passenger service being offered to Bridgeport residents, many took advantage of this opportunity to take day excursions or travel across the country from the hometown depot. There were three local lines that traveled to Waurika, Oklahoma, Graham, and Fort Worth. The line that went to Graham was also known as the Jack line or Doodlebug. This particular line also serviced the large ranching operations west of Bridgeport. The Romanger ranch and Cherry Holmes ranch would load hundreds of cattle to be sent to feedlots and packing plants. The south local that went to Fort Worth was a popular way to spend the day shopping at some of the large department stores downtown.

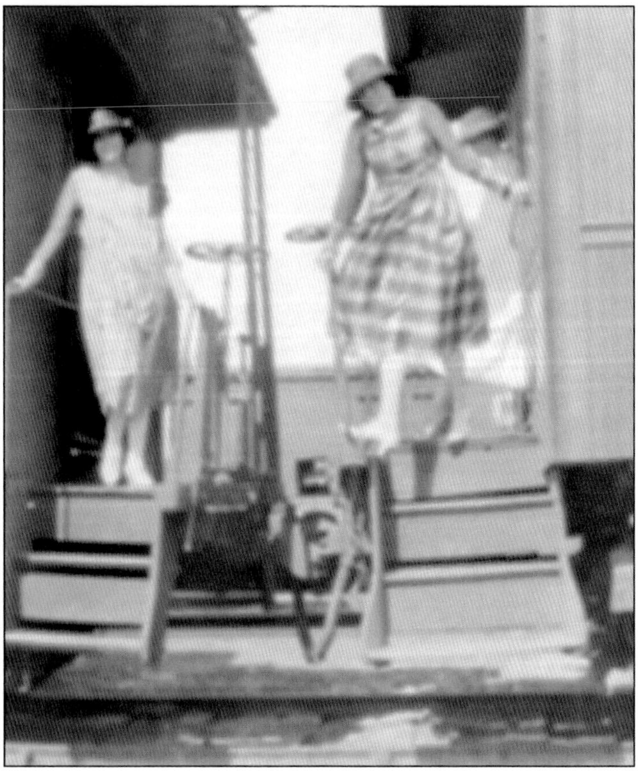

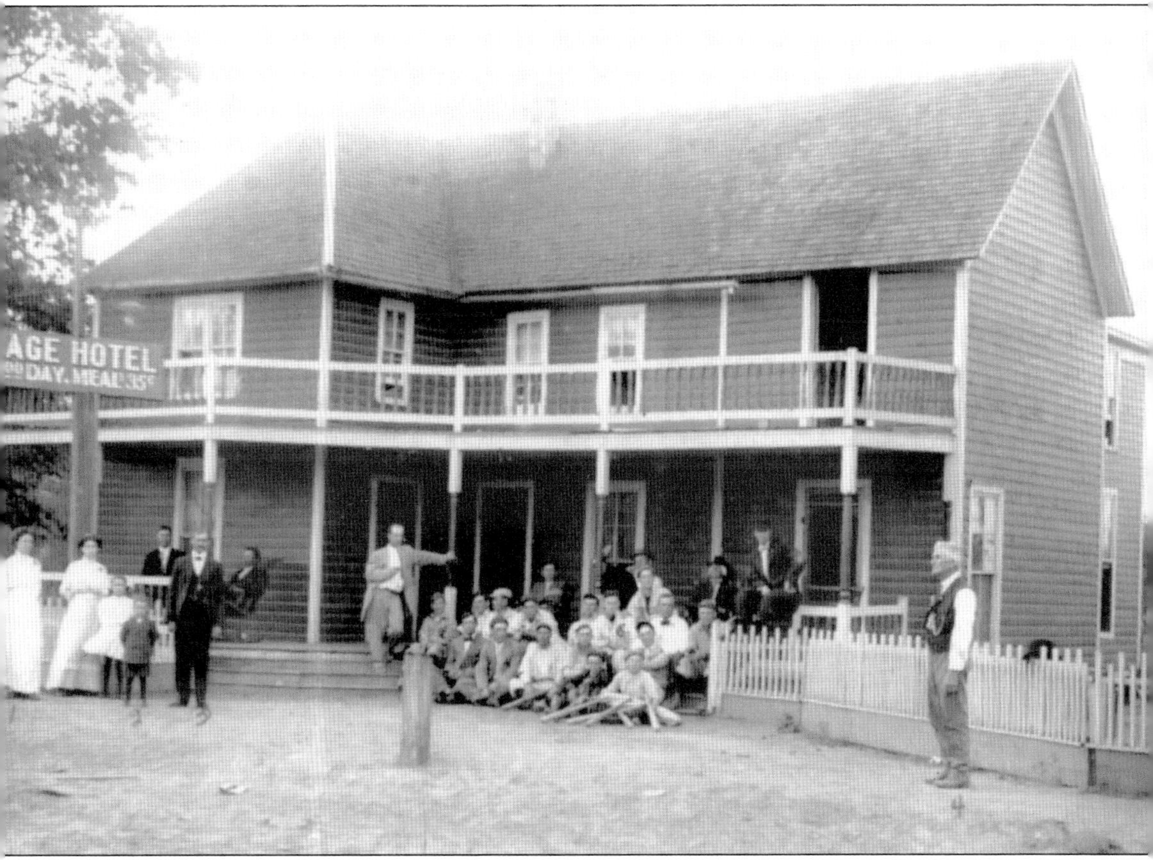

Soon after the railroad became established and the town began growing, boardinghouses and hotels were built to service the railroad workers and traveling salesmen who called on the local retail businesses. The salesmen, or "drummers" as they were sometimes referred to, routinely visited the grocery, hardware, and clothing stores to ensure they were properly stocked. A room could be rented for $1 and a meal cost 35¢. The Cage Hotel was located on Cates Street just west of the depot and railroad tracks. It was owned and operated by J. W. Cage and his wife, Dovie. The Cages are pictured in the front left with their two children. The local baseball team is assembled on the front steps, and the gentleman on the right next to the picket fence is T. J. Palmer, the father of Mrs. Cage. Palmer ran a secondhand store nearby. (Courtesy Frank G. Bordner.)

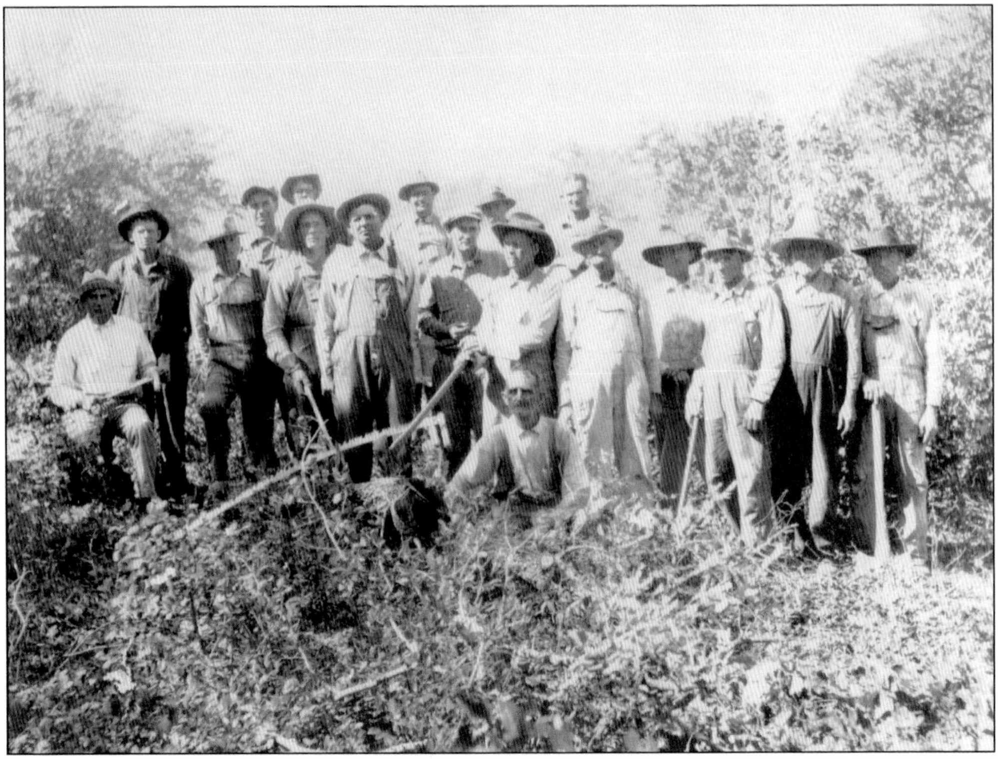

Even though the Model T Ford was introduced in 1908, automobiles were still infrequently seen in the country. And the roads between towns were little more than two ruts in the ground. In these 1910s photographs, county road crews can be seen clearing the way for what became Texas State Highway 114. Most of the work was done by hand with the assistance of large draft animals. The photograph below was taken south of Bridgeport near the Kaker farm. (Both courtesy Ann Kaker.)

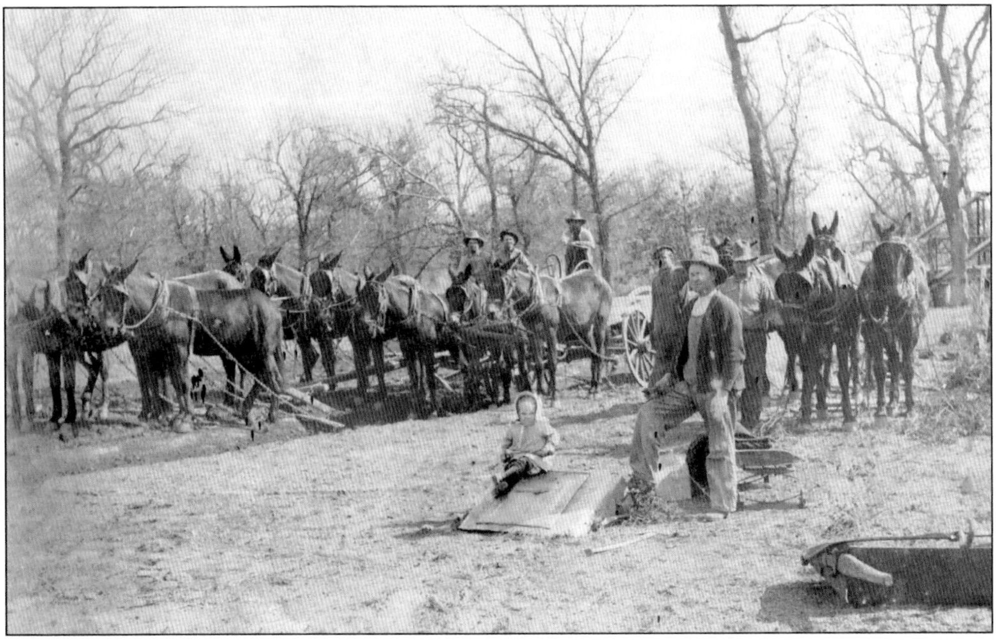

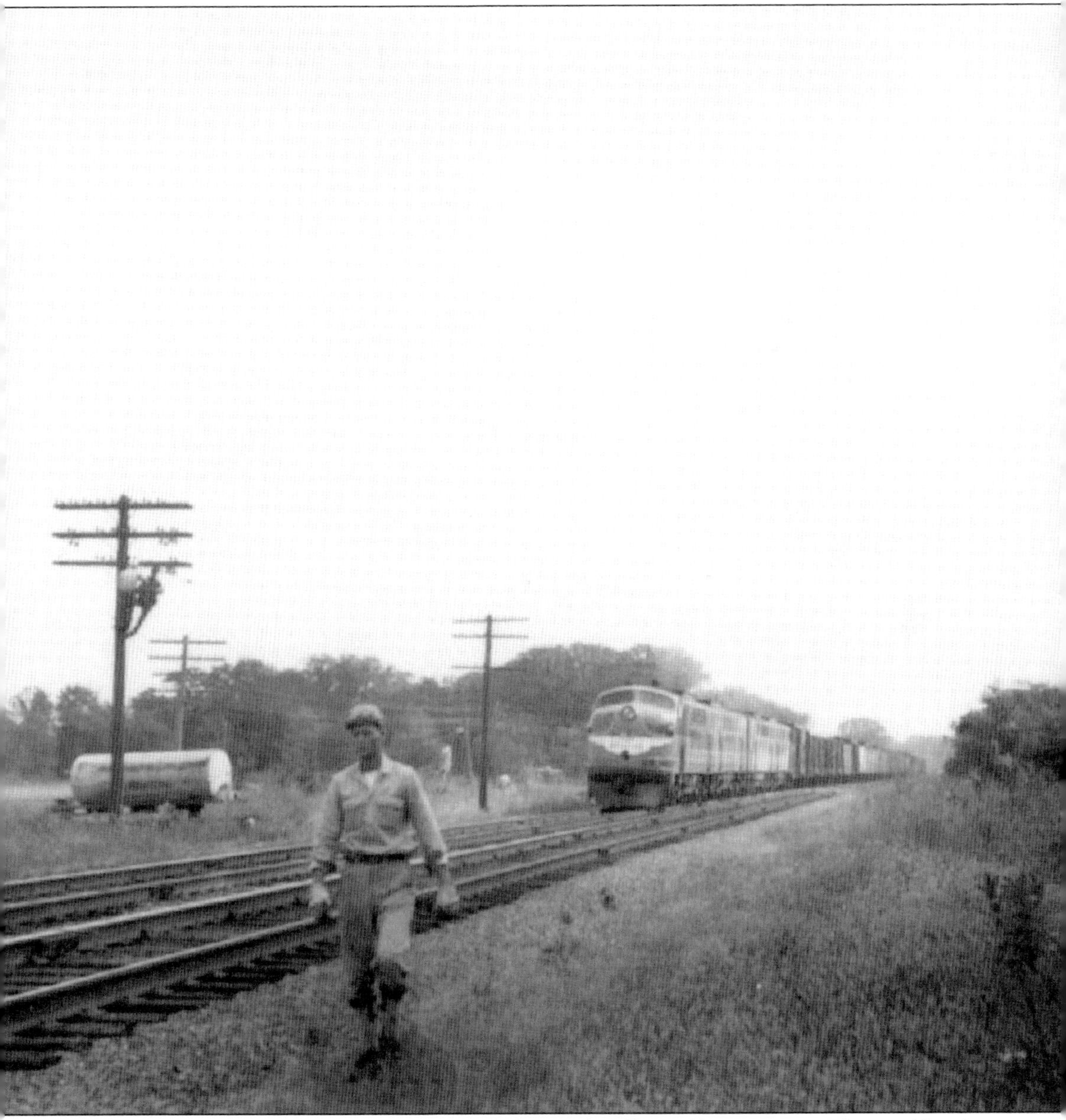

In 1941, the Rock Island Railroad introduced the Rocket fleet of locomotives. The profile of these powerful engines was a sleek, modern appearance, which was a departure from the old-looking steam engines of the past. These new trains created quite a stir when they roared into town. Crowds gathered at the depot in anticipation of getting a good look at these smart-looking vehicles. There were attendants onboard to help make the trip more comfortable and respond to passenger requests for service. So impressed by this new fleet, a restaurant near the depot changed its name to the Rocket Cafe.

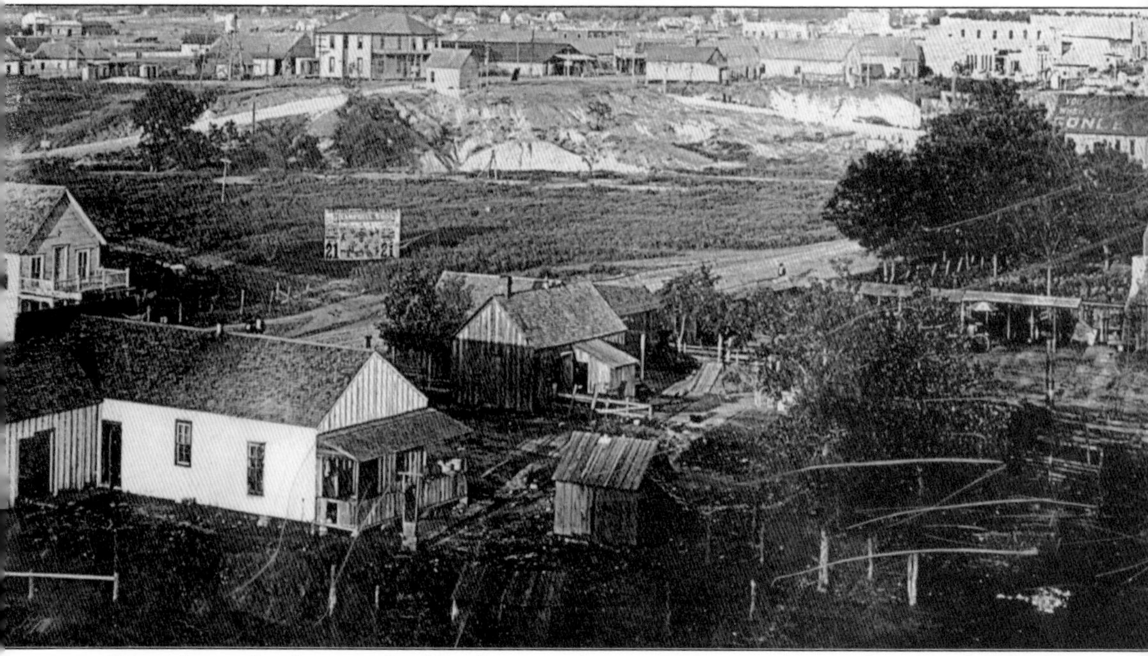

From this early photograph of Bridgeport taken in 1908, it is obvious that the railroad had a significant impact on the growth of the relocated Bridgeport. Looking east from the vicinity of the Rock Island Freight House, Cates Street is seen in the foreground and Halsell Street in the background. It is clear that the town familiar today is taking shape. While the future home of the visitor's center and museum is a vacant lot in the middle of the photograph, there is ample evidence of many homes, businesses, and hotels that have already been constructed. Also visible is the school and Methodist church. (Courtesy Dr. Robert Marlett.)

Three

Buried Treasures

Throughout the exploration period of the new world, expeditions were launched in an effort to find riches that the hardy adventurers thought were hidden in the vast continent of North America. One of the first to venture into Texas was Spanish explorer Francisco Vásquez de Coronado, who traveled throughout the Southwest in search of the fabled Seven Cities of Gold. While he never found what he was looking for, the seeds of future settlements were planted along his trail of discovery.

Several hundred years after the first Europeans journeyed through this territory, one legend still lingers regarding a $200,000 cache of gold hidden in a cave tucked away in a rugged canyon called Devil's Den. This hard-to-find spot is a source of numerous tales and located on the west side of Lake Bridgeport on the Sid Richardson Boy Scout Ranch. This unverified story related that a vast sum of gold coins was buried there during the Civil War. Unfortunately this wealth was never found; however, less than 100 years later, a new kind of buried treasure has been discovered nearby.

The day in 1860 that Charles Cates broke through a thin vein of bituminous coal while digging a water well set the stage for retrieving valuable products from the earth that has continued into the 21st century. In 1882, the Wise County Coal Company opened for business by sinking a shaft in the northeastern part of Bridgeport. At least 14 coal mines operated with varying degrees of success until the start of World War II.

Just a few miles northwest of Bridgeport and resting only several feet underneath the topsoil, one of nature's prizes is found. Winchell limestone, which is a hard, dense variety and found in only a few places in the entire world, is quarried here and found in countless construction and building sites throughout north Texas. Extending hundreds of feet down, the use of explosives breaks the limestone into large boulders. These large rocks are then crushed up to meet customer needs. The concrete used in building the Dallas/Fort Worth International Airport and almost all the highways in the area used crushed limestone that came from Wise County.

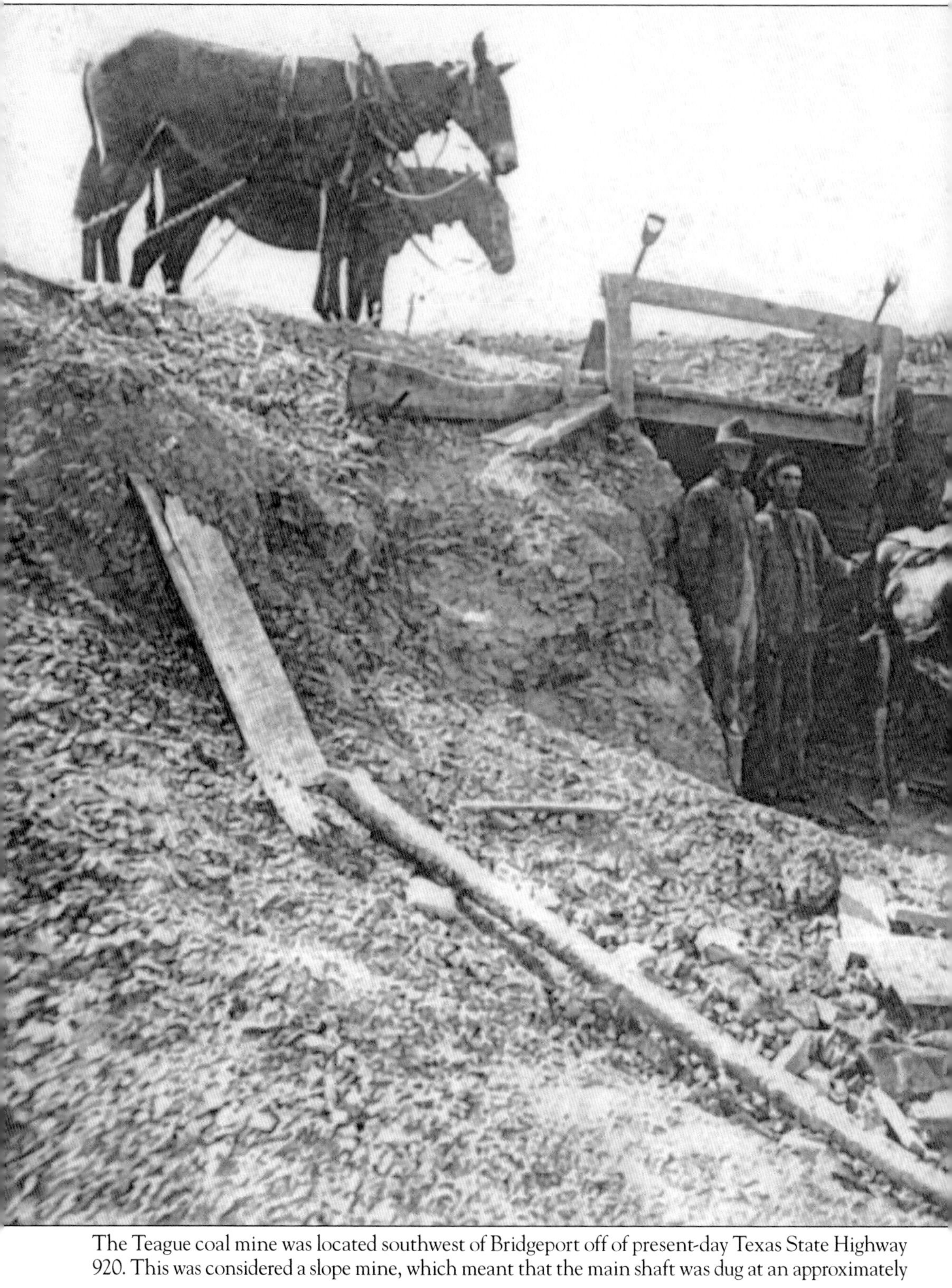

The Teague coal mine was located southwest of Bridgeport off of present-day Texas State Highway 920. This was considered a slope mine, which meant that the main shaft was dug at an approximately

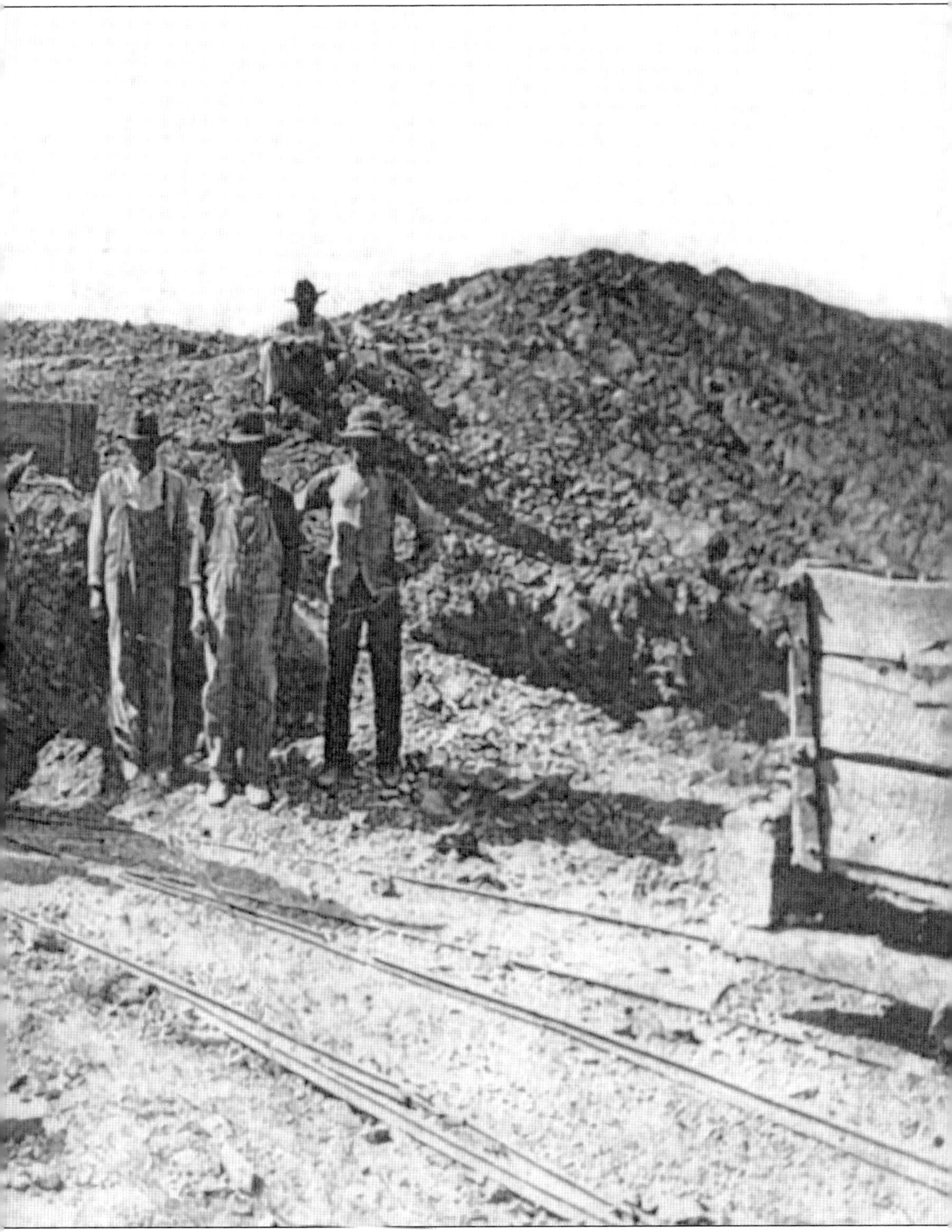

20-degree angle down into the ground. Mules were used to pull the coal cars up from the mine, and all mining work was done by hand.

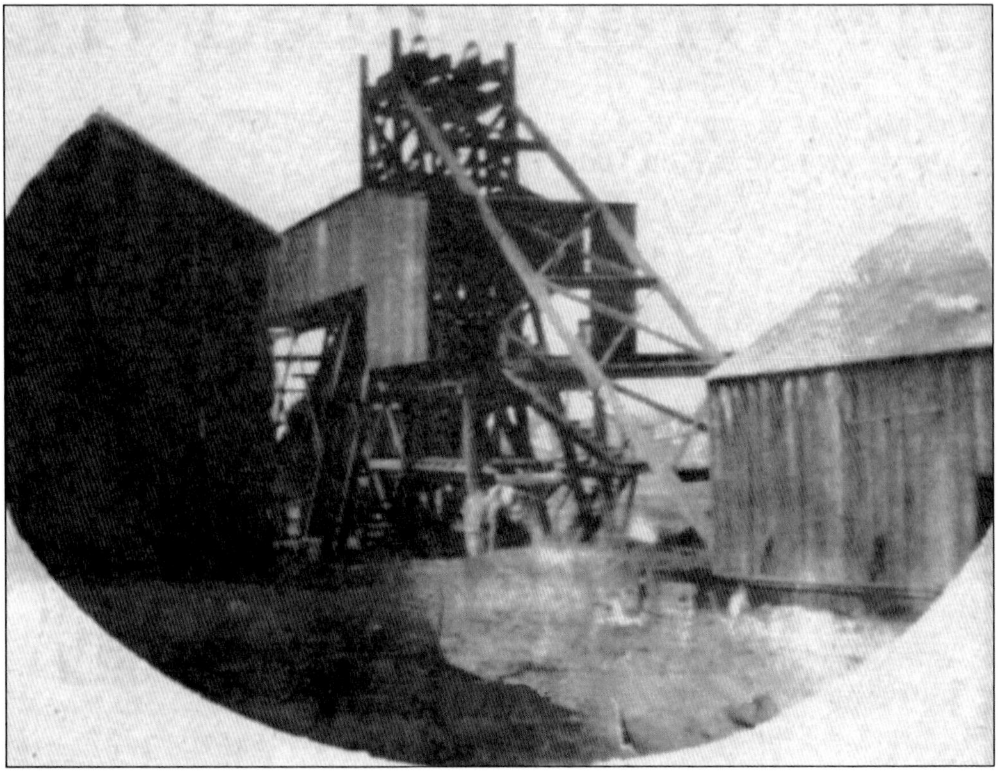

Bridgeport Coal Company Mine No. 4 was a shaft mine believed to be close to the railroad tracks south of U.S. Highway 380.

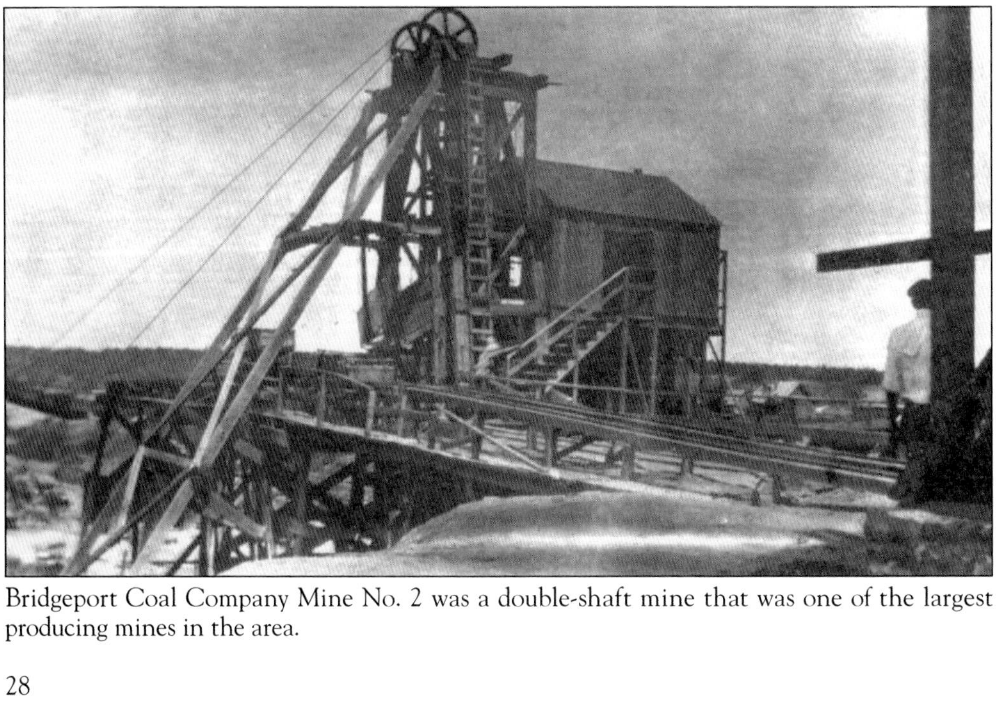

Bridgeport Coal Company Mine No. 2 was a double-shaft mine that was one of the largest producing mines in the area.

The Bridgeport coal seam crops out over an area approximately 16 square miles in Wise County. Most of the mines were located within the city limits of Bridgeport. In 1860, a thin strip of bituminous coal 17 to 20 inches thick was found 60 to 125 feet below the surface.

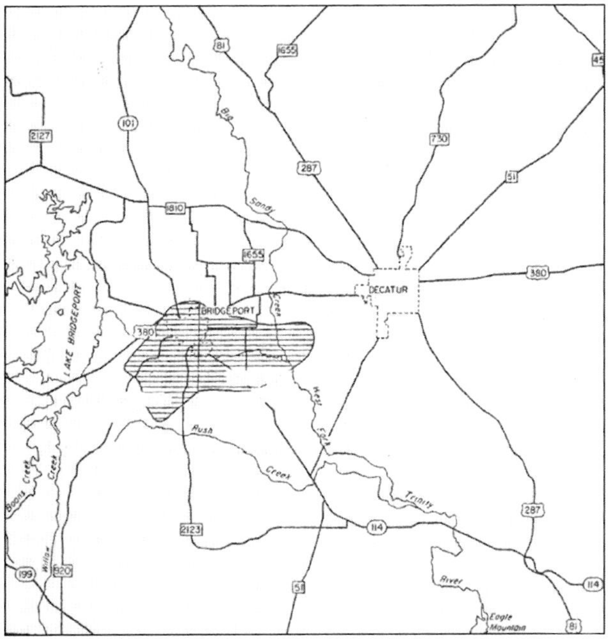

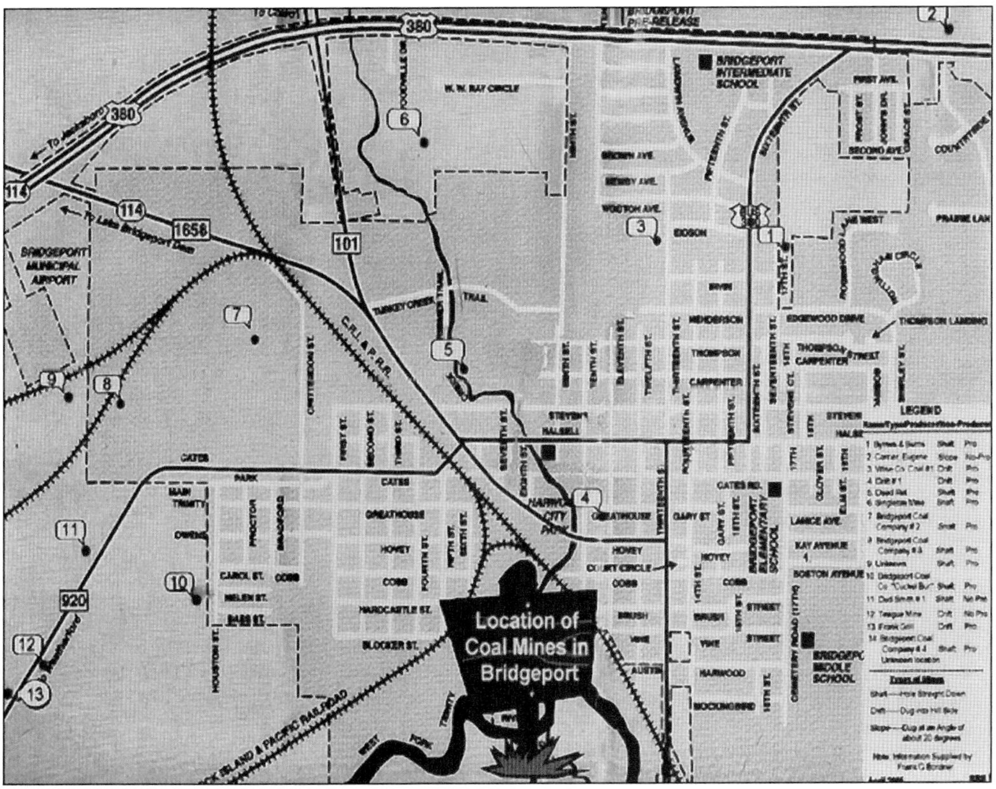

The town of Bridgeport is honeycombed with coal mines and tunnels beneath the surface. All the mines have been filled in, and there is very little trace that they ever existed. However, there are buildings in parts of town that have sustained foundation damage as a result of the soil settling where the tunnels were dug. (Courtesy Royce Raven.)

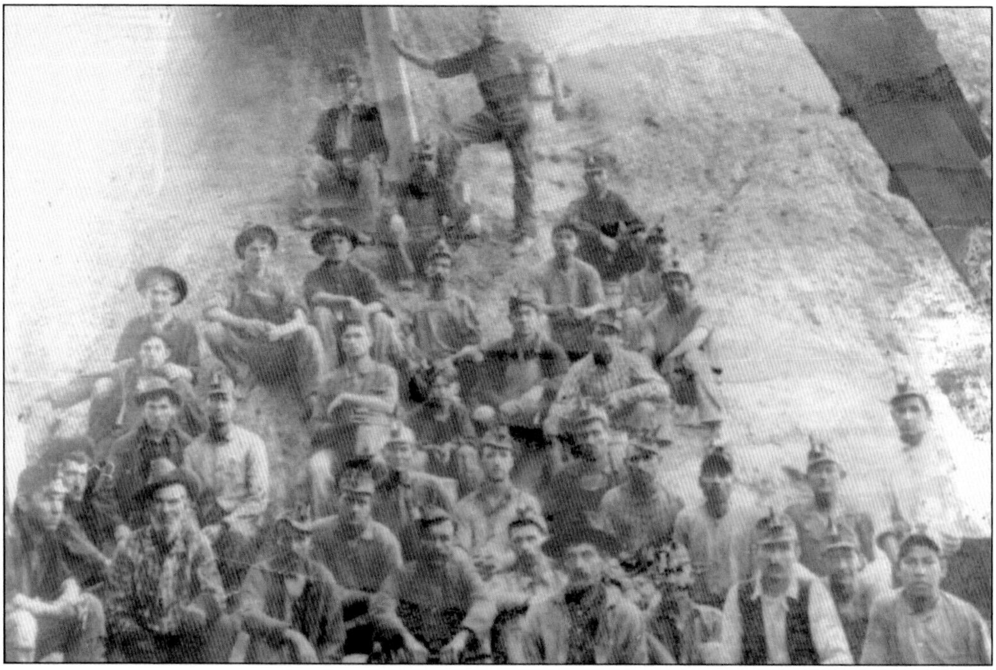

Over 75 percent of the miners were immigrants from Mexico. Most of them stayed in small houses or tents located near the mines. Superintendent W. H. John donated a building for a school, because the Mexican children were not allowed to attend the public school. John also helped organize a church for his workers. Today many of Bridgeport's residents can trace their heritage back to the coal mine workers from Mexico.

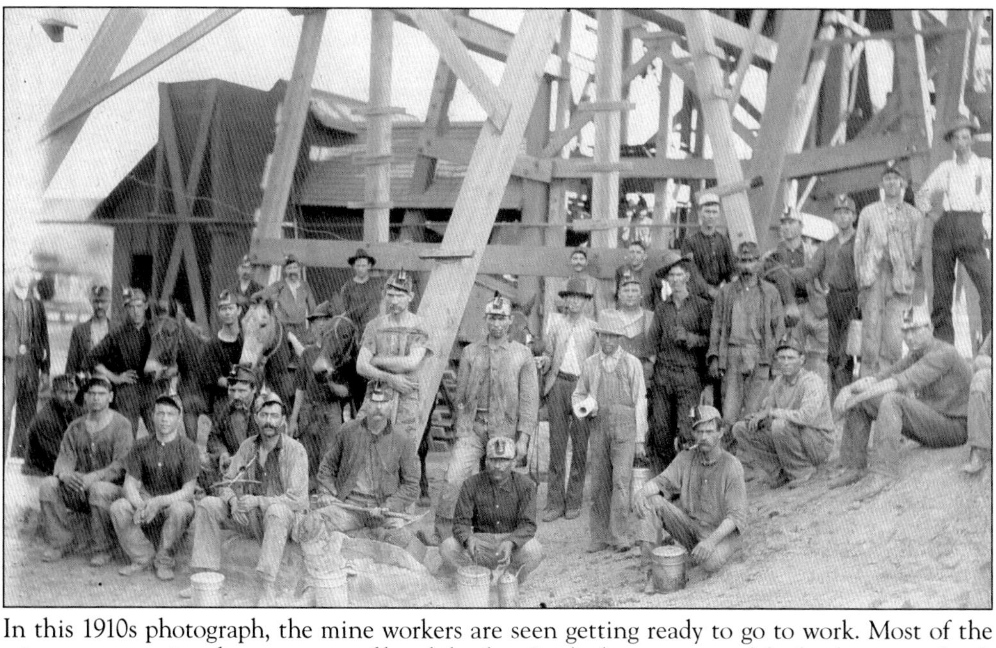

In this 1910s photograph, the mine workers are seen getting ready to go to work. Most of the miners are carrying the same type of lunch bucket. In the bottom part of the bucket was a drink such as coffee or tea. Located in the middle of the lunch bucket was a sandwich, meat, or cheese. The top part contained a dessert and usually a piece of fruit.

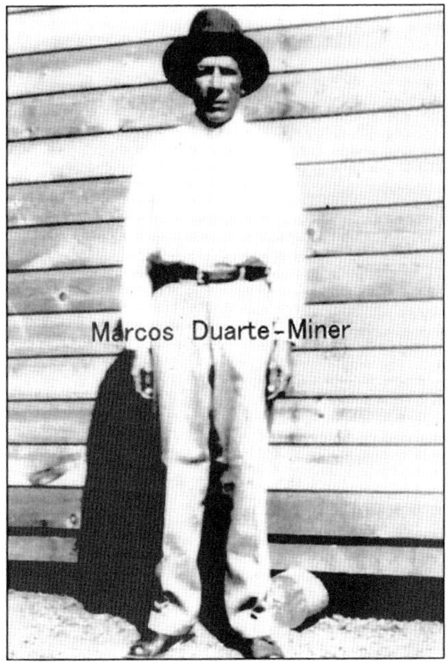

In these 1920s photographs are miner Marcos Duarte and his union card issued in 1919. In 1929, the coal miners went out on strike due to rising prices on their equipment, including blasting powder. The strike, weak American economy, and the increasing use of oil as a fuel spelled doom for the coal industry in Texas. Most all of the mines in Bridgeport closed shortly after the strike.

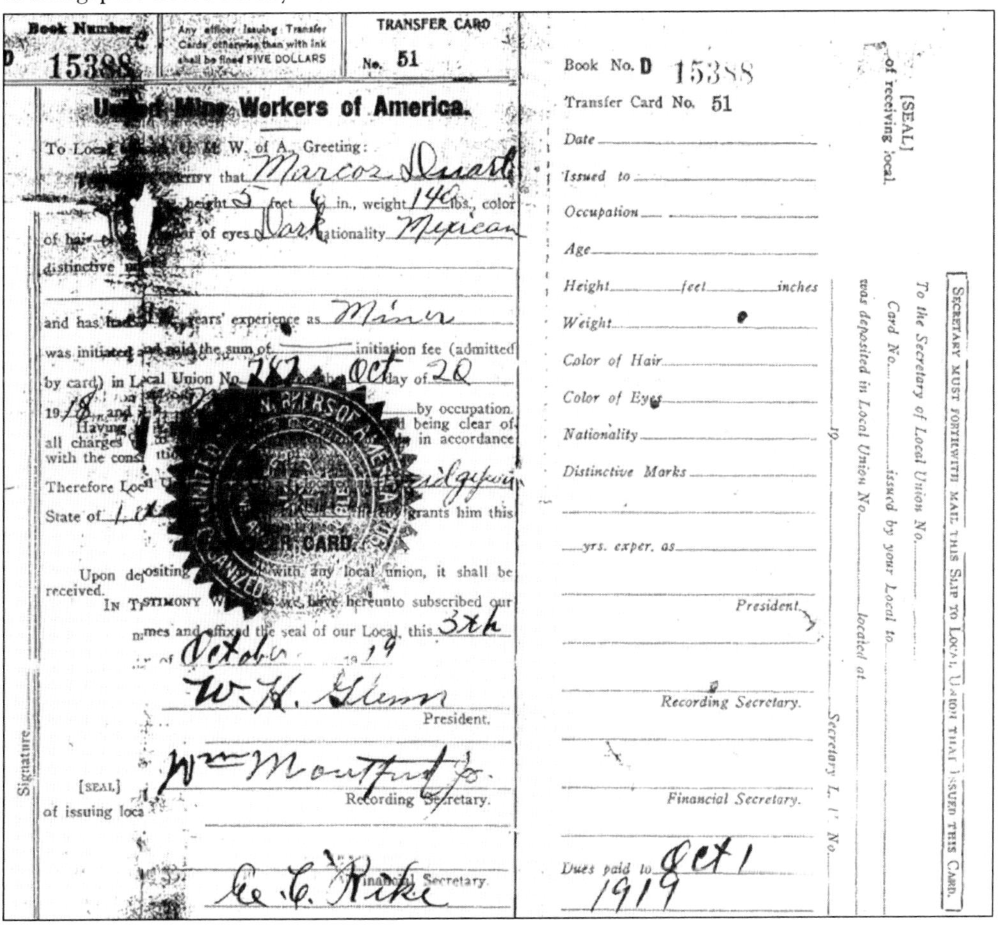

Book Number D 15388 | Any officer issuing Transfer Cards otherwise than with ink shall be fined FIVE DOLLARS | TRANSFER CARD No. 51

United Mine Workers of America.

To Local [illegible] U. M. W. of A., Greeting:

[illegible] that Marcoz Duarte [illegible] height 5 feet 6 in., weight 140 lbs., color of hair [illegible] of eyes Dark nationality Mexican distinctive [illegible]

and has [illegible] years' experience as Miner was initiated and paid the sum of ———— initiation fee (admitted by card) in Local Union No. 787 [illegible] Oct day of 20 1918 and [illegible] by occupation. Having [illegible] being clear of all charges [illegible] in accordance with the cons[illegible] Therefore Local [illegible] Bridgeport State of Tex [illegible] grants him this [illegible] CARD.

Upon depositing [illegible] with any local union, it shall be received.

In Testimony W[illegible] have hereunto subscribed our names and affixed the seal of our Local, this 3th [illegible] of October 1919

W. H. Glenn President.

[SEAL] of issuing local

Signature

Wm Montford Jr. Recording Secretary.

Ge. C. Rike Financial Secretary.

Book No. D 15388
Transfer Card No. 51
Date
Issued to
Occupation
Age
Height feet inches
Weight
Color of Hair
Color of Eyes
Nationality
Distinctive Marks
yrs. exper. as
President.
Recording Secretary.
Financial Secretary.
Dues paid to Oct 1 1919

[SEAL] of receiving local

Secretary L. U. No.

To the Secretary of Local Union No. Card No. issued by your Local to was deposited in Local Union No. located at 19

Secretary must forthwith mail this slip to Local Union that issued this card.

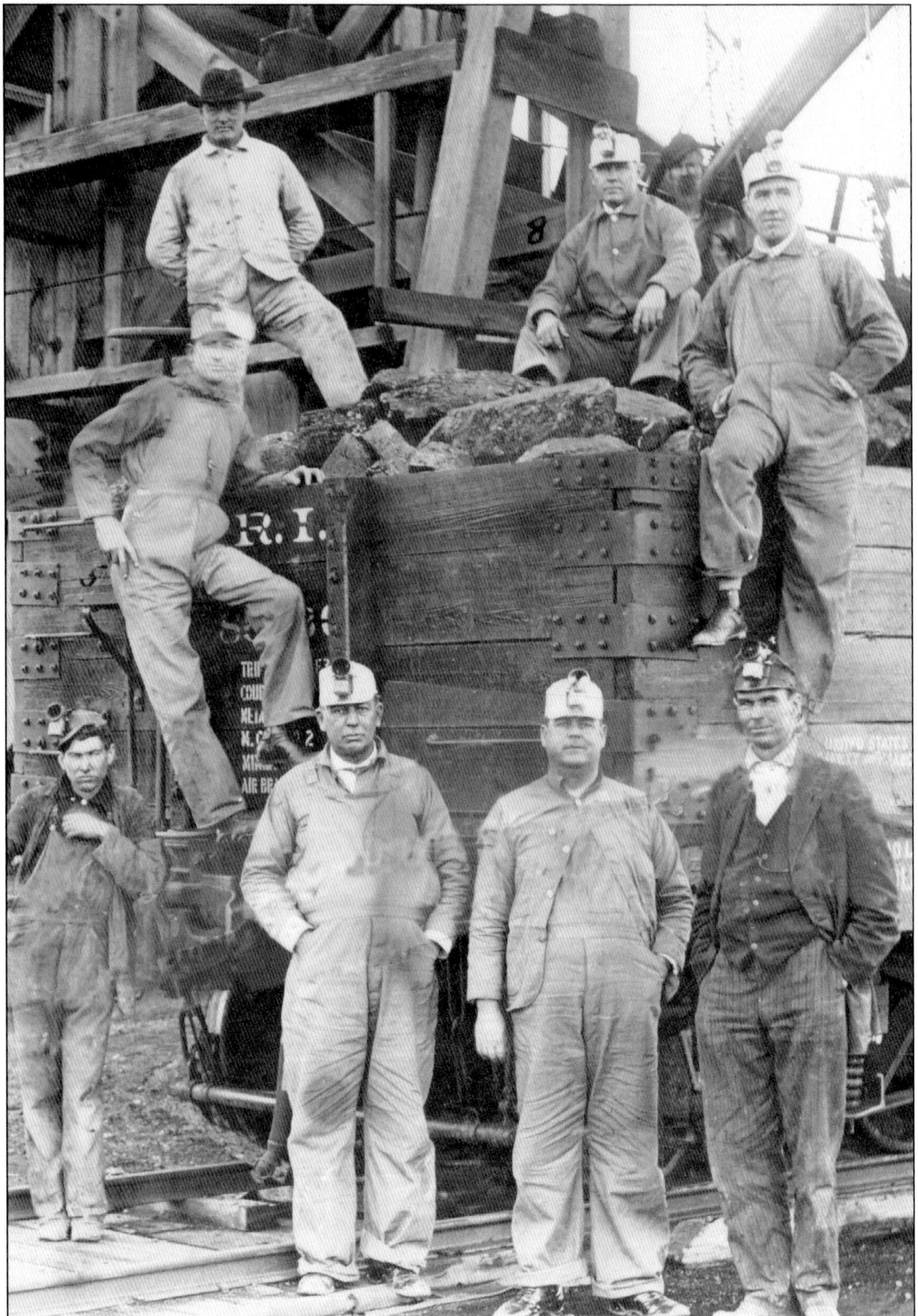

A loaded coal car is surrounded by, from left to right, (standing) foreman of Mine No. 3 Tom Byrnes, ? Holdemess, ? Gentry, and foreman of Mine No. 2 T. J. McAfee; (on car) ? Stevens, superintendent W. H. John, B. F. Austin, Jon Wright, and C. B. Whitehead.

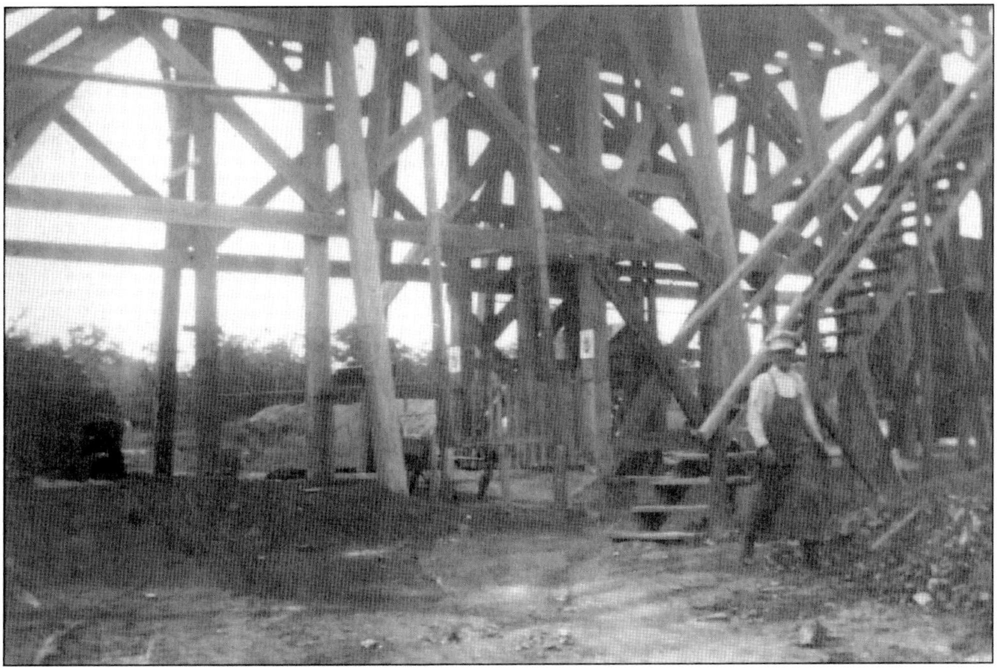

In this photograph, a worker has scampered down the stairs from the top of the tower where the elevator equipment is housed.

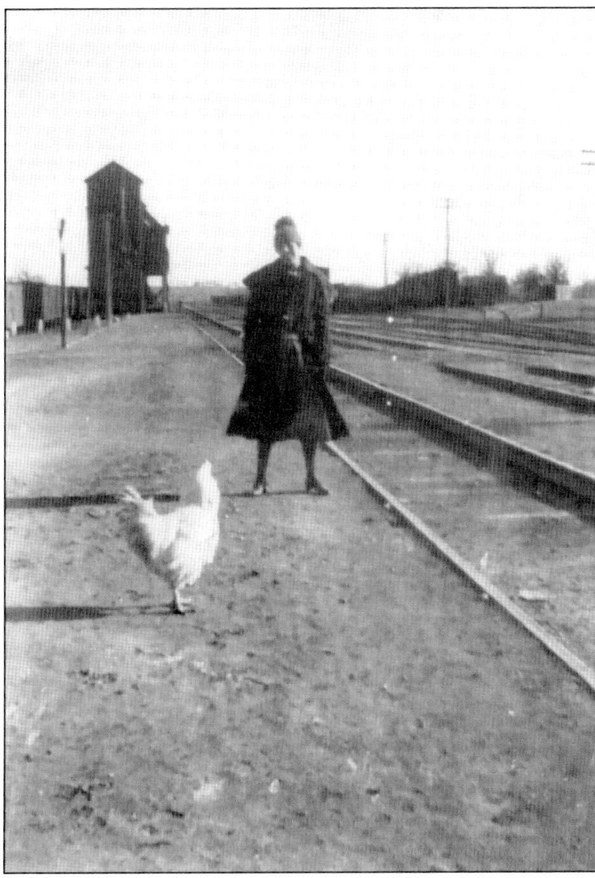

A young girl poses alongside the railroad tracks in front of the coal chute where the locomotive would stop and take on coal for fuel.

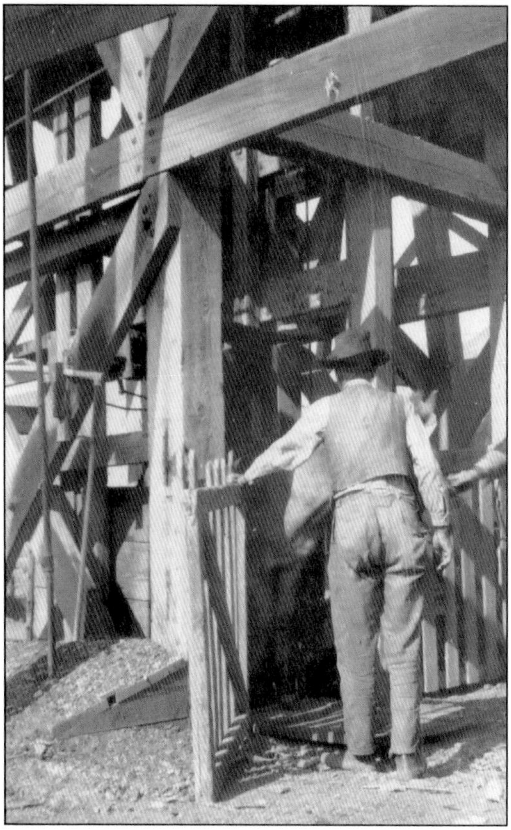

In this 1920s photograph, an employee checks on the horses and mules that were used in operating the mines. These animals would be lowered down the shaft, where they would then pull coal cars that the miners would load up. The miners would then take them to the main shaft, where the coal would be hoisted out. After complaints from the humane society, these animals were not left in the mines for long periods of time as they had been in the past.

Seen here is another livestock holding pen where mules were stabled when not working.

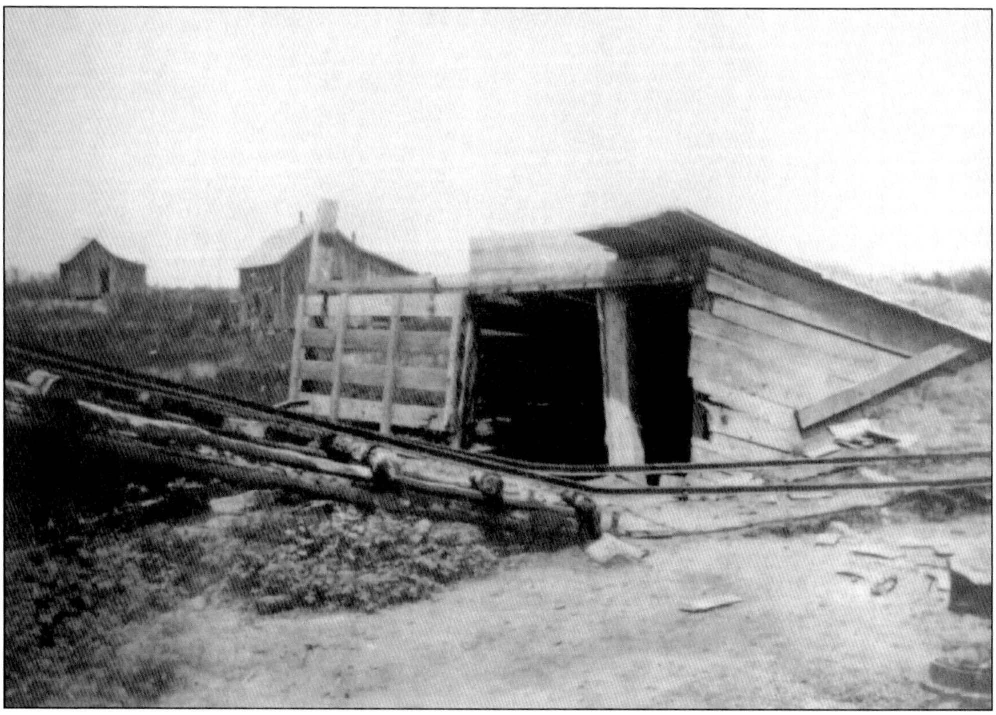

In this 1922 photograph, two generations of coal miners are featured. From left to right are (first row) John Bordner and son Frank Bordner; (second row) Mary Bordner Price and Helen Bordner. John emigrated from Czechoslovakia and also worked in the Thurber coal mines. (Courtesy Frank G. Bordner.)

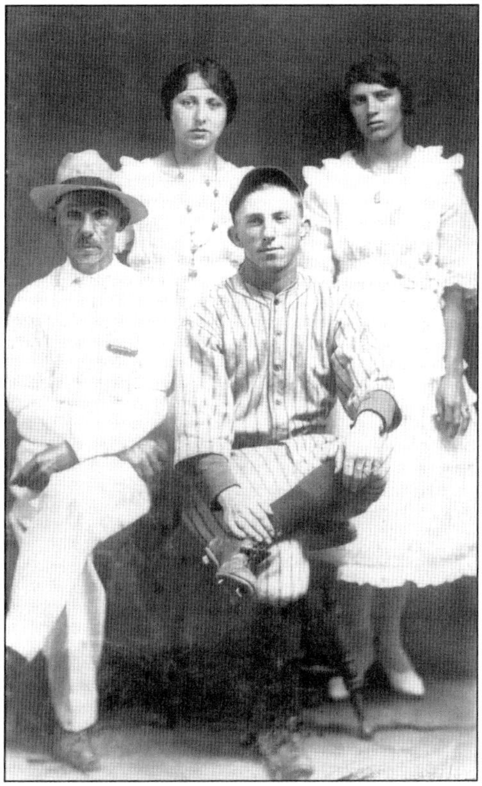

Seen here are the remnants of the company store, which was located on West Main Street but has since been torn down. The miners were issued company script and could buy necessary items at the store with the tokens. Groceries, clothes, and mining supplies were all available. A bank was also inside the store.

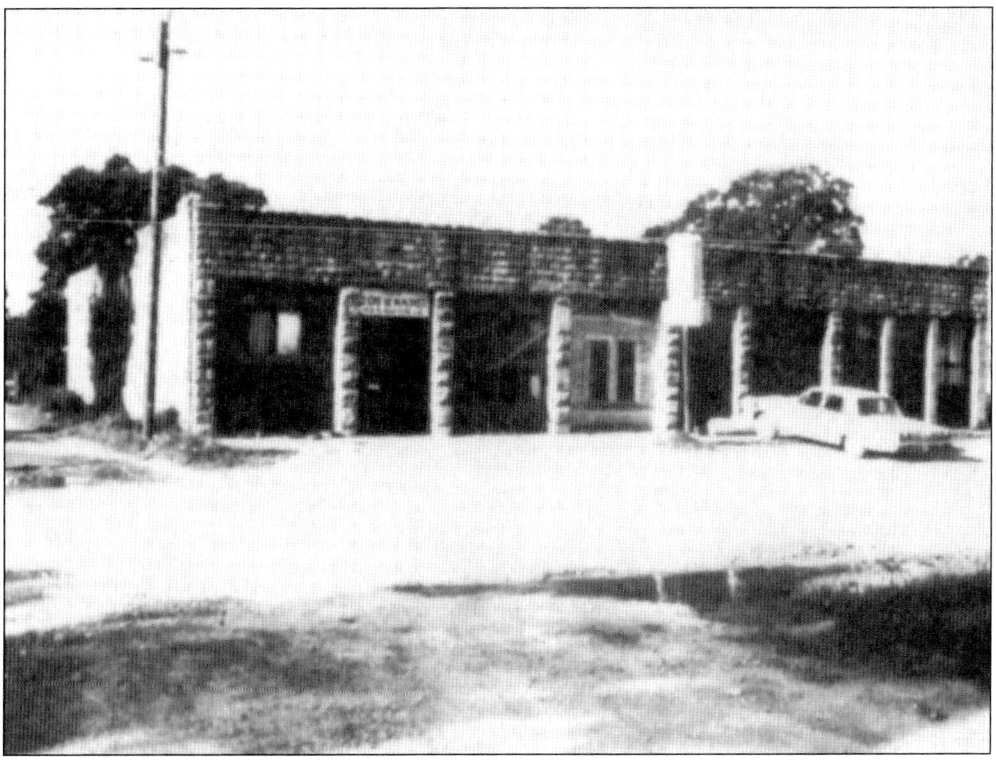

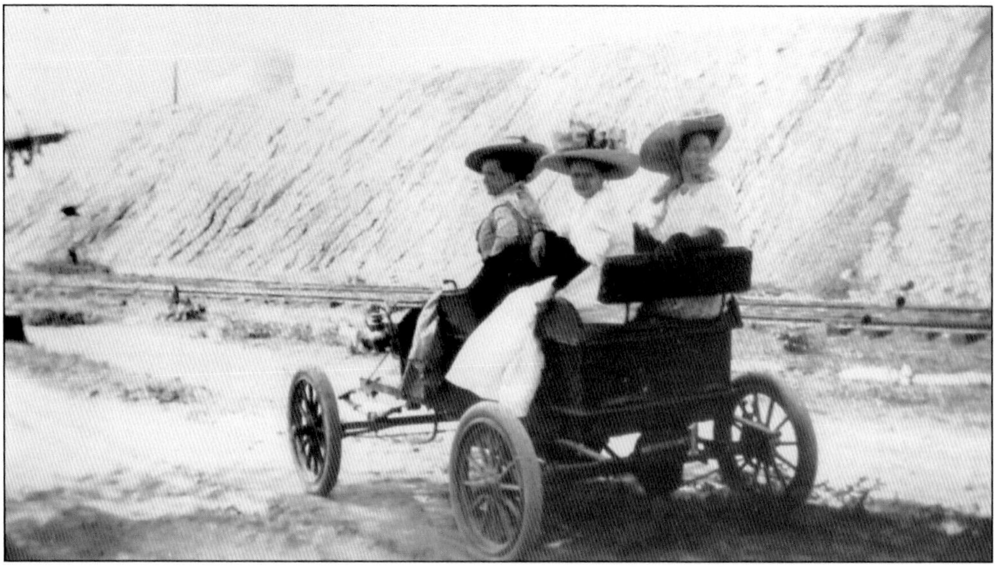

A coal mine was a dangerous place to work. However, it was an interesting place to visit on Sundays, which was the only day that the mines did not operate. Seen in this 1910s picture, curious ladies from town are inspecting the sites in some of their finest apparel.

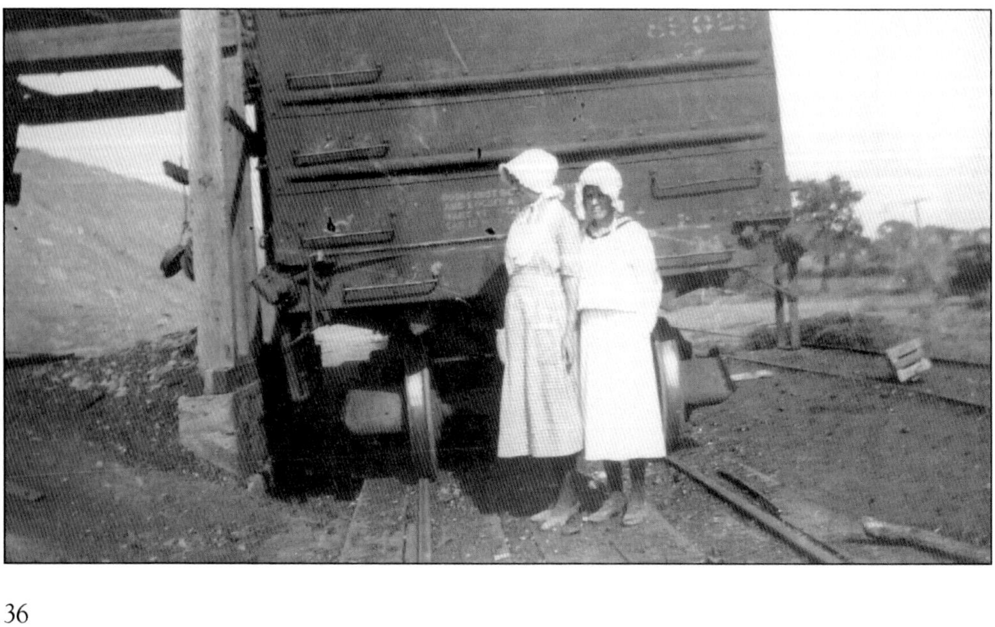

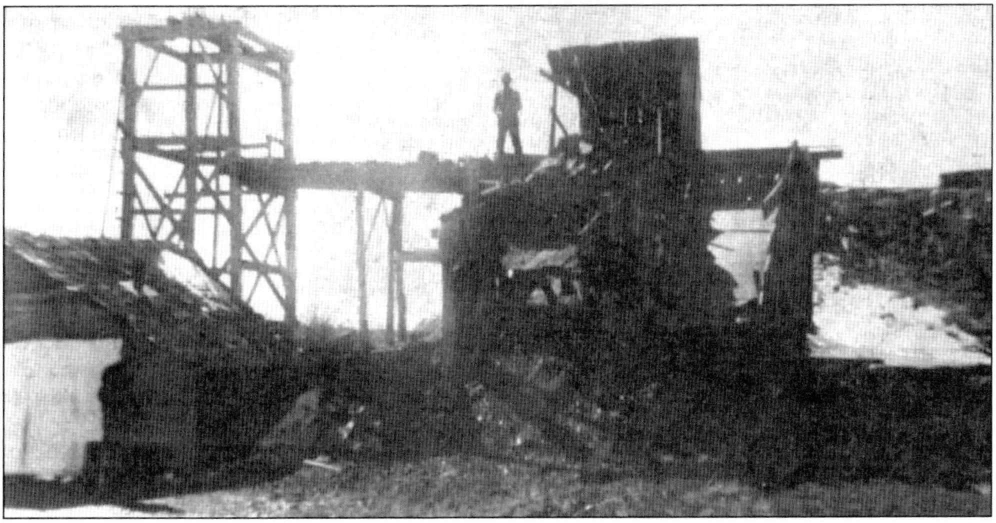

The Singleton mine was a shaft mine and one of the last coal mines to cease operations. The mine was effectively abandoned in 1941, leaving most of the equipment, including tracks and coal cars, in the shaft and mine. The new North Texas Community Hospital now occupies the spot where this mine was located.

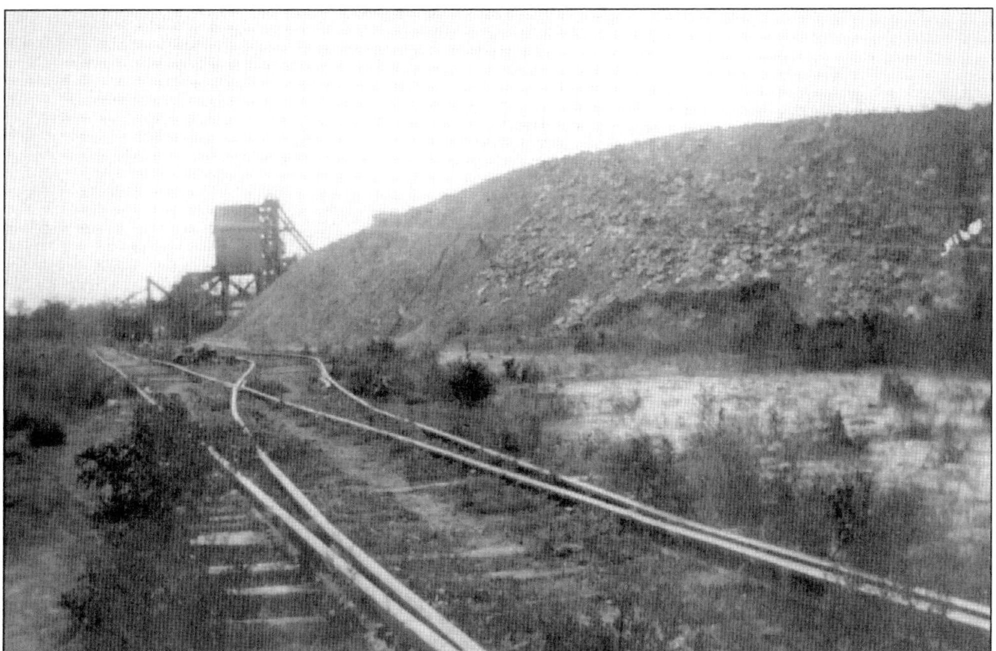

Most all of the larger mines had railroad spurs that connected the mine to the main railroad tracks in order to ship the coal on large rail cars. The tailings from the mine can be seen piled high next to the tracks. It was this shale that helped start the brick industry.

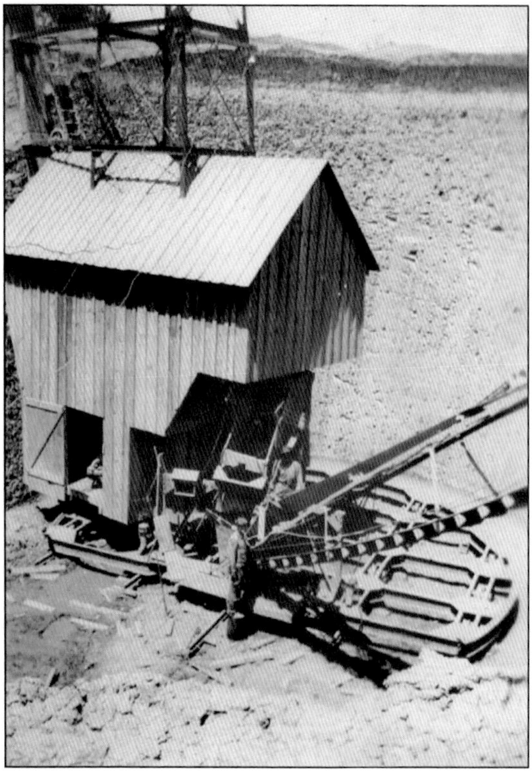

It was discovered that the shale tailings brought out from the coal mines could be made into brick. This waste from the mines was hauled by wagon to the first brick plant at Turkey and Ninth Streets where Fred's department store is located. The Wise County Brick Company started here in 1906 and used a dry-press plant method but soon changed to a stiff-mud operation.

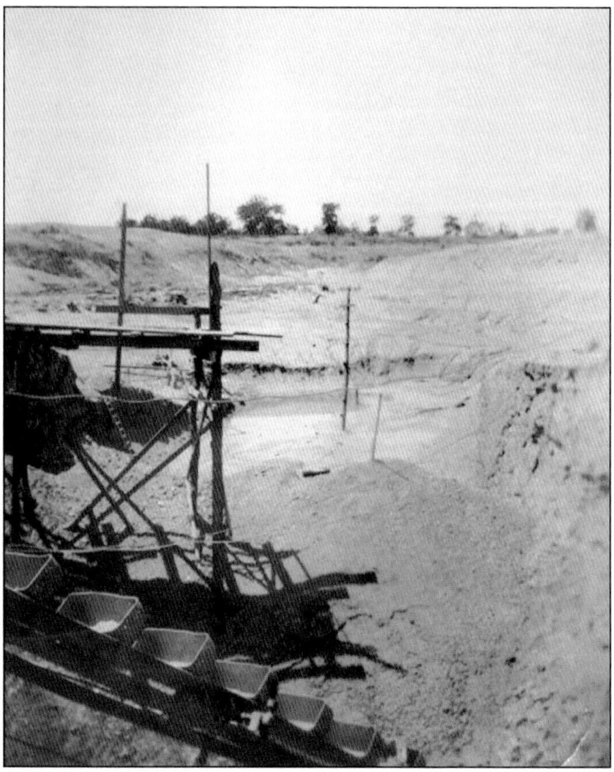

Once the ready supply of shale waste from the coal mines was exhausted, the brick plant began digging the shale from the ground with various mechanical buckets and steam shovels that allowed them to then manufacture the bricks from the material that was retrieved at the plant site.

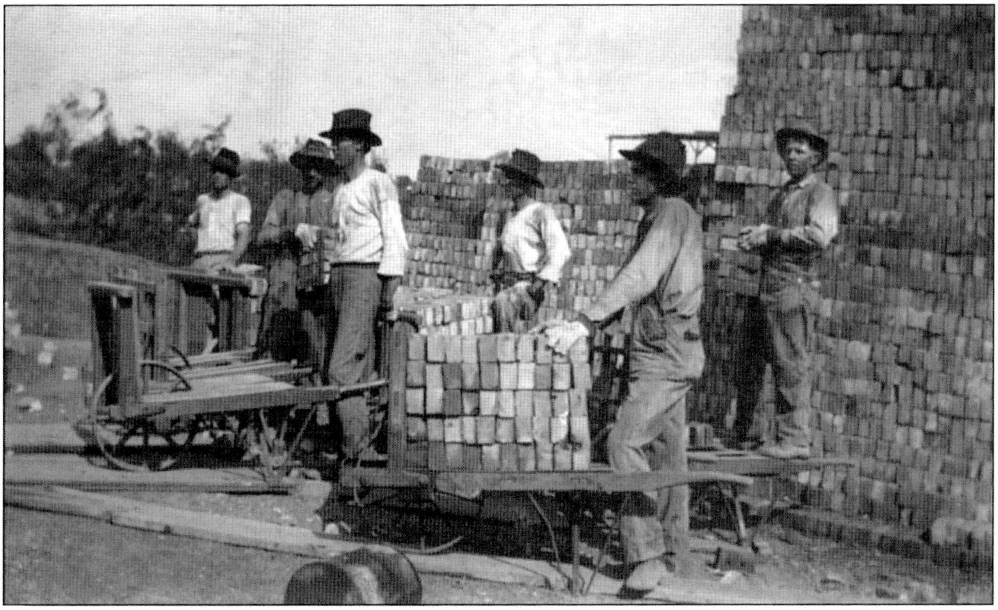

Seen here are workers in 1915 loading up the finished product. In 1916, the brick plant moved east across Ninth Street where there was additional land available to reclaim the shale used in manufacturing the bricks. This area is still undeveloped, and it is possible to see the pit where the soil was removed.

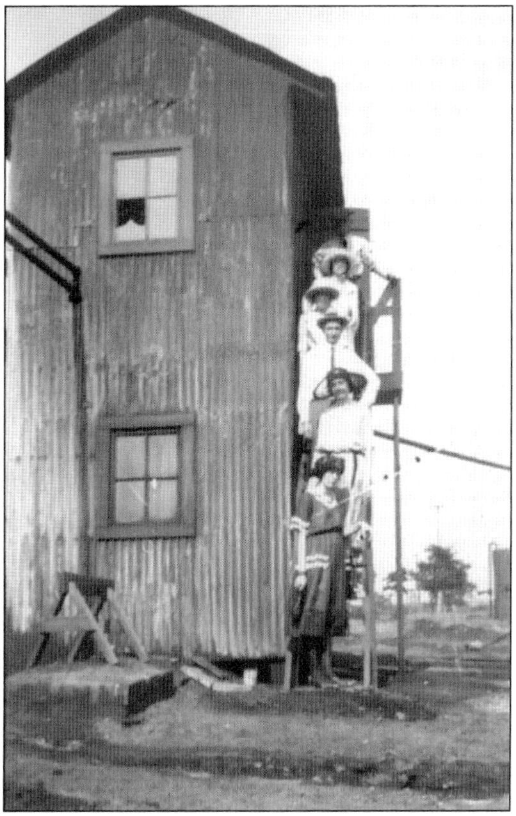

In 1918, a third plant opened on the west side of town at the present Acme Brick location. The company was bought in 1921 by C. W. Martin but failed in 1930. After sitting idle for several years, Acme Brick assumed control of the bankrupt company and went back into production in 1935.

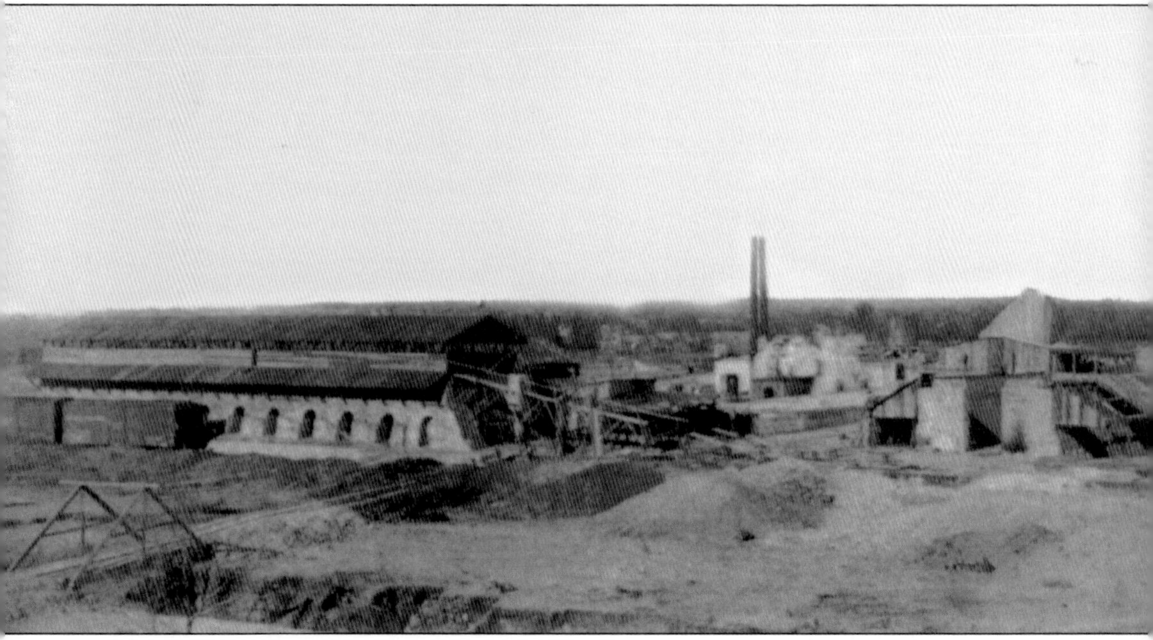

The Acme Brick Company made brick continuously for the next 70 years from the Bridgeport plant. The familiar red-with-black-specks brick has graced thousands of homes all over Texas. At the height of production in 2000, over 50 million bricks per year were being made in Bridgeport. With the downturn in residential construction, Acme ceased operations in Bridgeport in 2007.

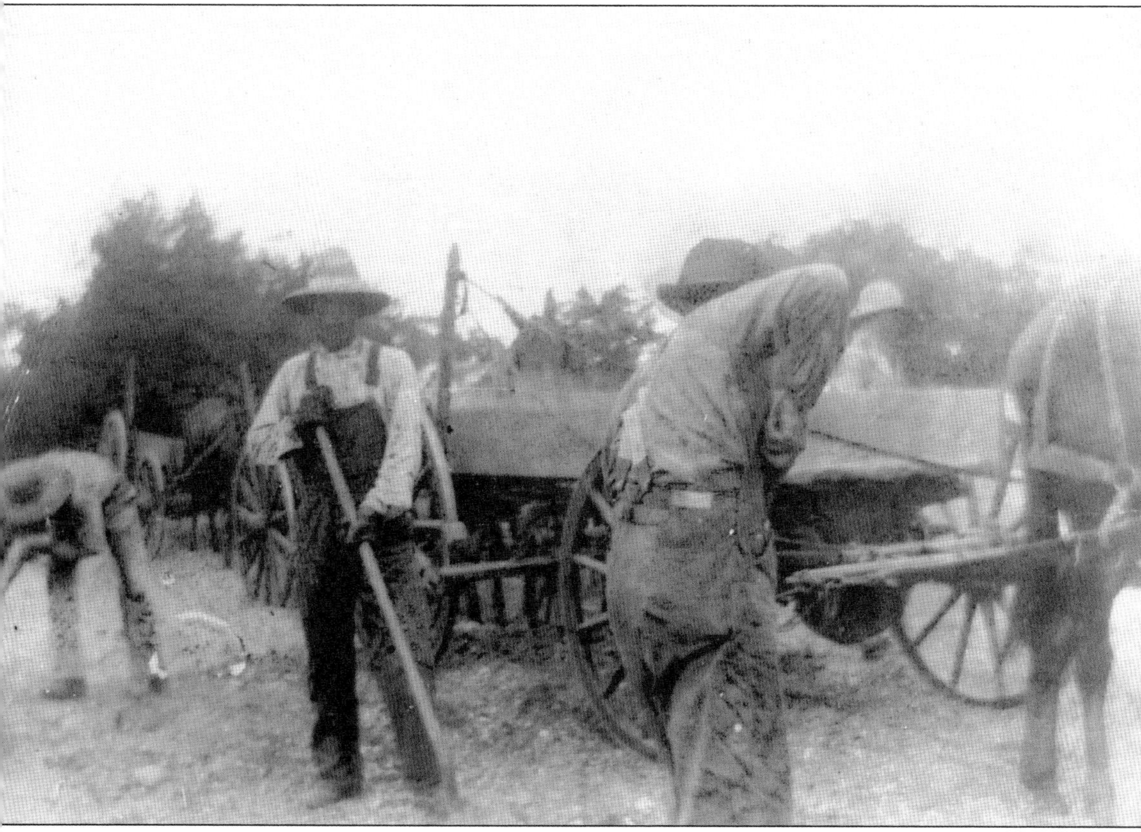

The crushed limestone business in Wise County began in 1919 when Chico Stone opened a plant about 5 miles north of Bridgeport. The primary market at that time was for railroad ballast and concrete used in road building. Initially much of the work was done by hand as depicted in the photograph, but increasingly larger equipment was introduced through the years as the operations expanded. Today millions of tons of crushed limestone are used throughout the north Texas region. Almost all the highways built in the area have used material that came from Wise County. The Dallas/Fort Worth International Airport is also the recipient of this valuable commodity.

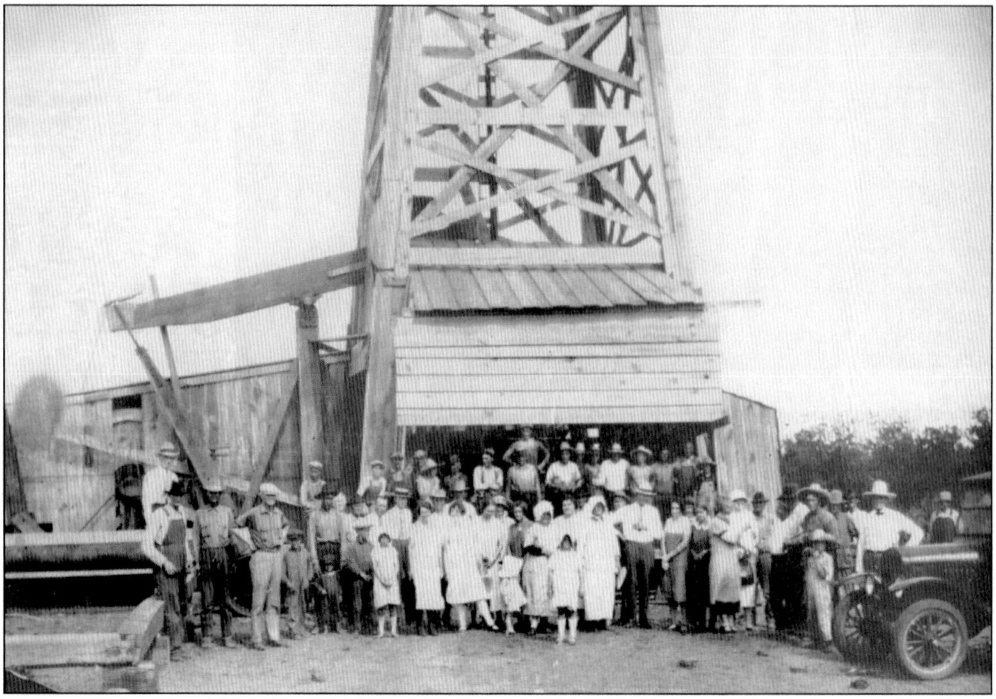

In this 1930s photograph, local residents are seen gathering around an oil well located off Cuba Road east of town. While drilling for oil was always a speculative venture, the real value of what was beneath the surface was the natural gas that was found thousands of feet underground.

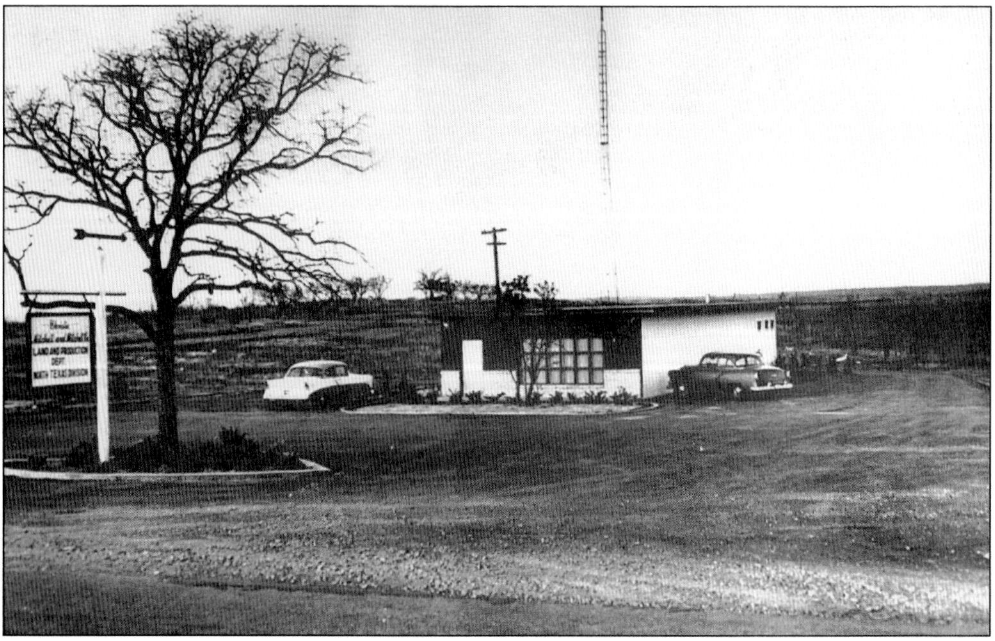

This 1956 photograph shows the humble beginning of George Mitchell and his exploration and production company that eventually had an enormous impact on the country's search for energy. The vast and profitable Barnett Shale gas play was developed nearby. Mitchell's model of extracting the gas from this formation has served as a model for retrieving gas throughout the world.

Four

A Dam Good Thing Happened in 1931

In 1927, Tarrant County voters passed a bond election that approved the funds to build Eagle Mountain Lake and Lake Bridgeport. Lake Bridgeport was completed in December 1931 and Eagle Mountain was finished the next year. However, it took a decade before Lake Bridgeport was full.

Situated only a few miles west of Bridgeport and with flood control now vastly improved and over 10,000 acres of water to play on, recreation opportunities began to develop around the 129 miles of shoreline of Lake Bridgeport. The area south of the dam was subdivided, many lake cabins were built, and eventually the small town of Lake Bridgeport came into existence as a result of the lake.

Other developments on the lake include the Bridgeport Camp and Conference Center, which is affiliated with the United Methodist Church. Using 142 acres of land donated in 1947 by the City of Bridgeport, the camp is located on a beautiful portion of the lake and home to many activities and provides facilities available to the general public as well.

The Sid Richardson Scout Ranch is 2,640 acres of rugged country and 19 miles of beautiful shoreline that is used in a variety of ways. Camping, water sports, and other outdoor activities are enjoyed by more than 20,000 scouts who come from across the United States and several foreign countries each year.

The Wise County Park and privately owned Bay Landing provide additional access to the lake. Situated at opposite ends of the lake, these facilities offer more than 200 RV hook-ups, rental cabins, campsites, and other water-related opportunities.

Located on the southwestern shores of Lake Bridgeport lies Runaway Bay. Started as a resort destination in the 1960s, it sits on rolling, wooded hills overlooking the lake. Runaway Bay has evolved into an incorporated city offering year-round boating, fishing, and golfing.

Bridgeport has benefited in numerous ways as a result of the construction of Lake Bridgeport. The Trinity River meanders much as it has for centuries above and below the lake; however, it yields to the wishes of the people who enjoy the bounty it has to offer.

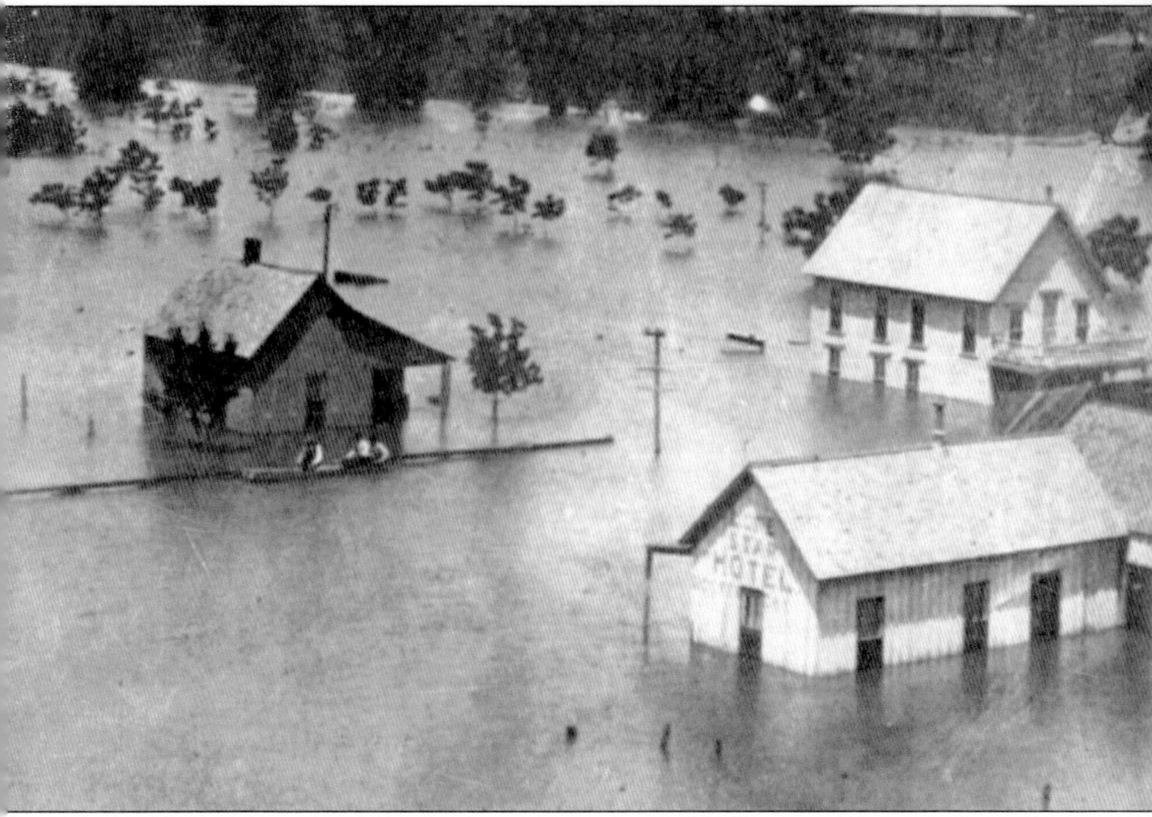

When the West Fork of the Trinity River flooded in 1908, parts of the town were inundated with floodwaters for over a week. Flowing over 400 miles from north Texas to the Gulf of Mexico, the Trinity River is the longest river that flows entirely in the state of Texas. Its drainage basin is almost 18,000 square miles. The upper region of the river is comprised of the East Fork, Elm Fork, Clear Fork, and West Fork. The West Fork travels approximately 145 miles through Jack, Wise, and Tarrant Counties.

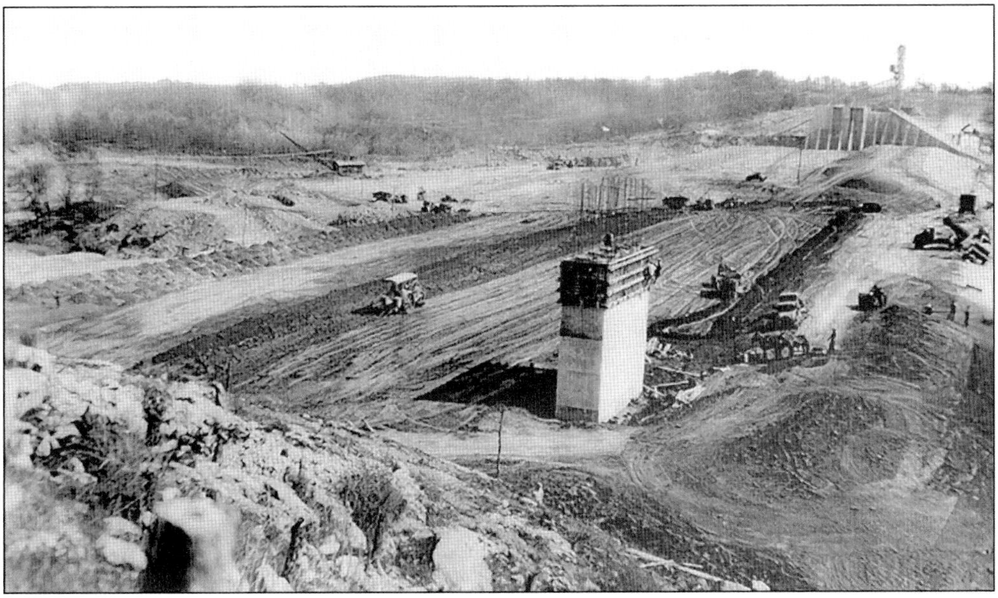

The dam was constructed by the wetted-and-rolled fill method with materials placed in layers approximately 12 inches thick and then thoroughly wetted and rolled to ensure proper compaction of the mass. (Courtesy TRWD.)

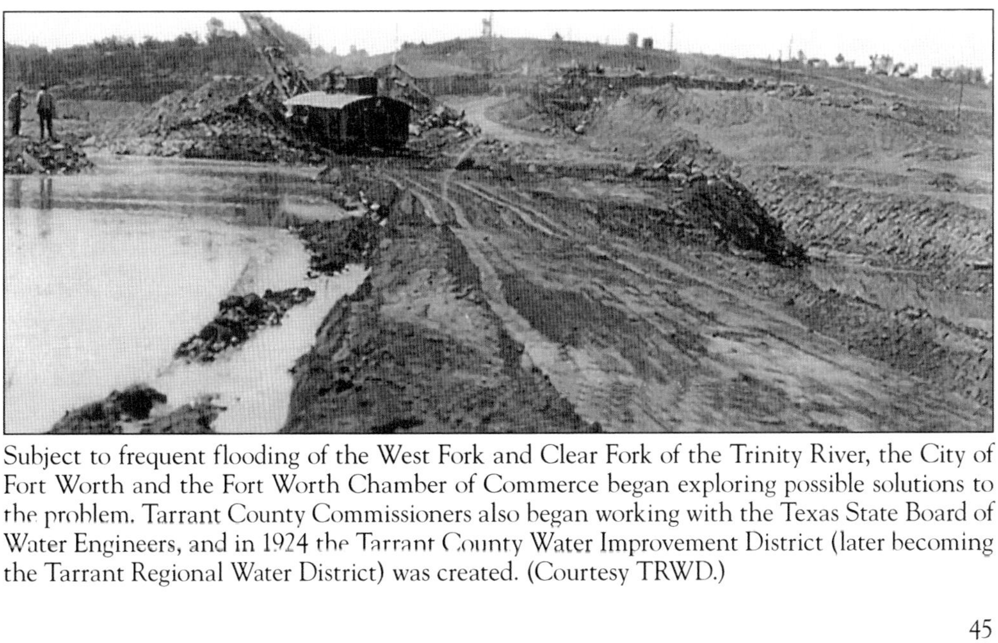

Subject to frequent flooding of the West Fork and Clear Fork of the Trinity River, the City of Fort Worth and the Fort Worth Chamber of Commerce began exploring possible solutions to the problem. Tarrant County Commissioners also began working with the Texas State Board of Water Engineers, and in 1924 the Tarrant County Water Improvement District (later becoming the Tarrant Regional Water District) was created. (Courtesy TRWD.)

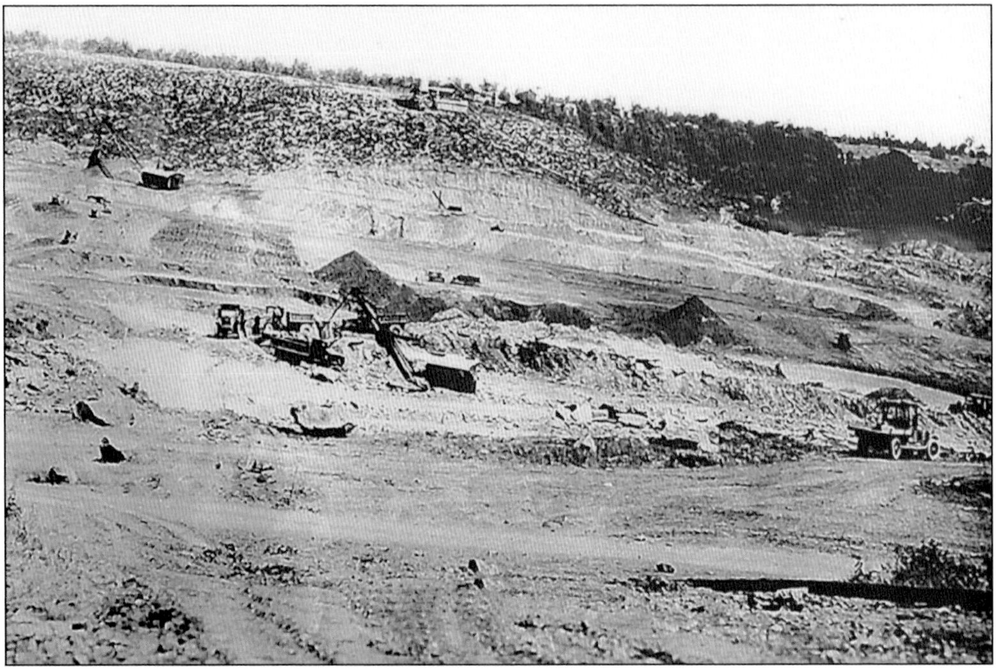

In the fall of 1927, the firm of Hawley and Freese was contracted to design and supervise the construction of Lake Bridgeport and Eagle Mountain Lake. The supervision of the construction of the Lake Bridgeport Dam was assigned to Marvin Nichols, a new member of the Hawley and Freese firm. Nichols became a partner in the firm in 1928, and the company name was changed to Hawley, Freese, and Nichols in 1930. Today the firm is Freese and Nichols Consulting Engineers. (Both courtesy TRWD.)

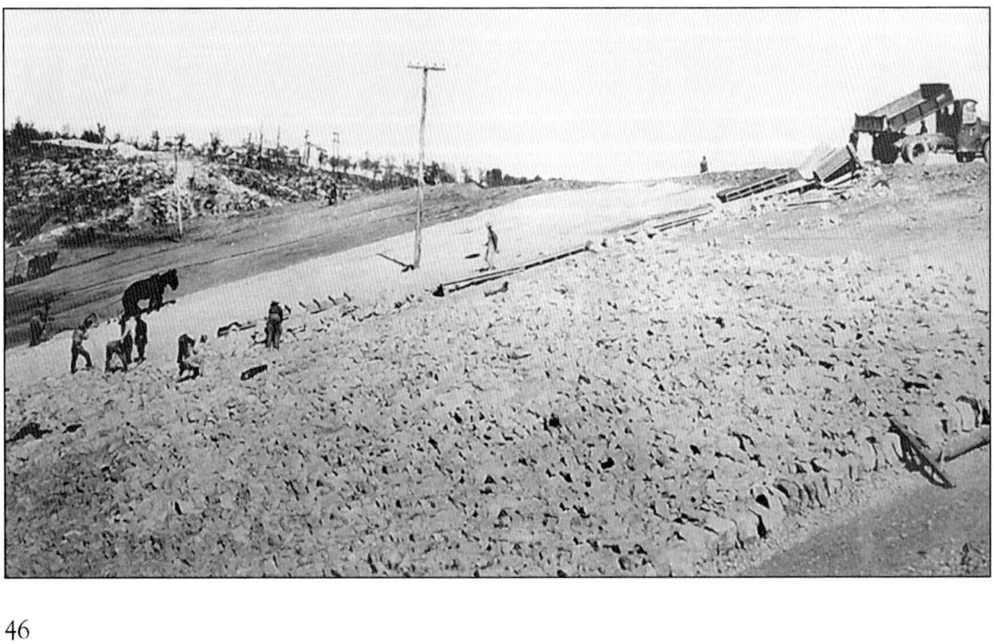

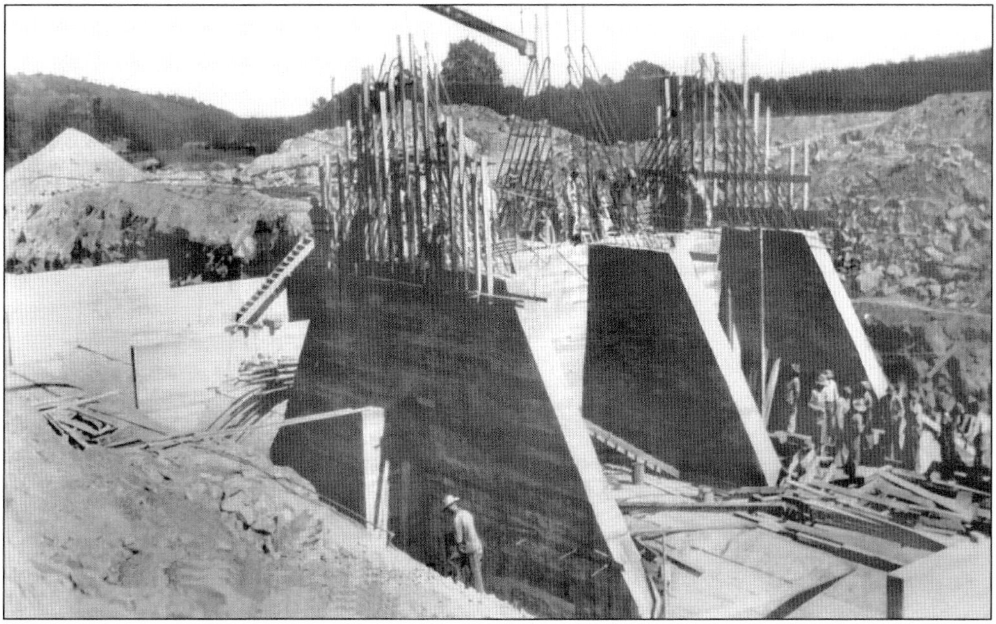

The original service spillway had three 20-foot bays; two were equipped with vertical lift gates and the third was left open. The outlet conduits in the bottom of the dam were equipped with 48-inch valves, two in each conduit. In 1969, the service spillway was eliminated and replaced with a 90-foot spillway equipped with eight roller gates. The conservation pool was raised from 826 to 836 feet above mean sea level. (Both courtesy TRWD.)

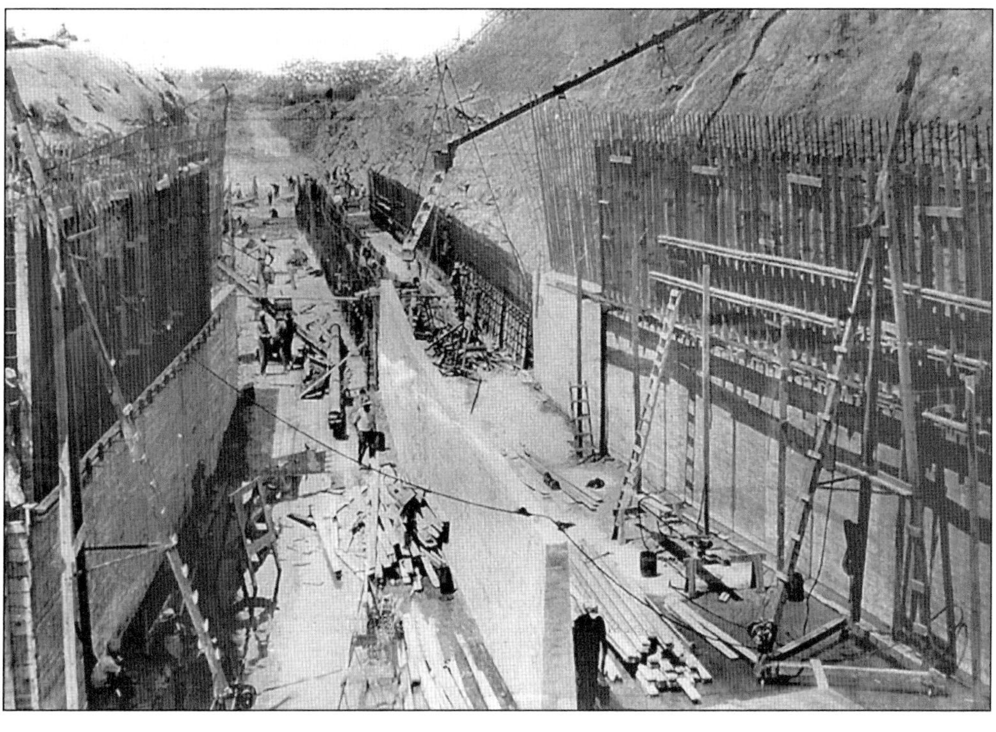

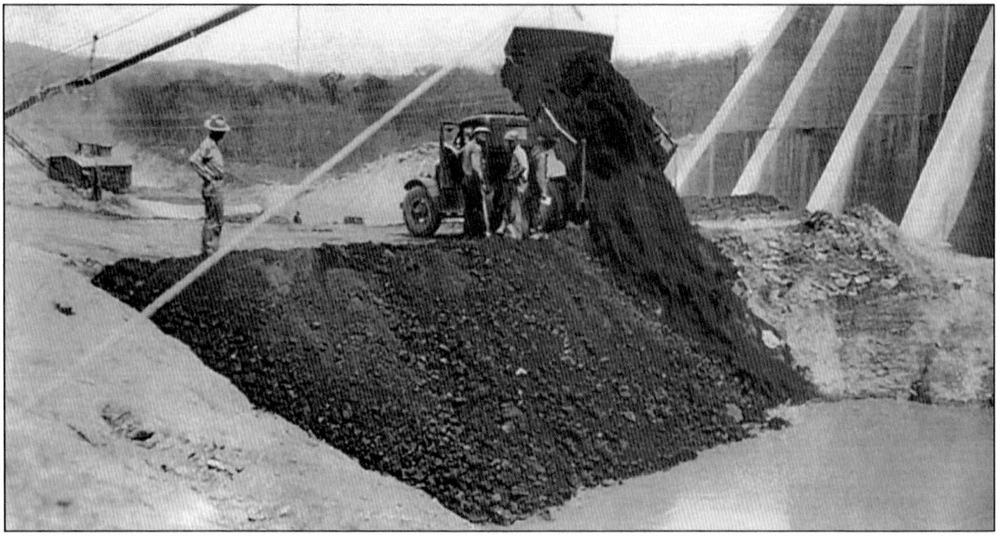

The Bridgeport Reservoir was built to have a flood-control capacity of 580,000 acre feet and conservation capacity of 290,000 acre feet. When the dam was raised, the conservation pool was increased to 366,236 acre feet of water. (Both courtesy TRWD.)

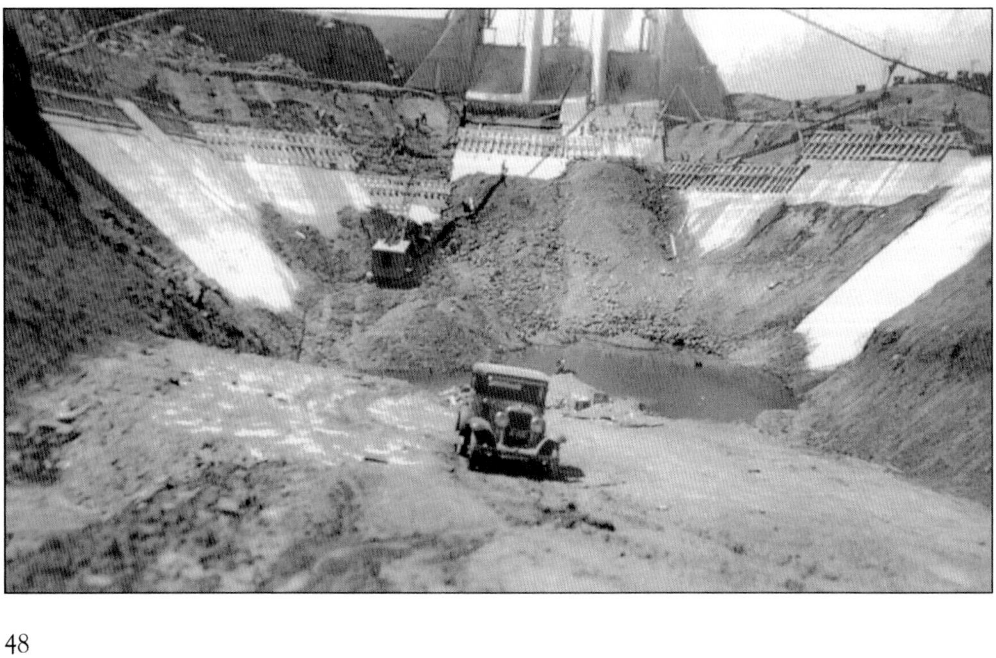

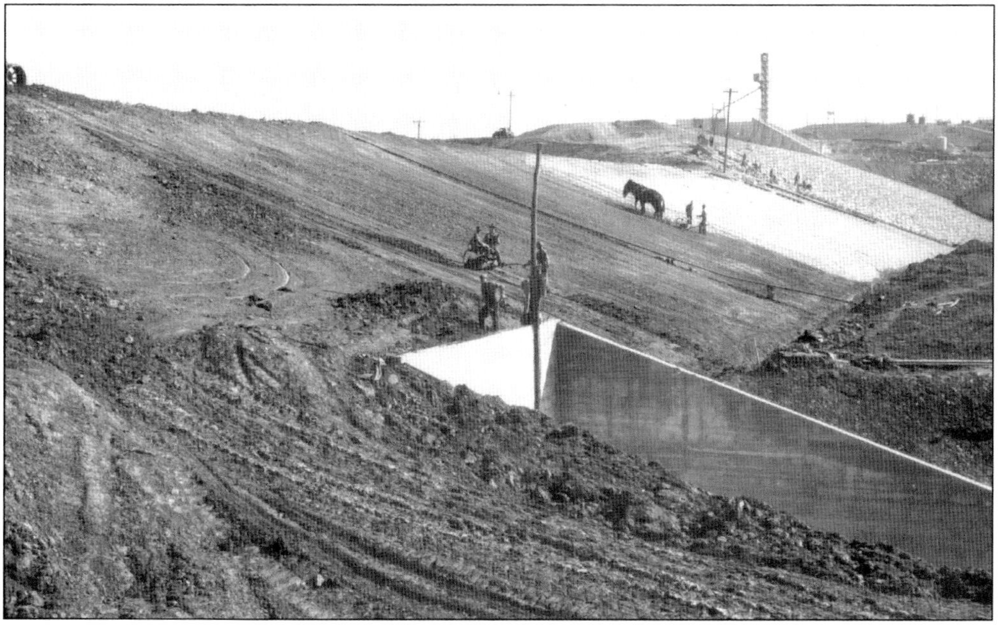

Much of the work clearing the land and laying the riprap rock on the dam was done by hand and with the use of animals. Lots were drawn for sections of land that required clearing with families often setting up tents and camping in the area. With the Great Depression sweeping the country, individuals were glad to get the opportunity to work. Trees were cut down by hand and then burned along with the brush. (Both courtesy TRWD.)

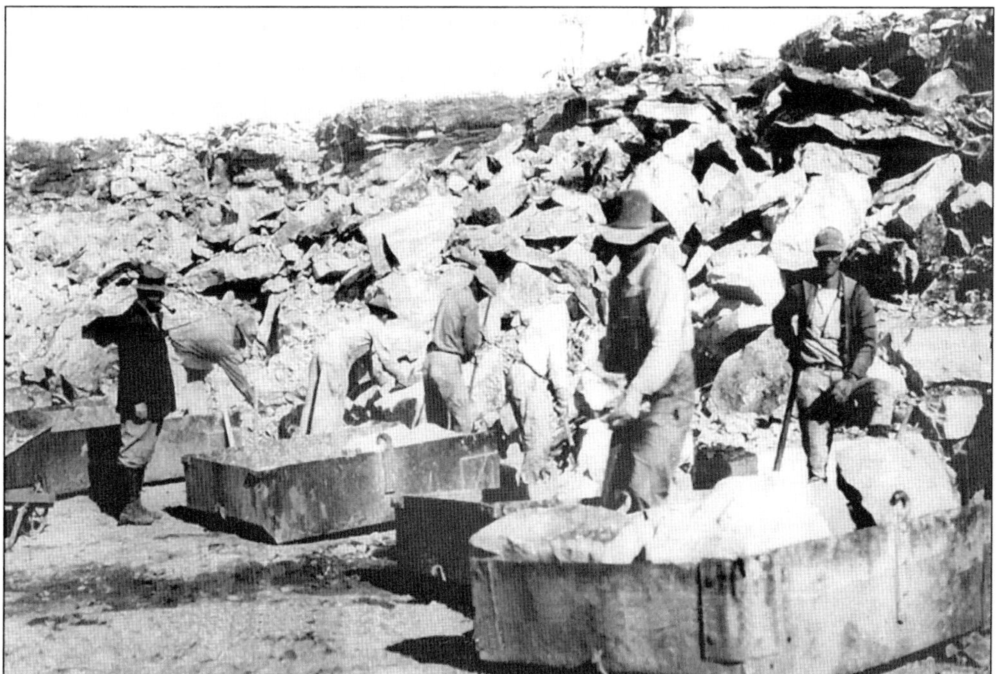

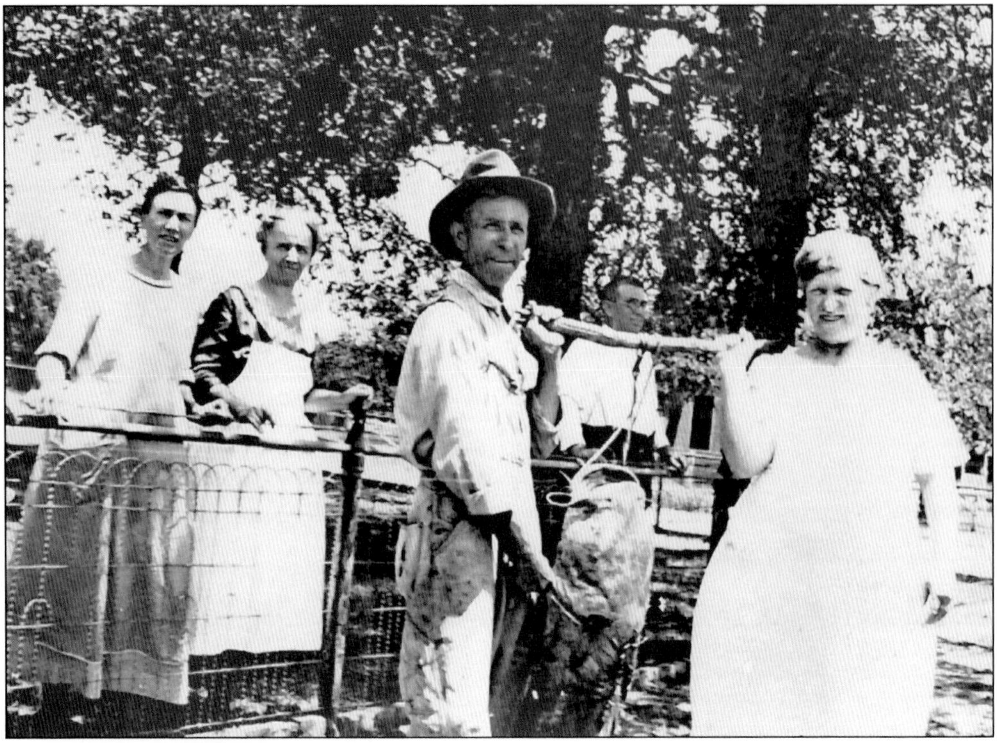

After the lake was full of water, the fishing began. This catfish was deep fried and served to many appreciative diners.

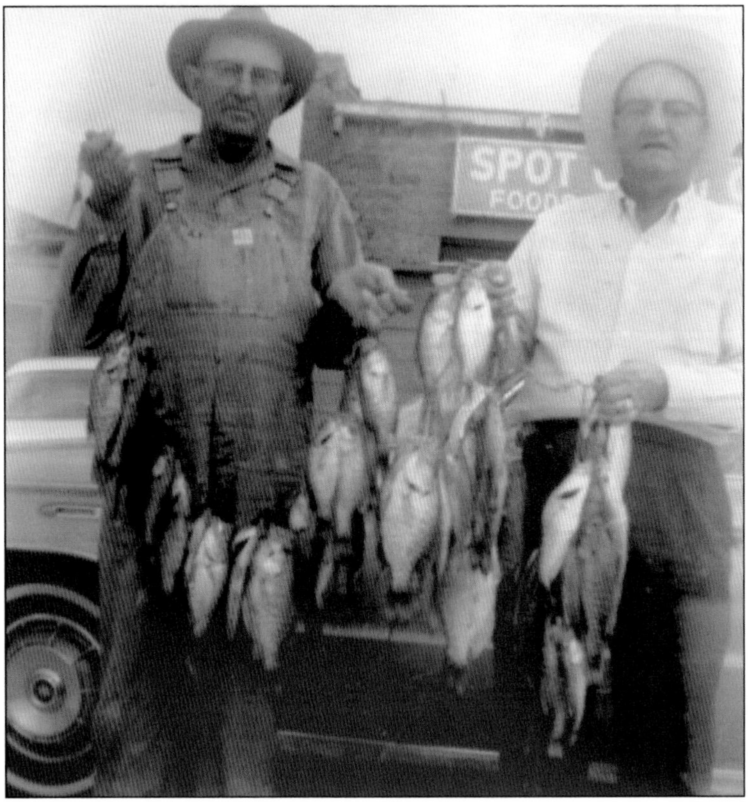

Best of friends Jess Tackel and Otis Meek show off their work for the day—a nice stringer of crappie.

Five

Living Off the Land is Hard

For most early pioneers in this area, self-subsistence was required. Agricultural practices varied with the type of land a farmer or rancher had, but the difficulty and challenges were the same. If a farm consisted of 120 acres, approximately 80 to 100 acres would be used to hunt, gather firewood, and raise cattle and hogs. Corn, which was consumed by the animals and people, was planted on any remaining land suited for crops. A home garden was also planted in the addition to an acre or two of cotton, which hopefully generated a small sum of cash for the farmer.

Mules and horses were used to plow the fields well into the 1930s until the advent of the all-purpose, gasoline-powered tractor became commonplace during the early 1940s. The life of a farmer is tenuous at best. After World War I, there was a surplus of farm commodities that drove crop prices down dramatically. Following this economic crisis was a number of years of drought and the ensuing Dust Bowl, which effected Wise County agricultural operations. The result of these years of bad luck was increased poverty in rural areas. During and after World War II, many good-paying, industrial-related jobs were found in the Dallas, Forth Worth area resulting in a decrease in the farm population.

The rancher has also had constant hurdles to overcome in order to survive. The type of land available dictated what kind of livestock was suitable and offered the best prospect of making a living. Much of the land around Bridgeport is rocky and semiarid, which is favorable to sheep and goat production, and many of the first settlers found raising sheep more profitable than the larger beef cattle. However, today there are many successful cattle-ranching operations found nearby.

Likewise, the dairyman has struggled with low prices and the demise of the small operator over the years. In the late 1950s, milk price wars broke out in Texas, and milk was shipped in from Minnesota and Wisconsin to drive prices down further.

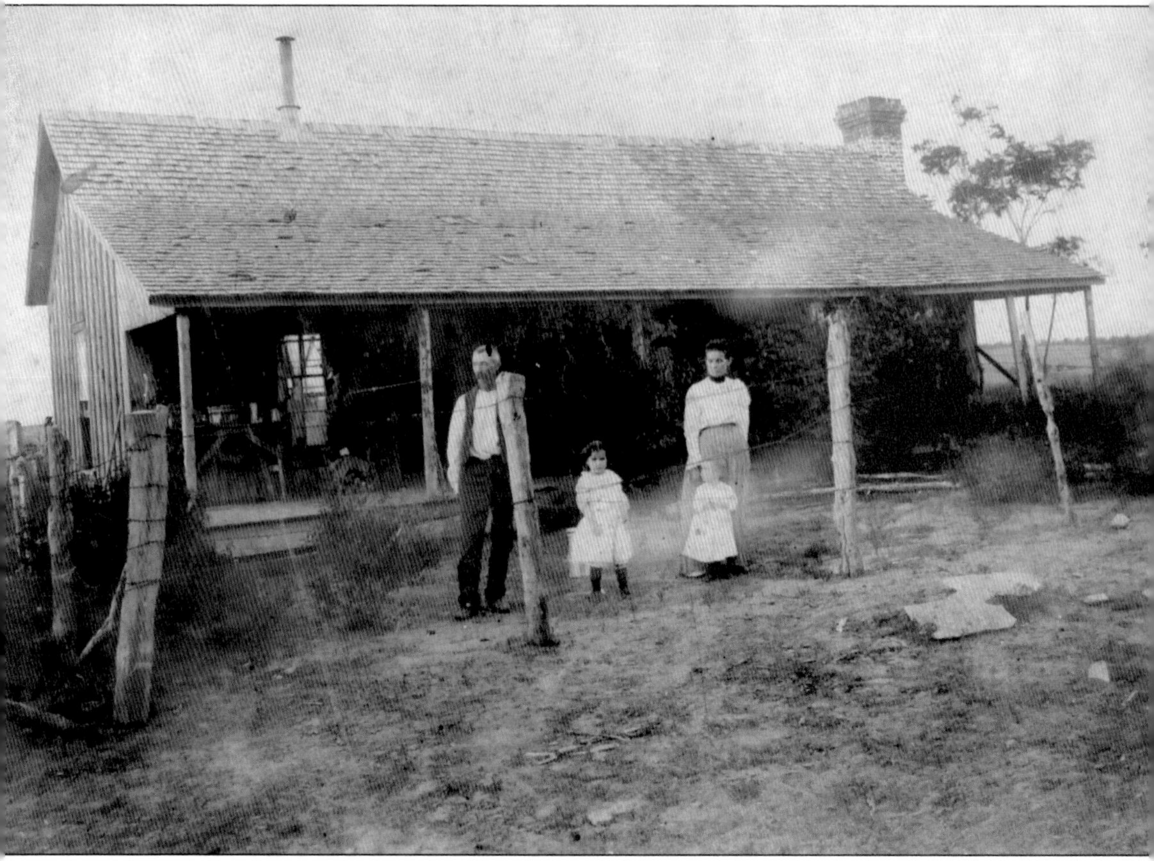

This late 1890s photograph depicts a typical farm that was found around the Bridgeport area. The farm was located south of town and was close to a small settlement of German immigrants who came to Texas after traveling through the Midwest. After farming for several years, many of these people moved into town and sought employment there.

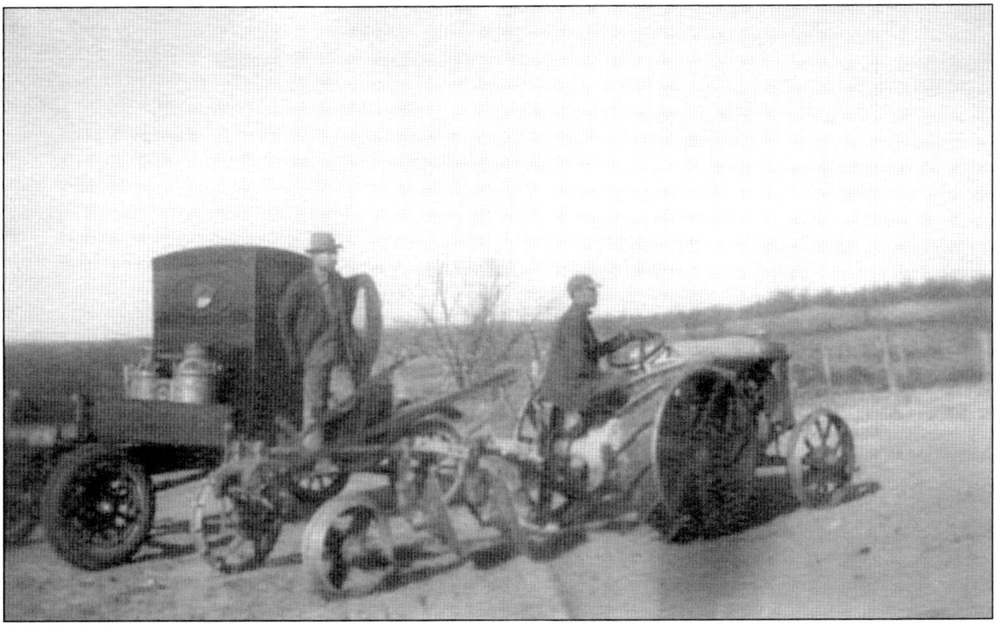

In this 1920s photograph, Ernest Jones and an unidentified man on a tractor are heading out for another day in the fields. This farm was located south of Bridgeport.

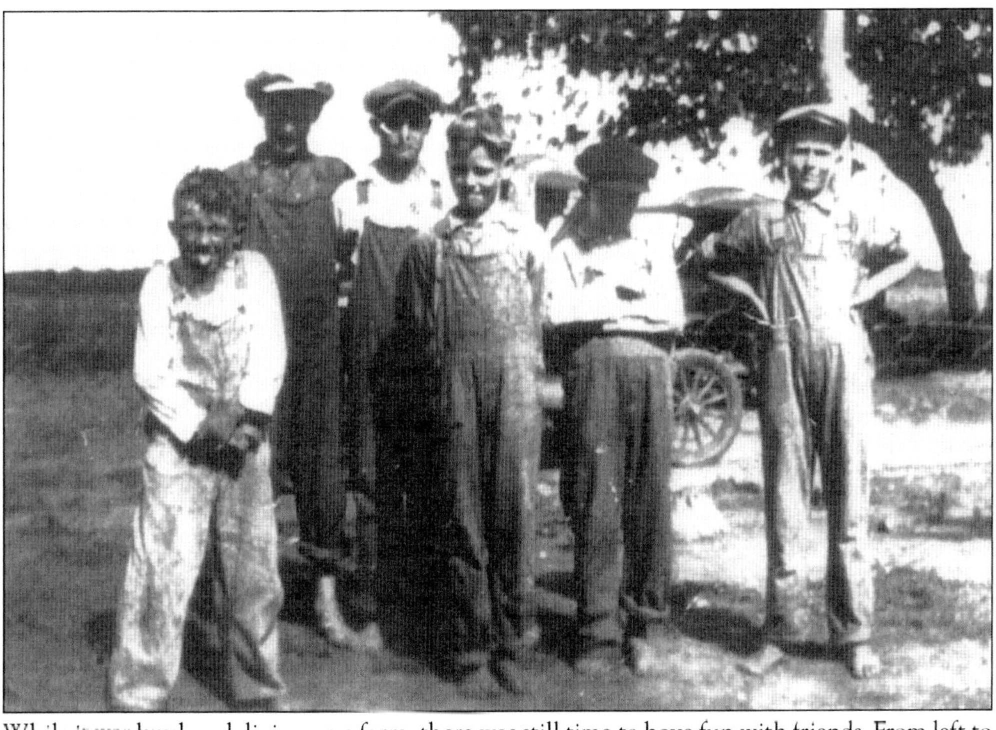

While it was hard work living on a farm, there was still time to have fun with friends. From left to right are Joe Motsenbocher, Carl Holt, Otis Meek, Royce Holt, Marvin Meek, and Bessel Holt.

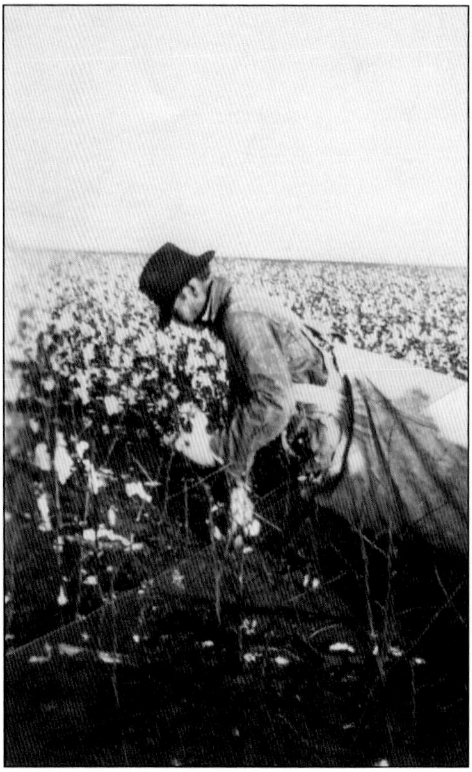

Cotton was king in the South, and the farms around Bridgeport produced its share. Jim Gossett (left) is surrounded by acres of the crop that has to be picked by hand. An unidentified girl (below) watches from the wagon that will be used to take the cotton to the gin in town.

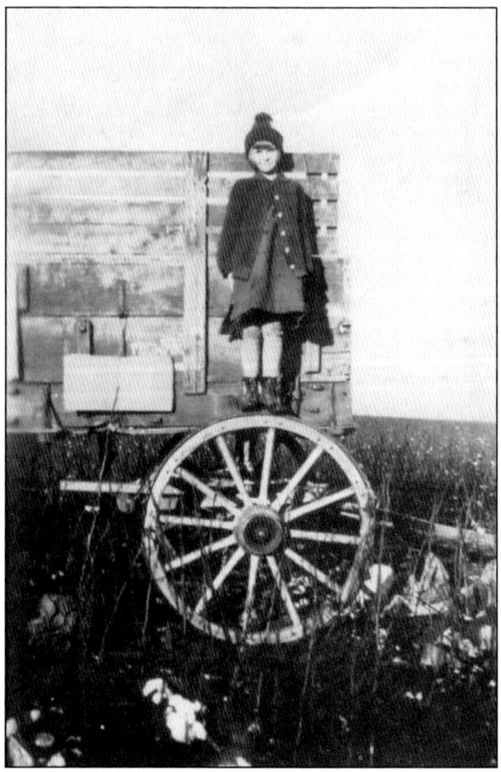

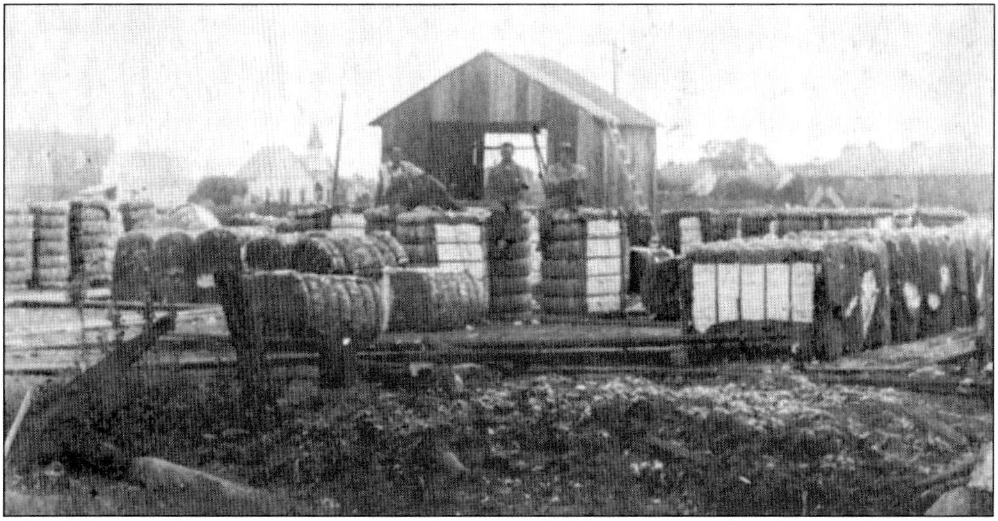

After the cotton has been processed at the gin, it is baled and taken to the loading station at the railroad, where it is then shipped to various factories in larger cities. Standing on the platform below are, from left to right, Jesse Power, unidentified, Ed Bingham, and unidentified.

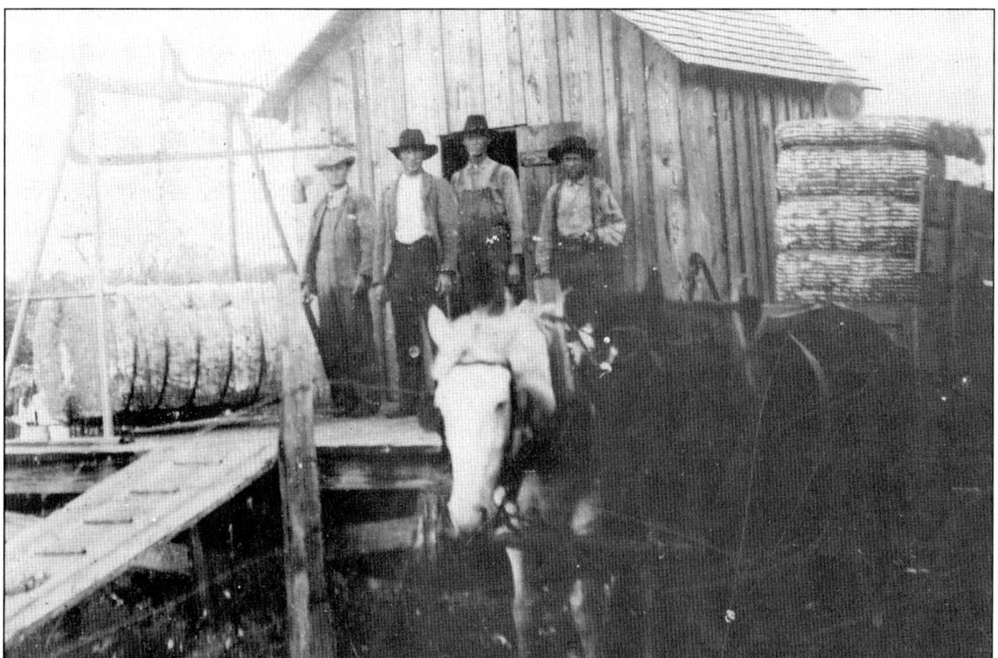

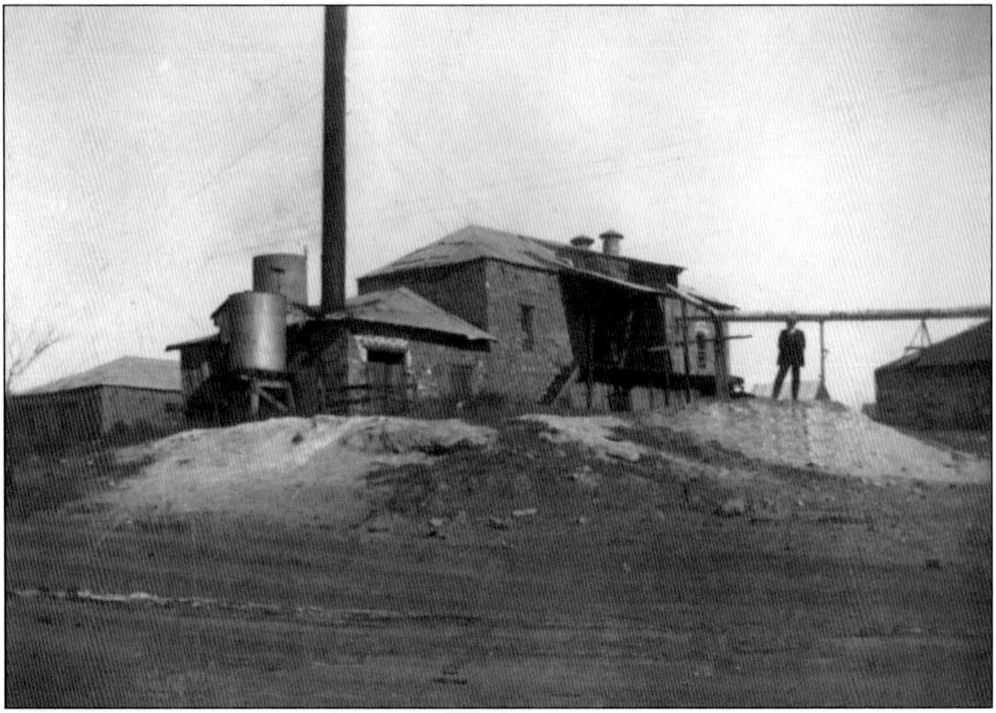

The Bridgeport cotton gin was located on Thompson Street at Ninth Street across from the present city hall building.

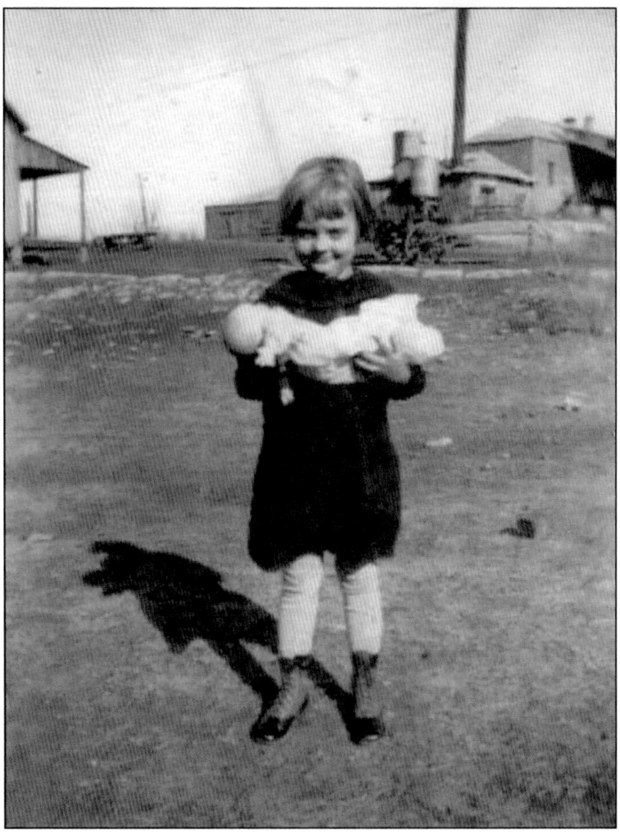

In this early 1930s photograph, Ione Counts is playing across the street from the cotton gin. Her house can be seen in the background. (Courtesy Ione Counts Smith.)

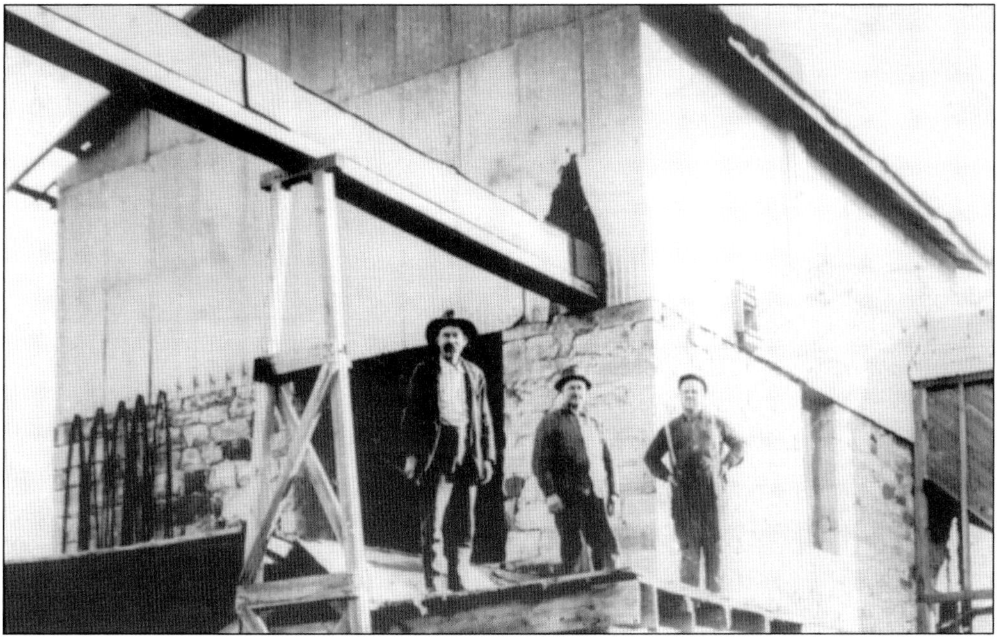

Frank Kaker (left) and two unidentified individuals are at the cotton gin. (Courtesy Ann Kaker.)

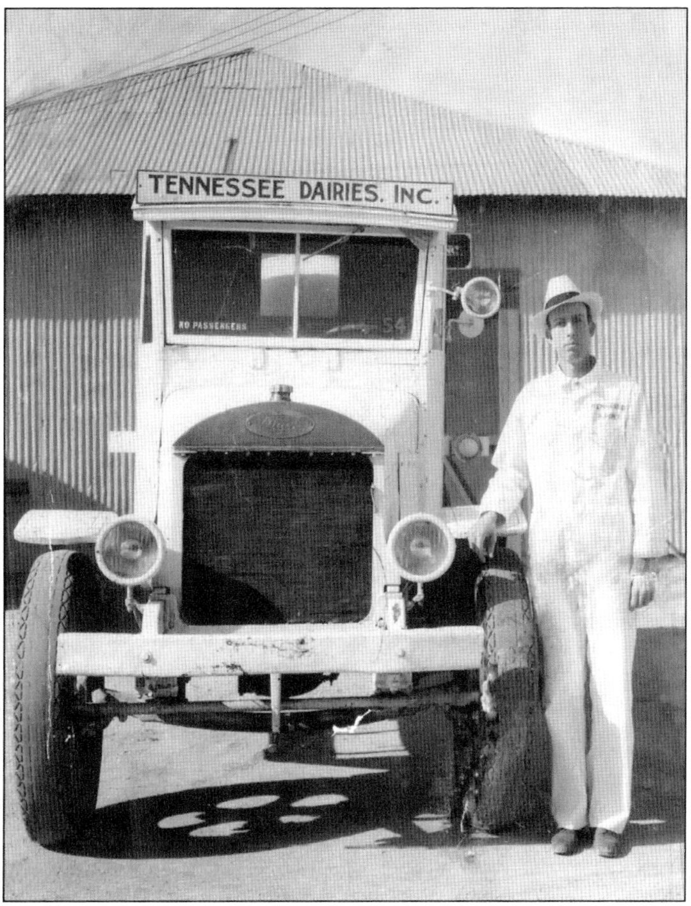

Bob Fry worked for the Tennessee Dairies, located at 502 Halsell Street, and would collect milk from the dairies all around Bridgeport.

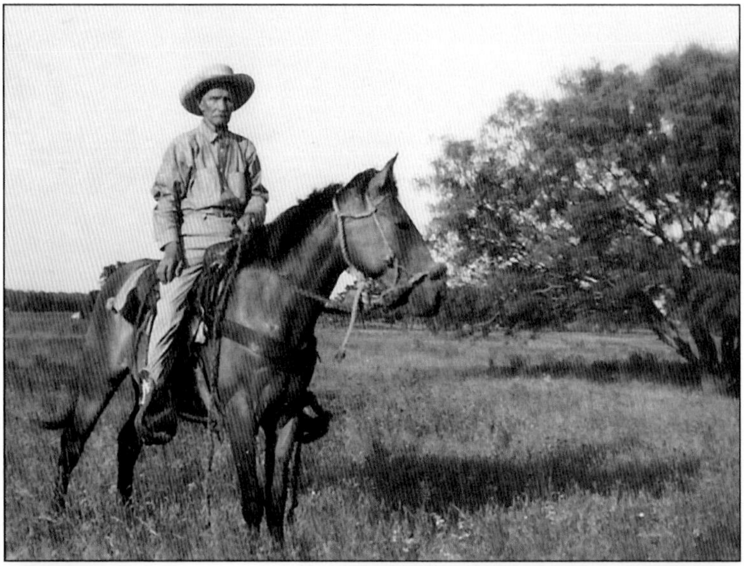

In this 1942 photograph, W. T. Jarnagan inspects his ranch while on horseback. William Temple and Emma Jarnagan moved to Bridgeport from Bryson, Texas, in 1917. The ranch was located south of Bridgeport, where they reared their 12 children. Ranching has been a staple of the Bridgeport economy since the town first began in 1860.

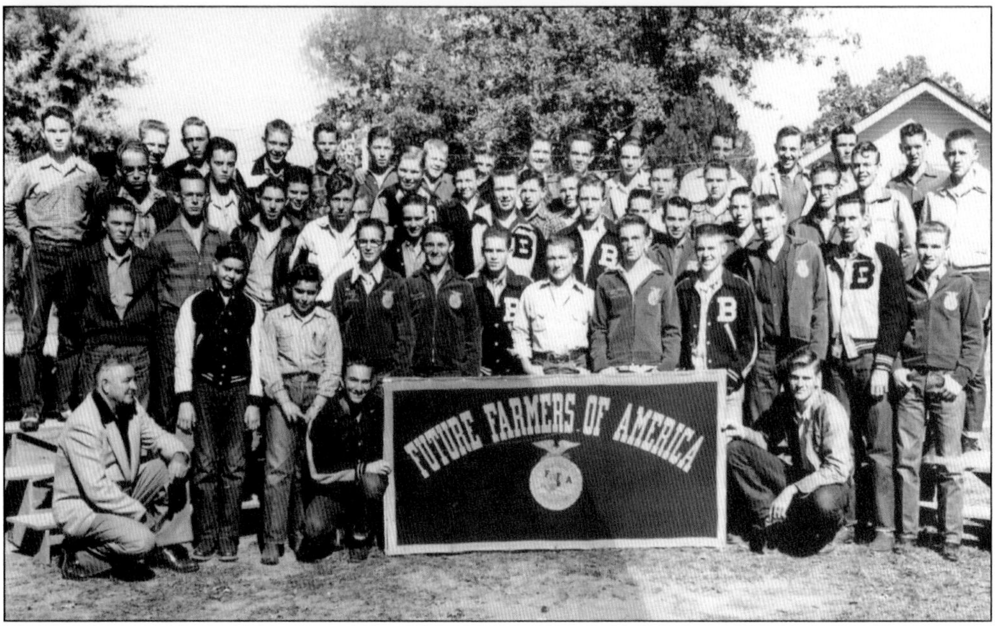

The role of agriculture is emphasized in school through an active Future Farmers of America program. Pictured here in 1955 are, from left to right, (first row, kneeling) teacher Zeb Tindel, Charles Strawn, and Billy Fred Walker; (second row) Ray Turner, Richard Blagg, Bobby Carpenter, Clarence Garrett, Jimmy Munn, Claude Pewitt, Johnny Beeson, Carl White, Charles Kaker, Eldon Kaker, and Thurman Sparks; (third row) William T. Smith, Paul McWilliams, Danny Chilton, Donald Roberts, Leroy Sparks, G. B. Funk, Thomas Wright, Rex Boulware, Robert Moody, Robert Phillips, and Jerry Counts; (fourth row) Dwight Green, Freddie Thomkin, William Slagle, Jerry Thetford, Ernest Largent, Victor Reynolds, Doyle Gene Smith, Gary Womack, Cecil Van Hoose, Harold Allison, Bill Ryan, and Kenneth Christensen; (fifth row) Johnny Herndon, Donald Lawrence, Billy Martin, Marshall Rainwater, Orville Munn, Lewis Hall, Kenneth Cansler, Troy Lutenbaker, Jerry Lowe, Albert Jones, Charles Walker, Carl Jackson, Carl Jones, Wayne Bradley, and Gary Early. (Courtesy Donna Munn.)

Six

Our Town

In his 1938 Pulitzer Prize–winning drama *Our Town*, Thornton Wilder takes people back to a small town shortly after the turn of the 20th century and examines how change is affecting its citizens. The audience is taken through a day in the life of the town, where daily routines and relationships are introduced as significant components of the human experience.

Bridgeport was a small town during this time and no doubt shared many traits of Wilder's fictional town. The fabric that is woven into any town's history is simply the stories of the people. Over time, traditional institutions such as school and church played a large role in the life of Bridgeport. Education has always been deemed important in the life of the community, and the role of dedicated teachers and involved parents has certainly made a positive impact. The function of the varied church denominations was of equal value. Serving as the conscience and moral compass of the community, church life was an integral part of Bridgeport's narrative.

Halsell Street is where most all the merchants were found. Grocery stores, drug stores, banks, hardware stores, gas stations, and dry good stores were some of the businesses anchoring this important road. This is where a boy could spend a Saturday afternoon watching Tom Mix, Gene Autry, or other western heroes of the big screen. Young girls could window shop for a new dress or hat. Young couples or singles could socialize at a drugstore soda fountain.

This is the place on Saturdays where families would drive and vie for a parking space for the entire day or evening. This is where friends were. This is where all the activity was. This was downtown.

And located not far from this bustling hub was the park. Every town needs a park to enhance its standard of living. Fortunately Bridgeport has recognized this need, and for many years it has provided this setting. Harwood Park has been the scene of numerous special events including festivals, county fairs, and the circus. Countless reunions have reestablished family ties, and children have happily played in the park for generations.

Bridgeport has certainly changed over the years but in some ways retains elements of an earlier era. And to borrow the famous line from *Our Town*, "This is the way we were."

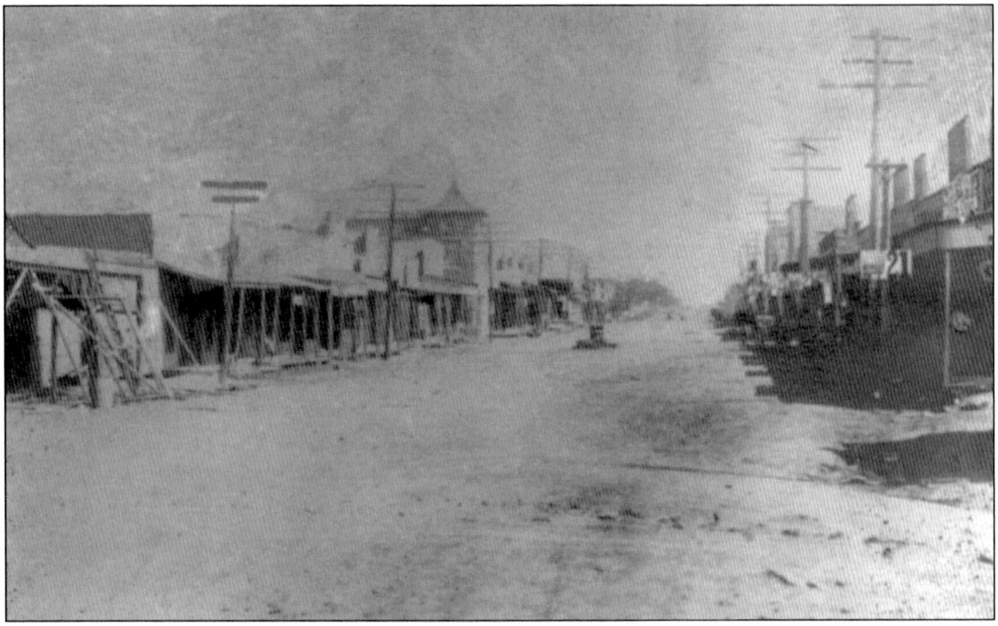

In these early photographs of downtown Bridgeport, the business district has already taken shape as many owners have built their stores on Halsell Street. Anchored in the middle of the block is the unmistakable First National Bank building with its distinctive Chinese-style roof. (Both courtesy Gilbert and Sue Williams Shawn.)

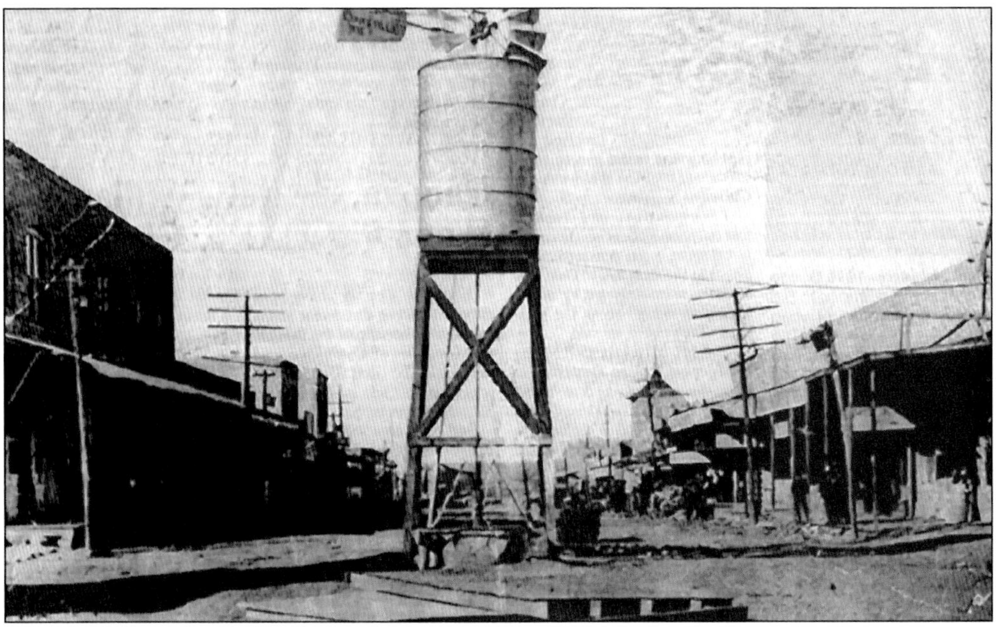

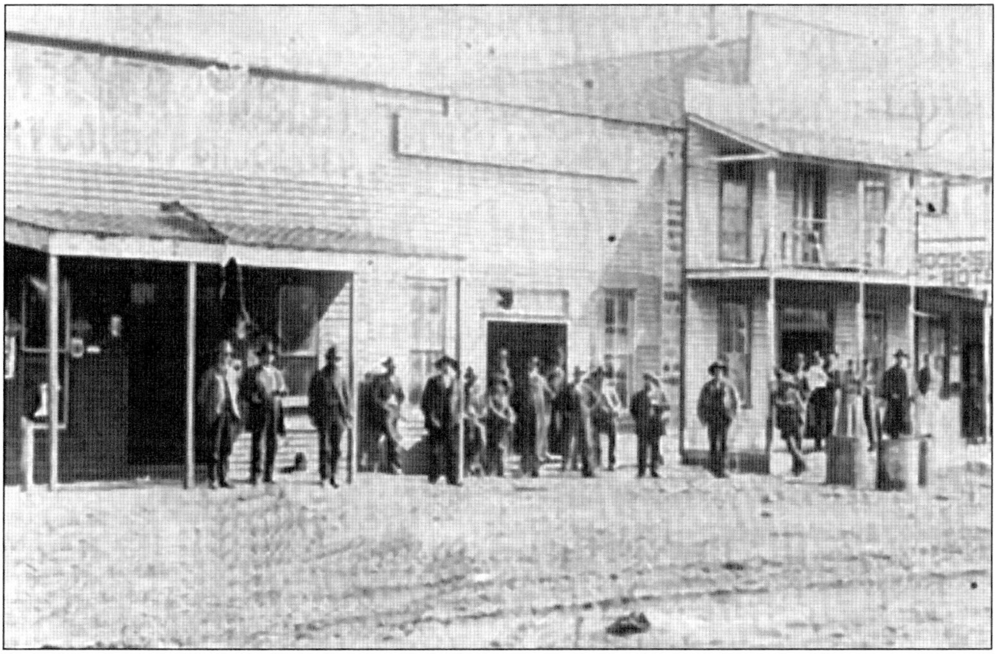

Located on Halsell Street, the Tinsley store was one of Bridgeport's first general stores.

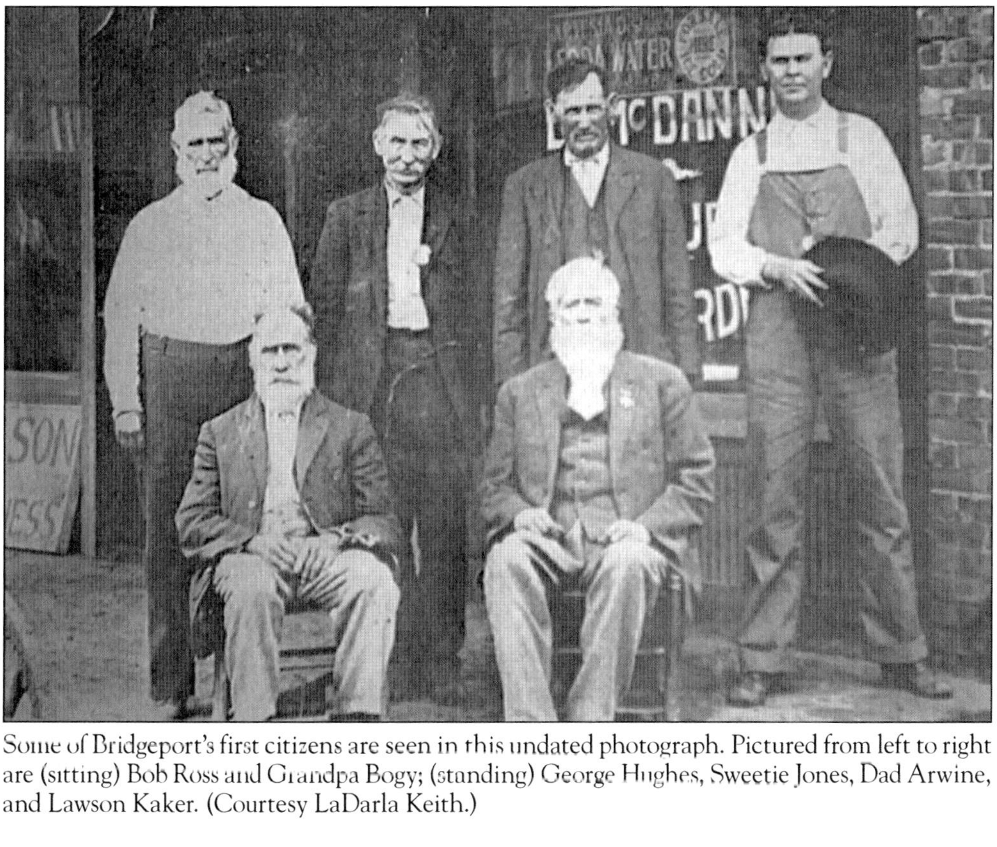

Some of Bridgeport's first citizens are seen in this undated photograph. Pictured from left to right are (sitting) Bob Ross and Grandpa Bogy; (standing) George Hughes, Sweetie Jones, Dad Arwine, and Lawson Kaker. (Courtesy LaDarla Keith.)

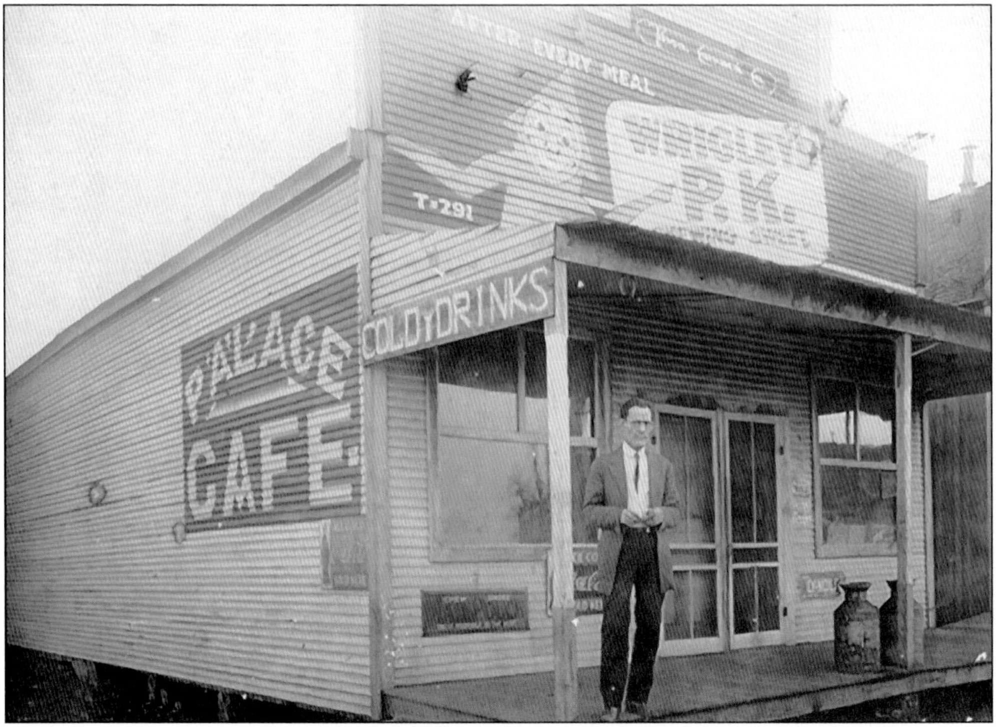

In 1912, a soda and snack could be bought at Sam Easly's store located on the west side.

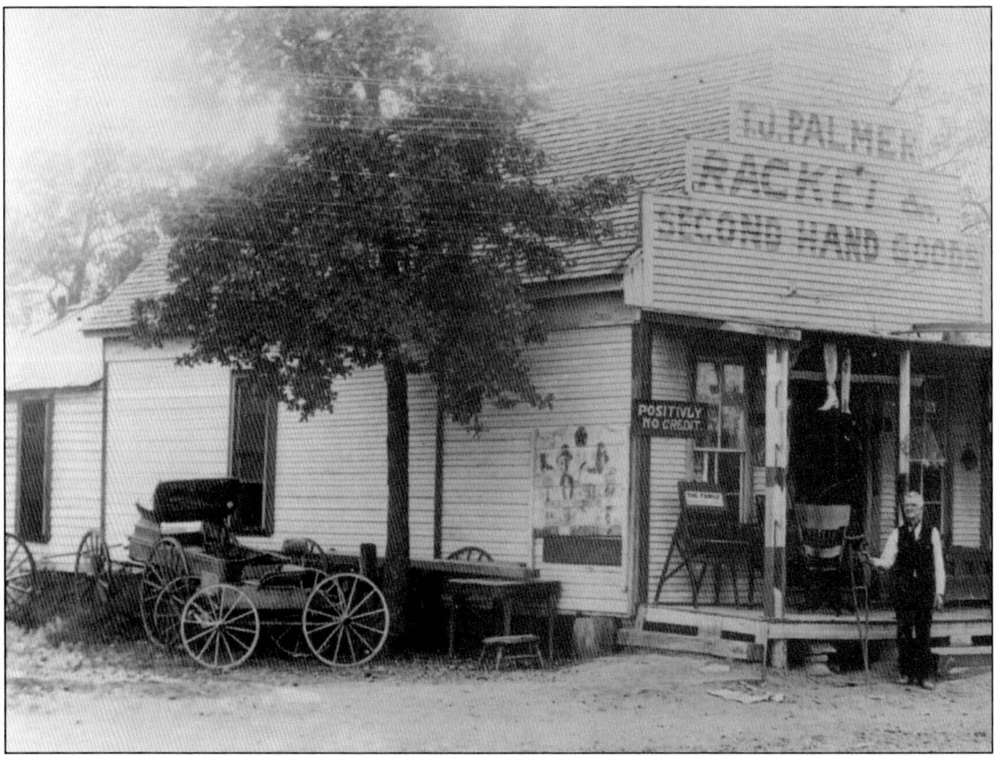

T. J. Palmer, seen here, operated a secondhand store on the west side near the coal company store.

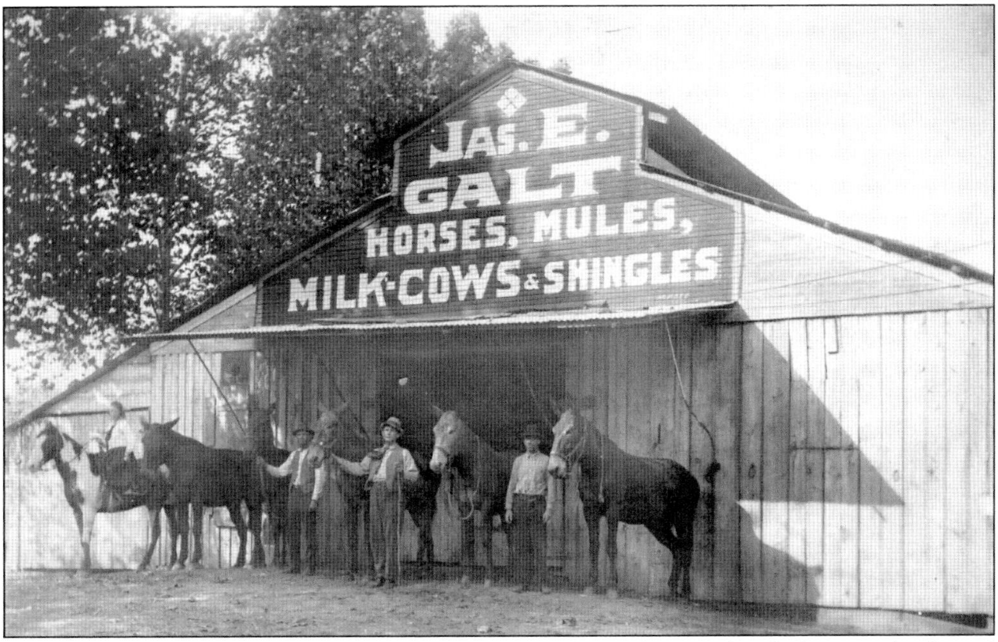

James Galt (center) is seen here trying to make a deal on a low-mileage mule. The horse trader thrived into the 20th century.

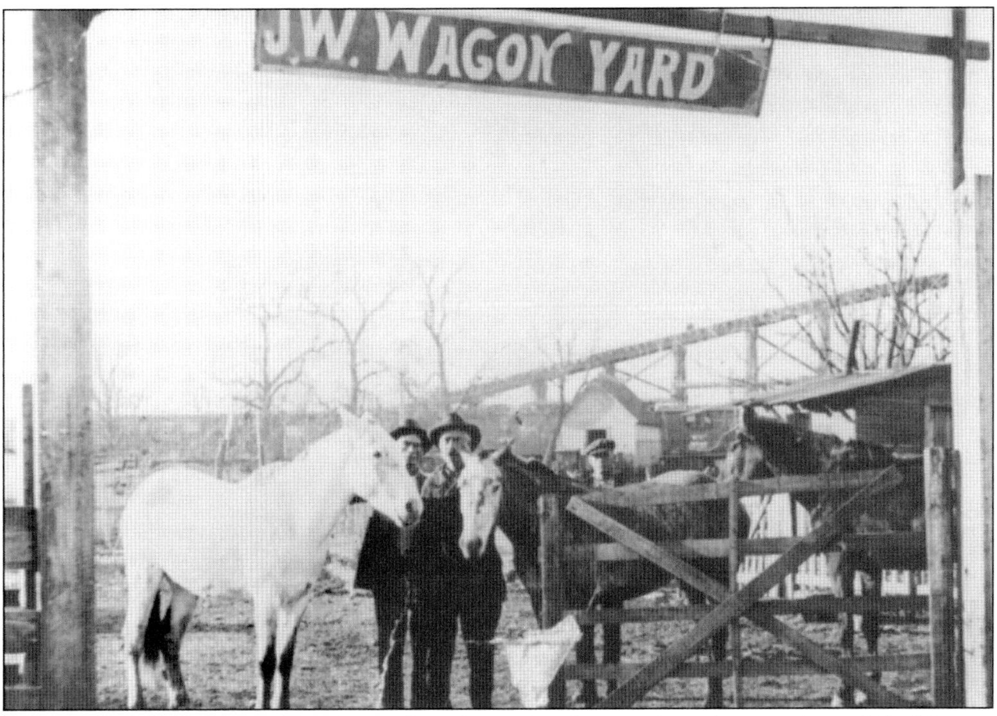

J. W. Morton owned one of the first parking lots in Bridgeport. Seen here in the middle, Morton ran a wagon yard close to where Cates Street and Eighth Street intersect. Whenever folks from the country came to town, they would pay Morton to park their horse-and-buggy in his yard while they conducted business.

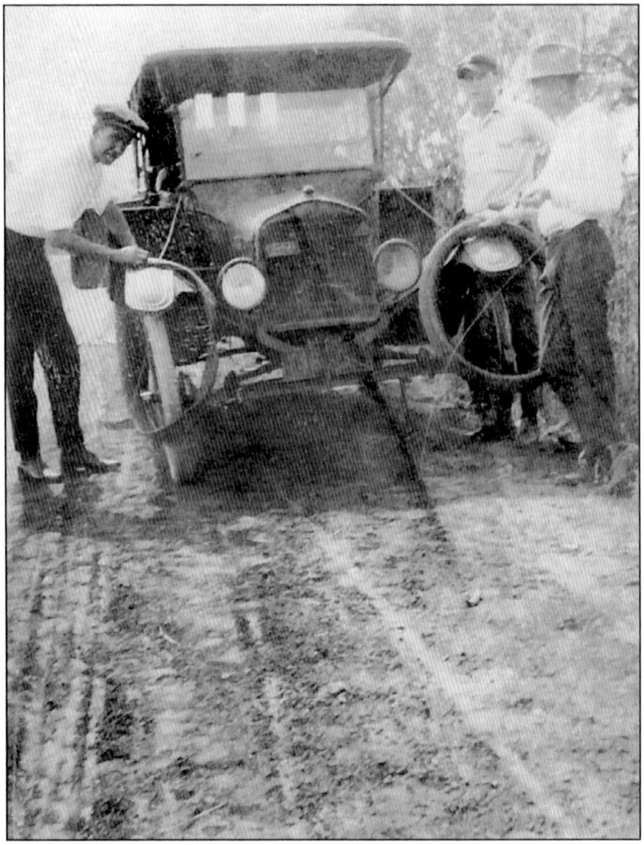

Changing a flat on a Model T Ford was an all-too-frequent occurrence. It is a good thing someone brought some patches along.

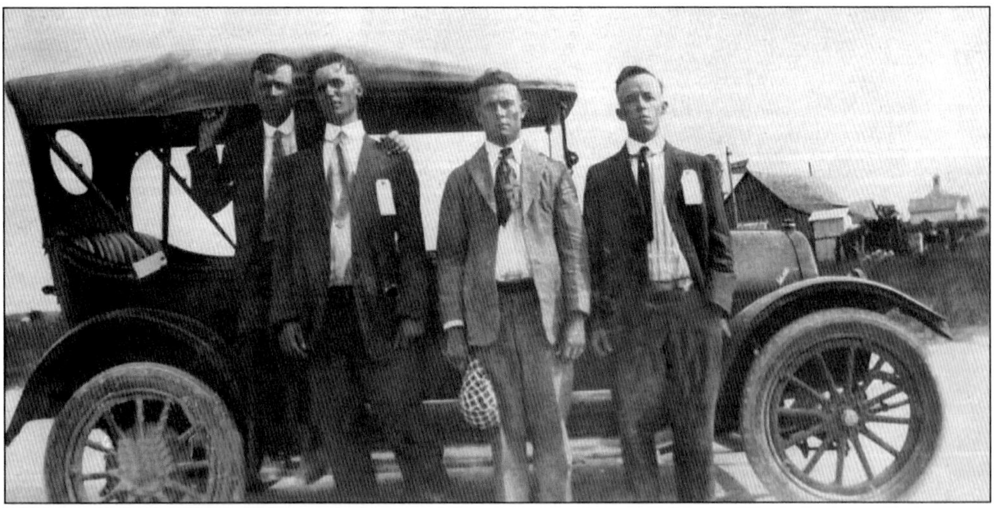

Standing in front of a Model T Roadster are, from left to right, Fernando Raven, unidentified, Sterling Leverett, and Roy Raven.

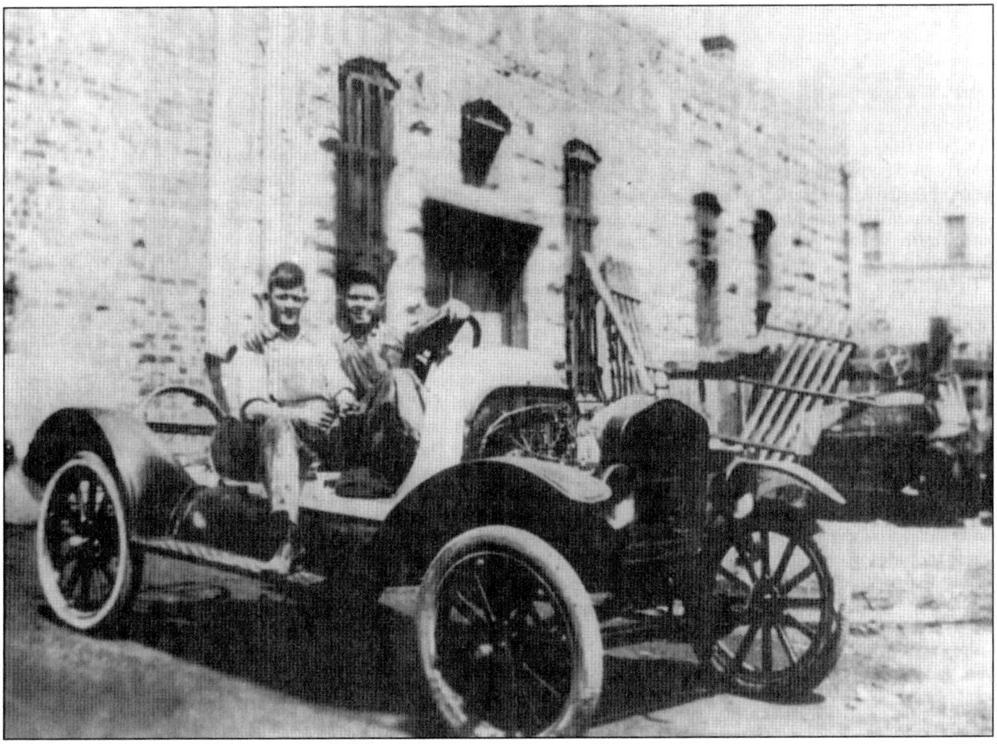

Henry Crawford (left) and an unidentified man are seen working on a Model T in the south alley of the 1000 block of Halsell Street.

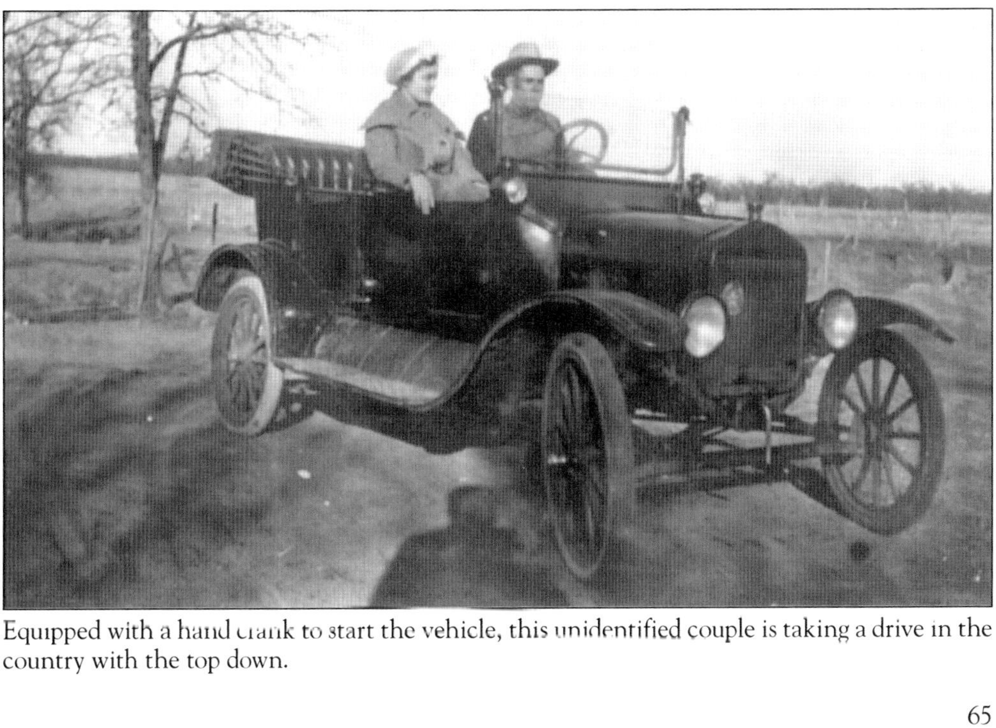

Equipped with a hand crank to start the vehicle, this unidentified couple is taking a drive in the country with the top down.

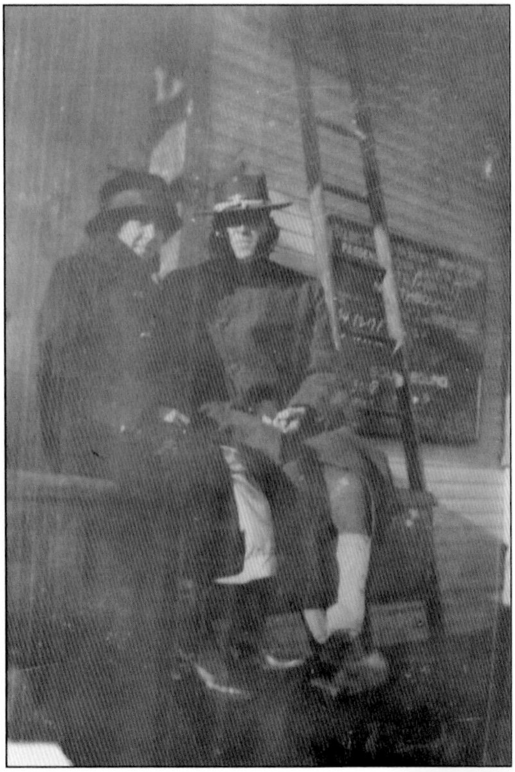

During World War I, many young men from Bridgeport fought in the war, and some never came back. Pictured here is a soldier waiting on the train to return to service.

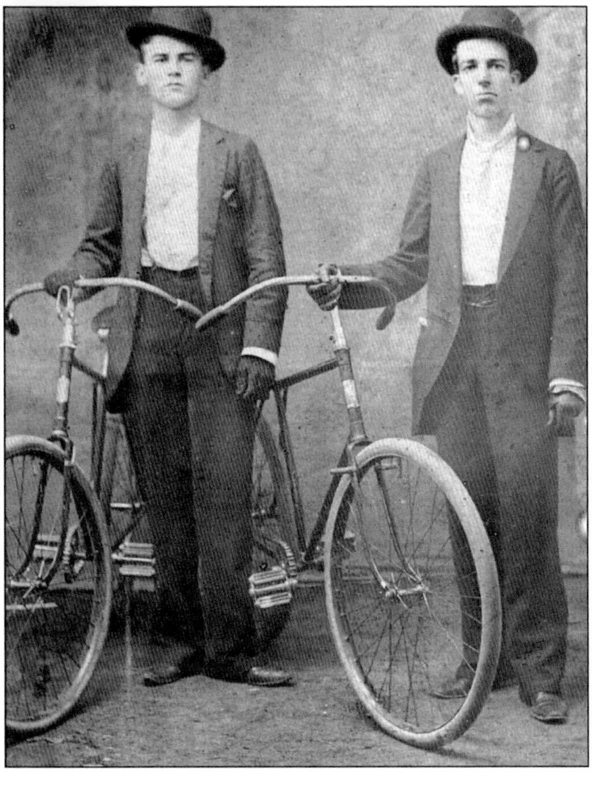

Cousins William Stevens (left) and Henry Leonard were both orphaned at early ages and came to Bridgeport to live with their uncle Bob Stevens in 1892. The boys worked for the Wise County Coal Company and the Coal City Bank as bookkeepers. In 1897, Henry married Natalie Edgar of Weatherford, who was the first music teacher in Bridgeport. William later married Lillian Kirkpatrick who was the daughter of the first mayor of Bridgeport. Stevens and Leonard established a dry goods and grocery store at 1023 Halsell Street and also assumed ownership of the Coal City Bank. (Courtesy Jerry Stevens.)

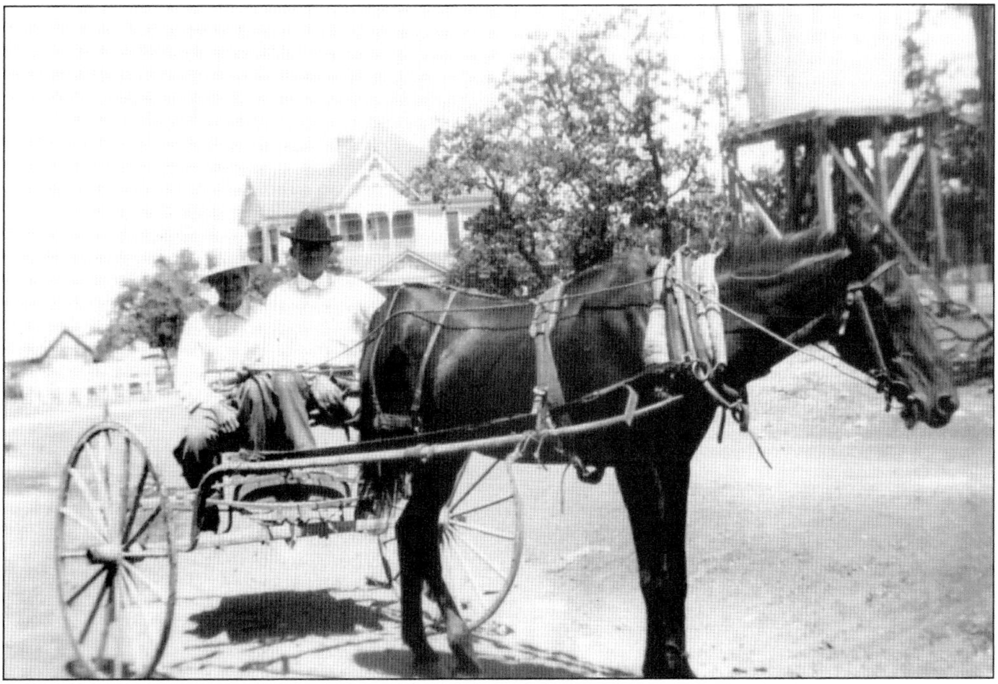

Pictured here is a couple getting around town in a horse and buggy.

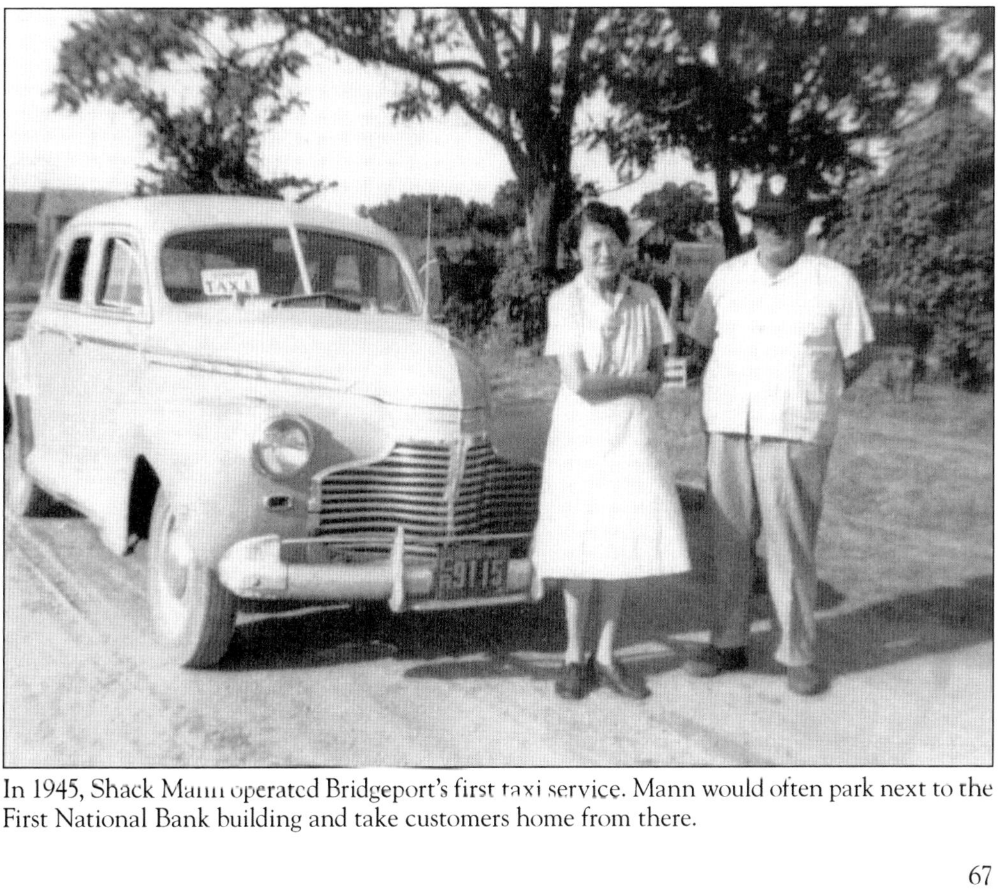

In 1945, Shack Mann operated Bridgeport's first taxi service. Mann would often park next to the First National Bank building and take customers home from there.

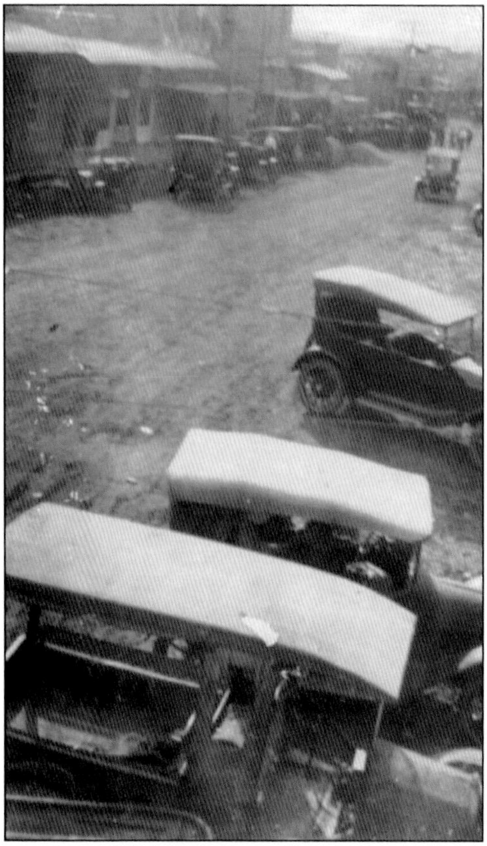

Halsell Street in downtown Bridgeport was bustling with activity in these 1918 photographs.

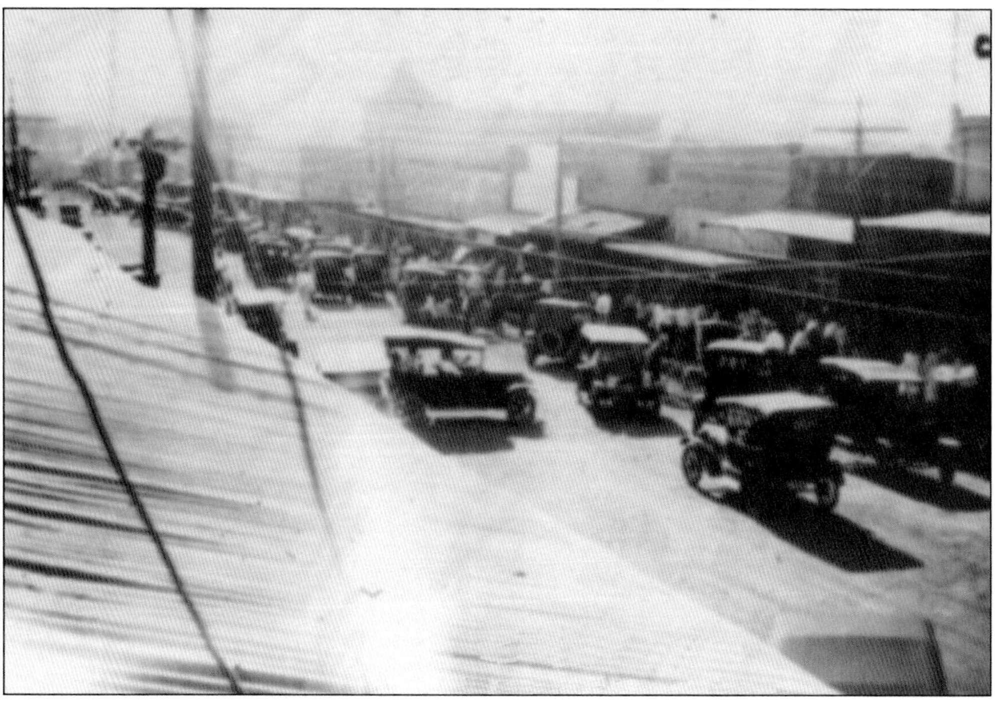

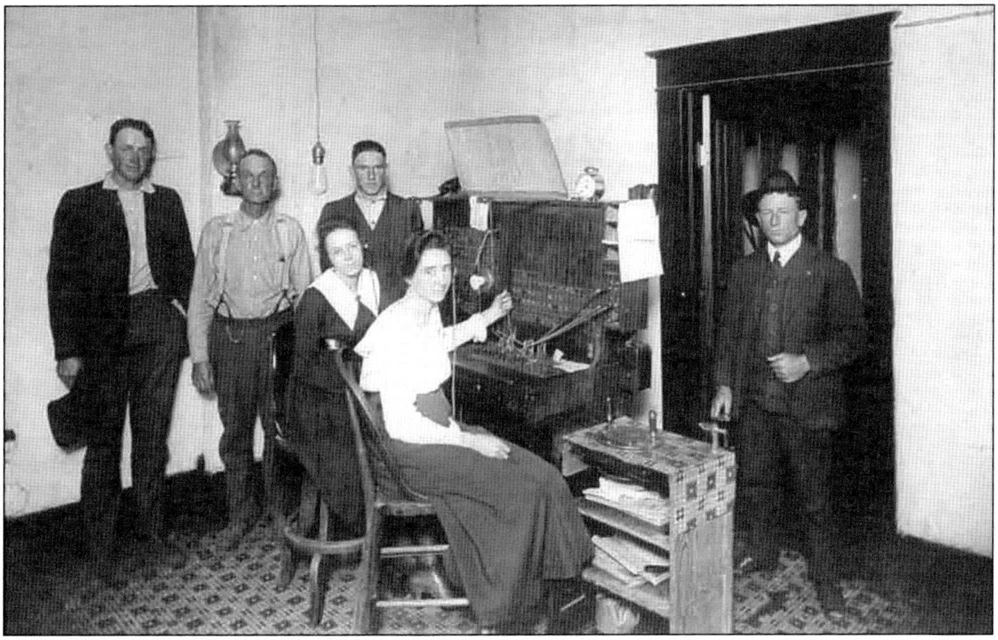

Bridgeport's first telephone switchboard was located above the First National Bank building. Standing from left to right are Oscar Raven, George Raven, Guy Smith, and S. G. Smith, who are visiting operators Mae Smith (front) and Della Raven.

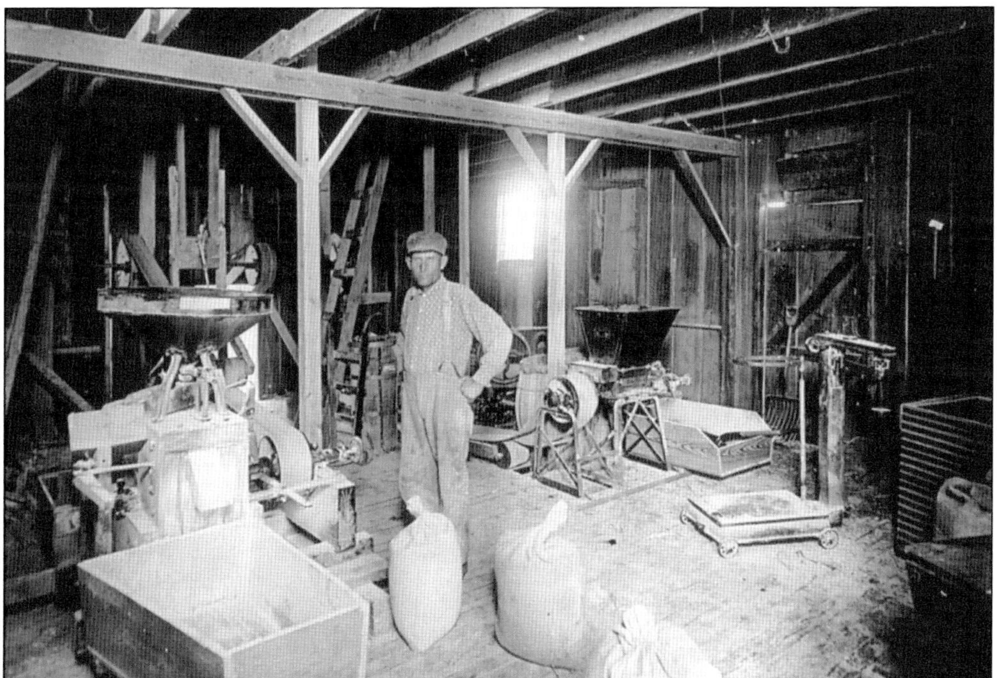

Pictured here in 1921 is William Tackel working in the feed mill, which was located at 800 Cates and Ninth Streets.

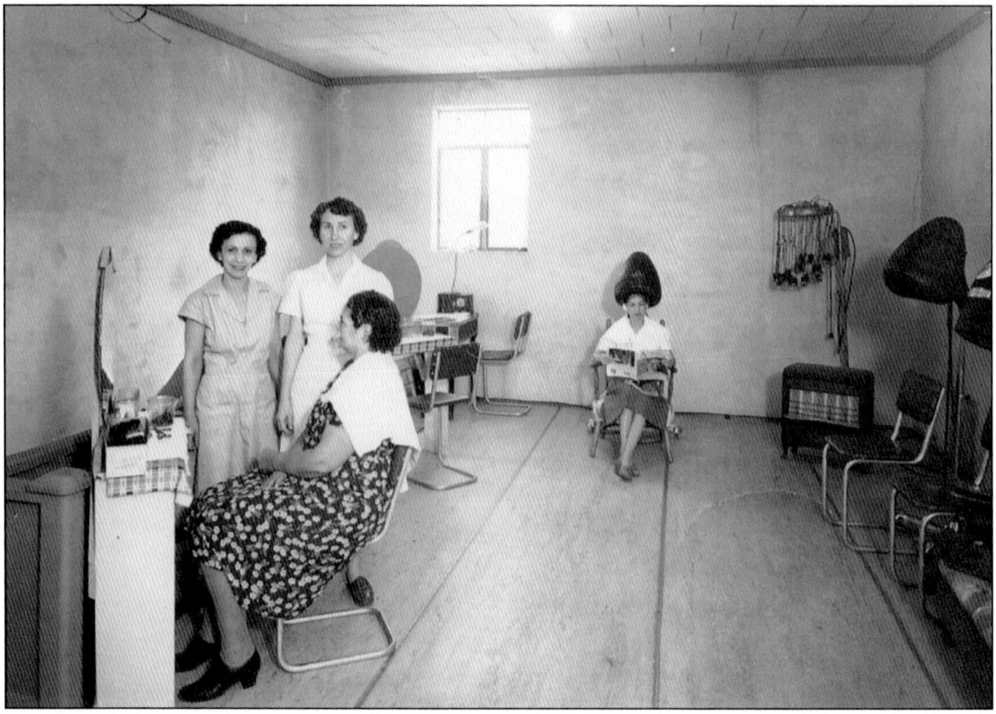

The ladies of Bridgeport always enjoyed getting their hair done at the beauty parlor. This beauty shop was located upstairs over the First National Bank.

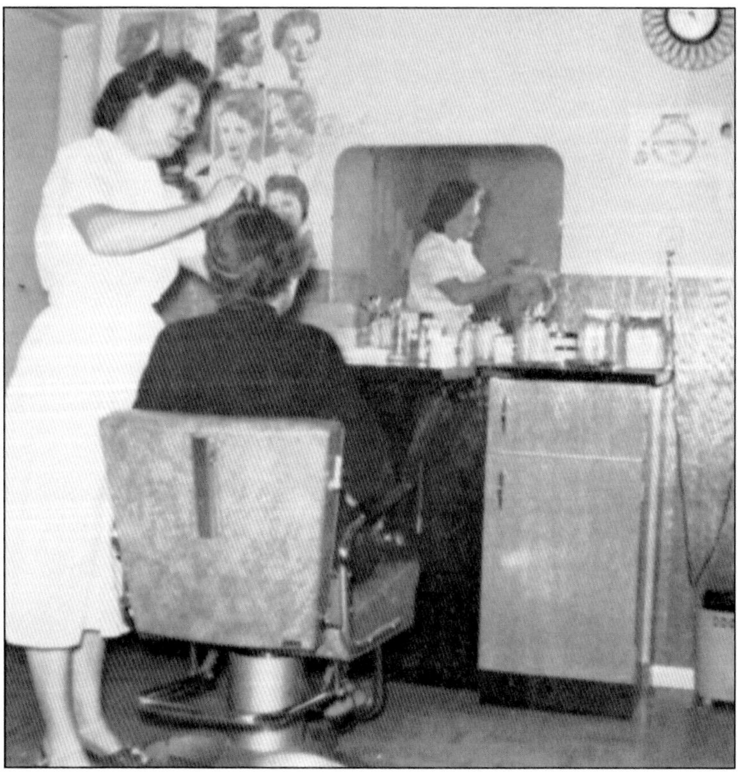

This photograph was taken in Jewel's Beauty Shop.

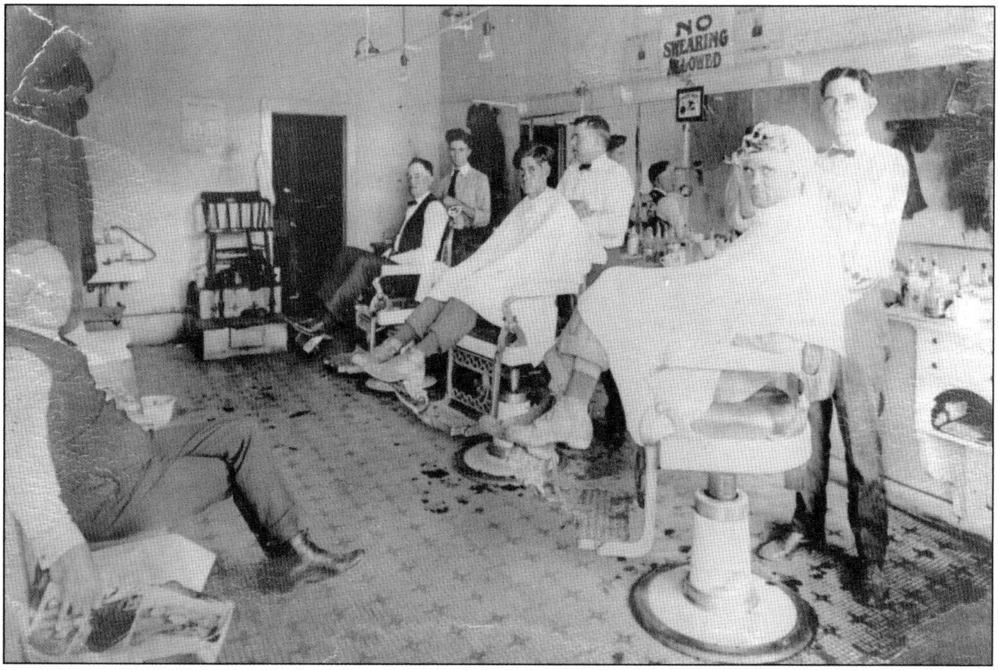

The gentlemen of Bridgeport always relished getting their hair cut at the barbershop. Seen here in the 1920s are, from left to right, Dr. P. C. Funk, Henry Pate, Sinclair Pate, unidentified, Tom Hudson, Earl Ward, and ? Matzinger. (Courtesy Dr. D. C. Sipes.)

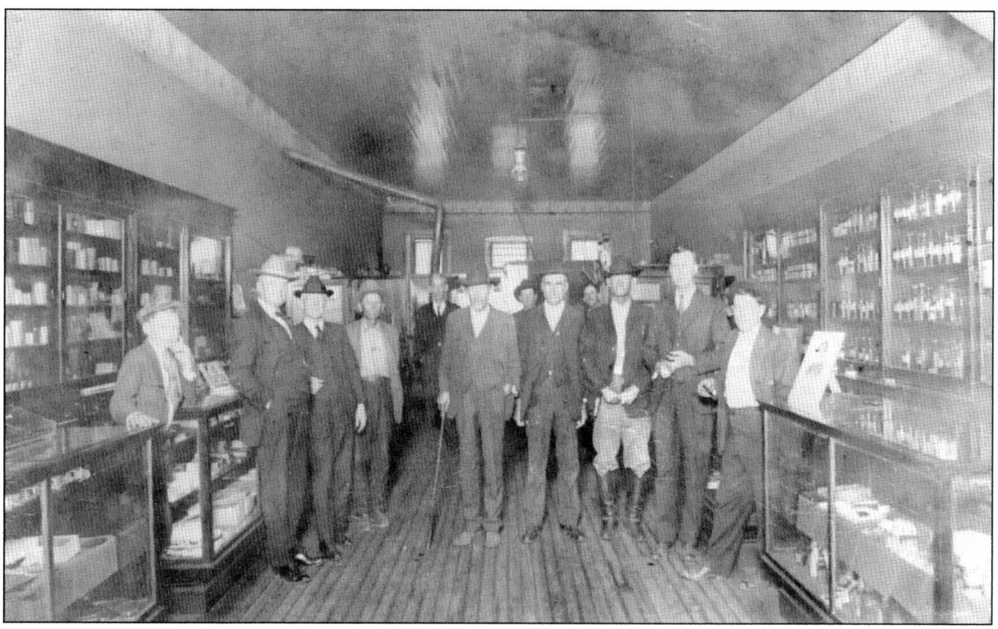

Pictured here in 1915 are, from left to right, Pete Alexander, Walter Bradford, Dr. P. C. Funk, Lee Phillips, Jim Alexander, six unidentified men, and Dr. Braselton inside the Alexander Drug Store located at 1021 Halsell Street. (Courtesy Dr. D. C. Sipes.)

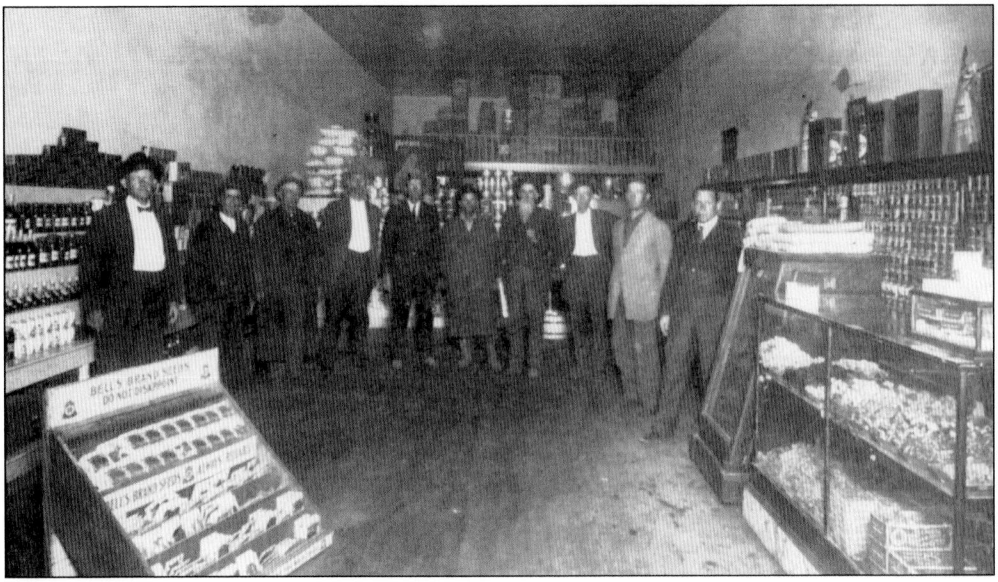

In this 1920s photograph, customers in the Brown Grocery store are, from left to right, Jake Green, Judge Foster, Jim ?, John McClain, John Thompson, Dave Young, Lee Phillips, Norton ?, Harry Hardy, and W. A. Brown. The store was located at 1005 Halsell Street from 1918 through 1948. (Courtesy Dr. D. C. Sipes.)

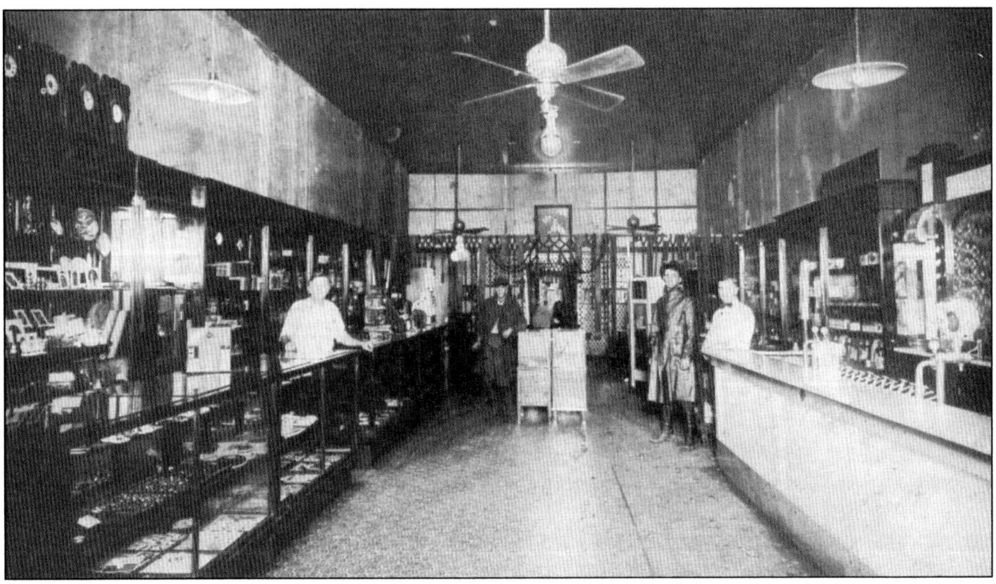

Pictured in the 1920s inside Poore's Jewelry are, from left to right, R. B. Robb, Gene Hoover, Barney Williams, and Oscar Poore. (Courtesy Dr. D. C. Sipes.)

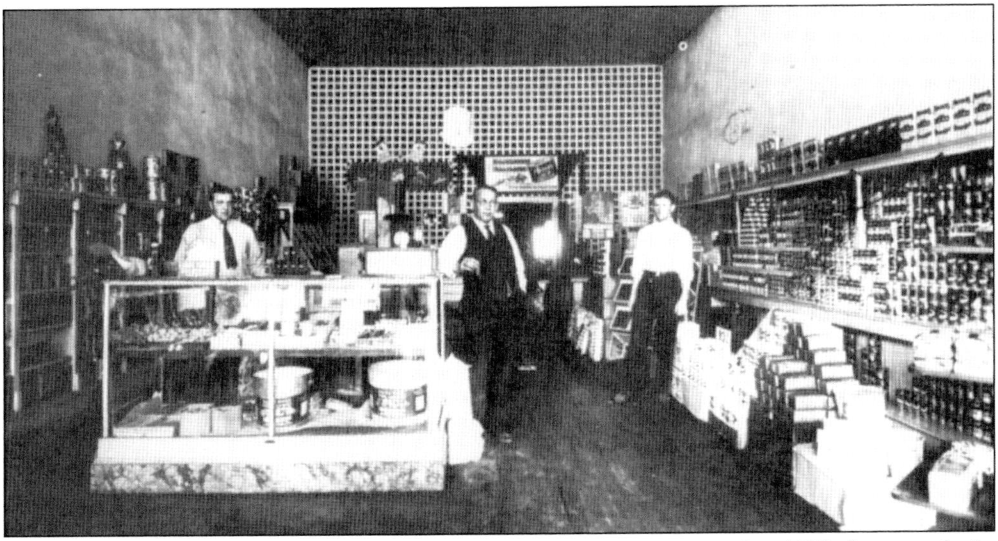

Fully stocked shelves greet customers in the Brown Grocery store in this 1928 photograph. In the photograph are, from left to right, Guy Brown Sr., W. A. Brown, and Red Littler. (Courtesy Dr. D. C. Sipes.)

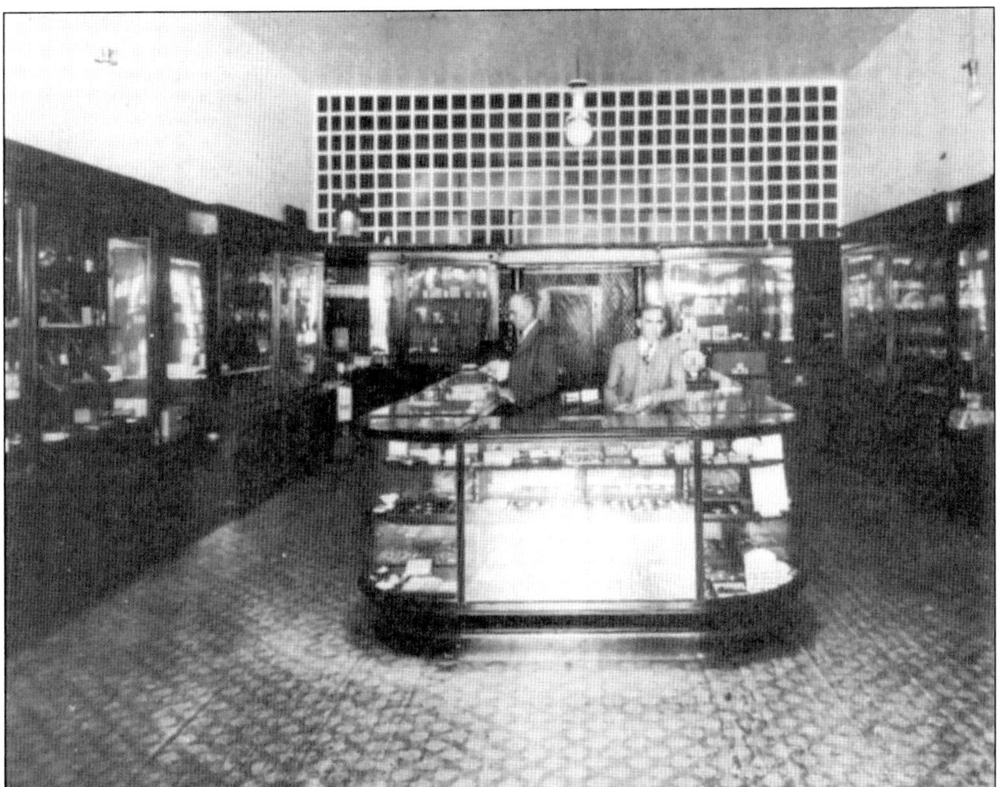

Assorted jewelry items were available in Poore's Jewelry store. Pictured in 1926 are B. B. Poore (left) and Roy Poore. (Courtesy Dr. D. C. Sipes.)

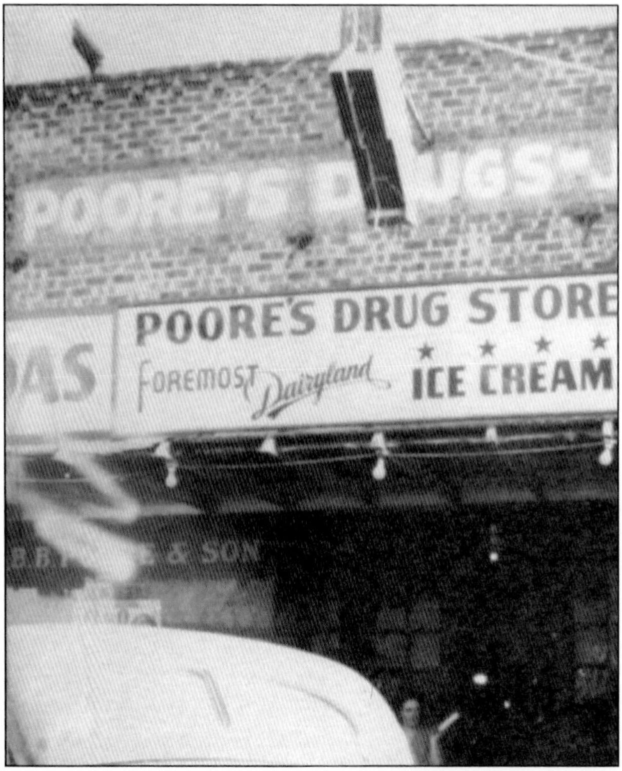

Downtown businesses often competed for customers next door or on the same block. Below is a booth in Poore's Drug Store.

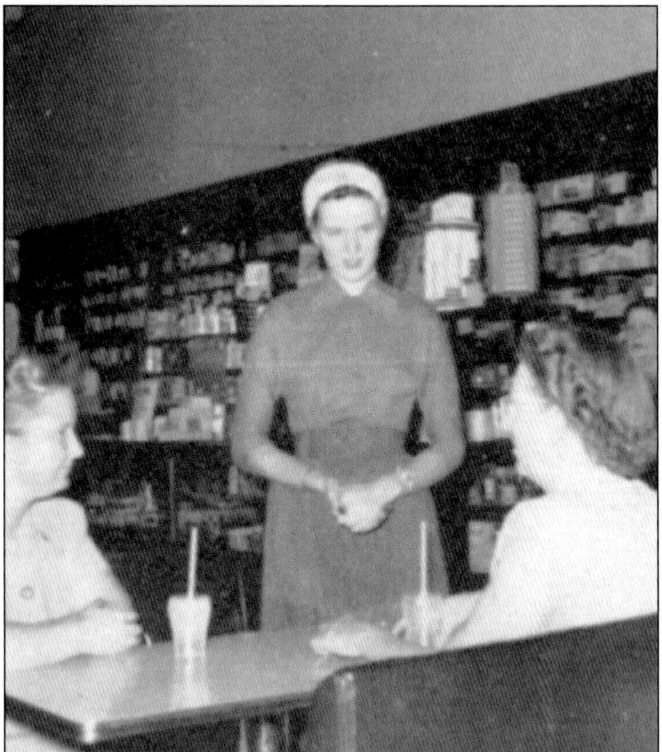

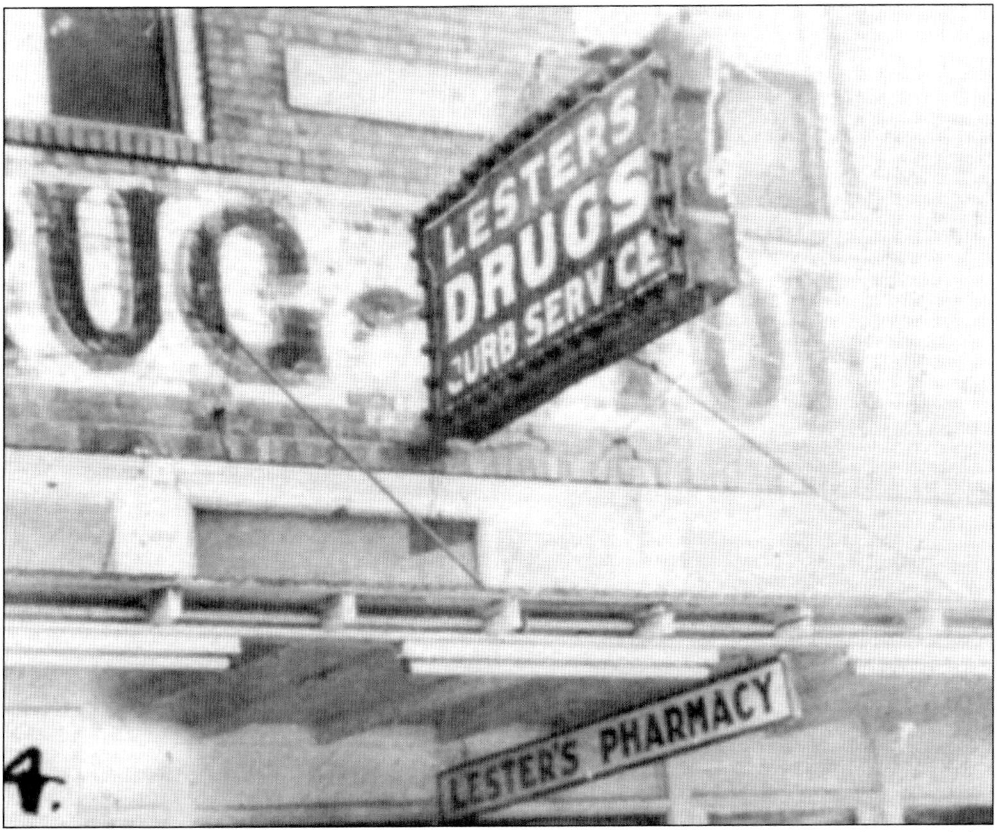

The sign out front of Lester's Drug Store is seen in the image above. Below, employees of the drugstore are depicted in a 1950 photograph.

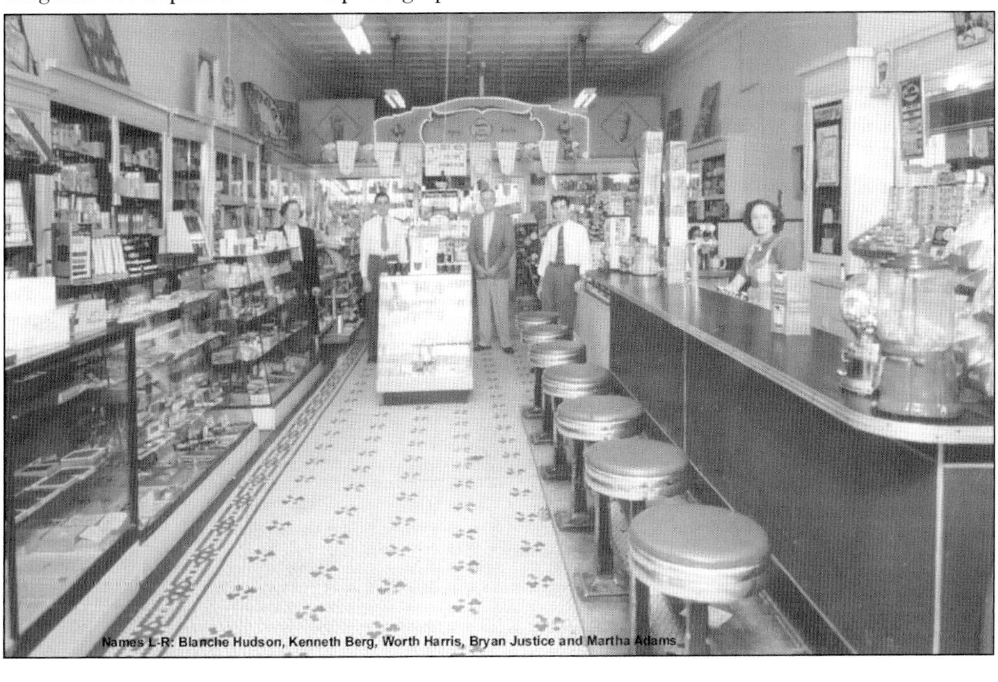

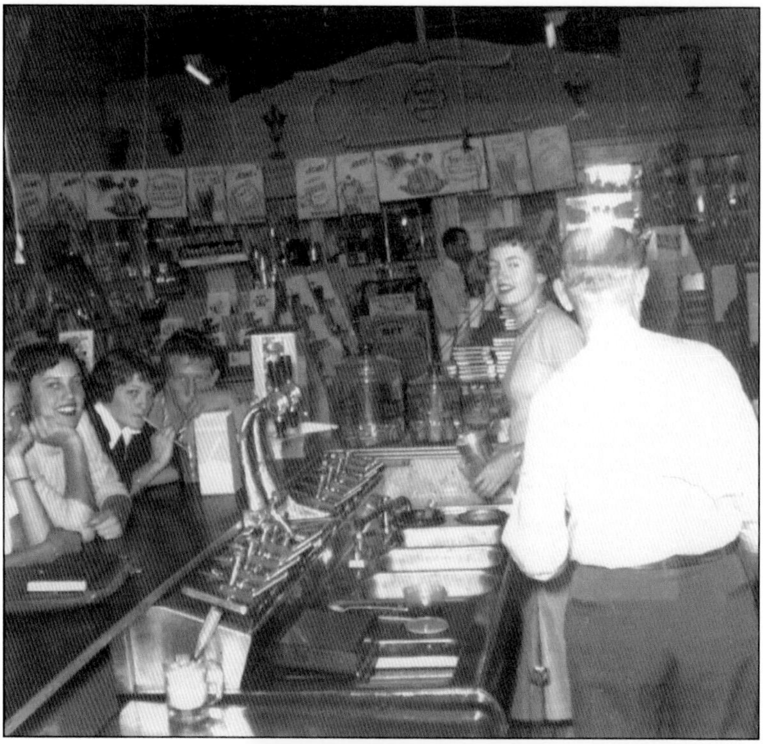

In this 1952 photograph of Lester's, Worth Harris watches Myrle Harlan Duncan mix a malt for her friends at the counter, from left to right, Joanne Shanks Beneke, Allene Garrett Cheves, and Walton Cox Gasaway. The man in the background is Bryan Justice. (Courtesy Joanne Shanks Beneke.)

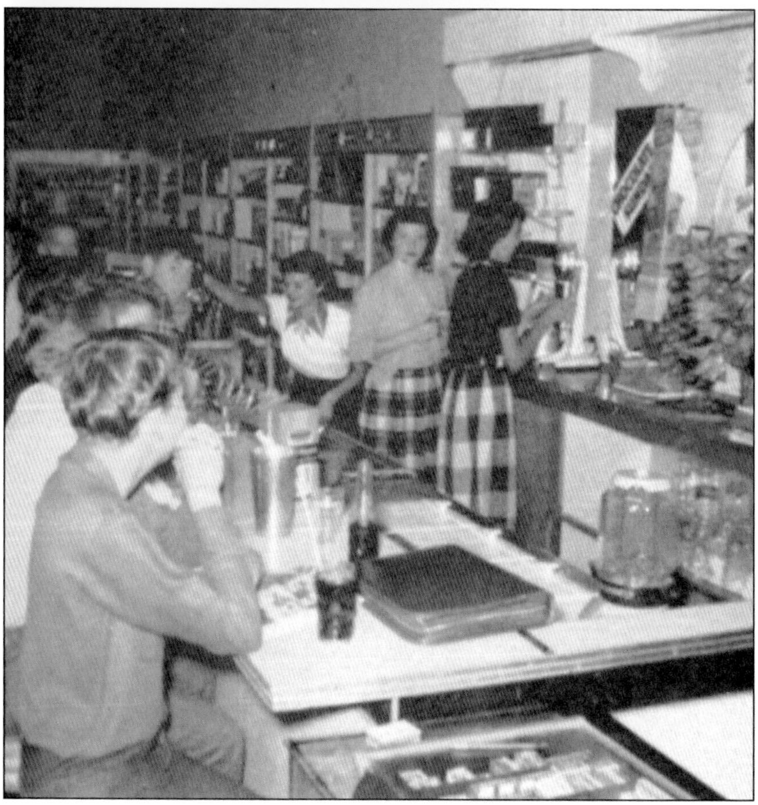

Lester's was a favorite place to gather after school.

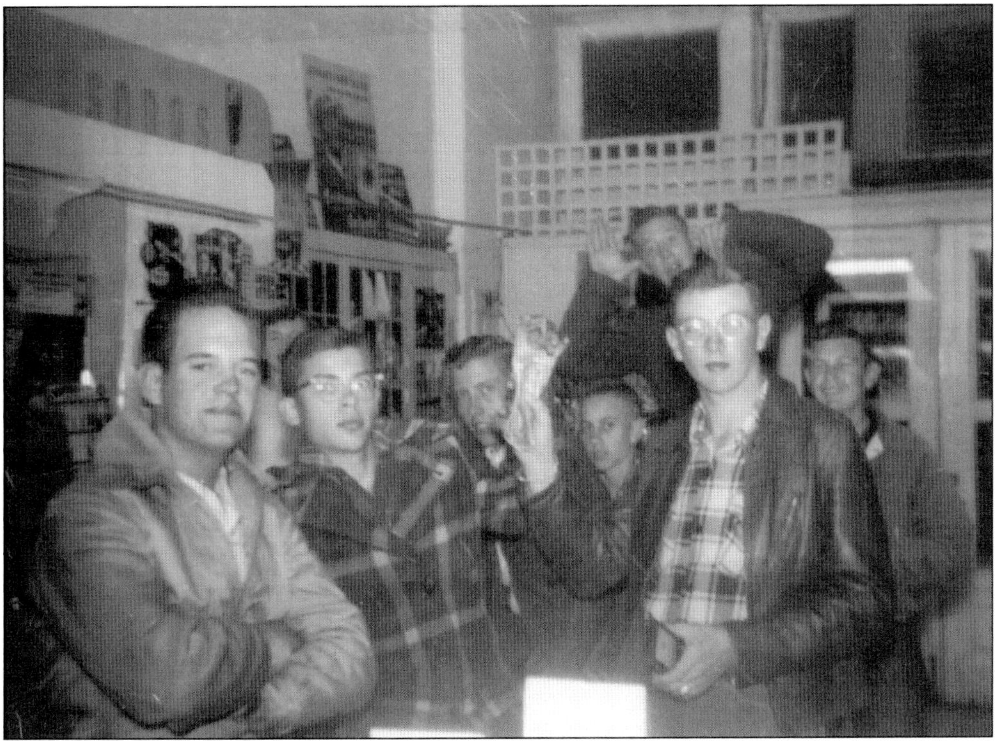

Pictured here in 1952 from left to right are Gilbert Shawn, George Favaron, Lawrence Holley, Carl Jones, Leon Foreman, R. L. Groves (holding an item), and James Orr. These students were regular after-school visitors at Lester's.

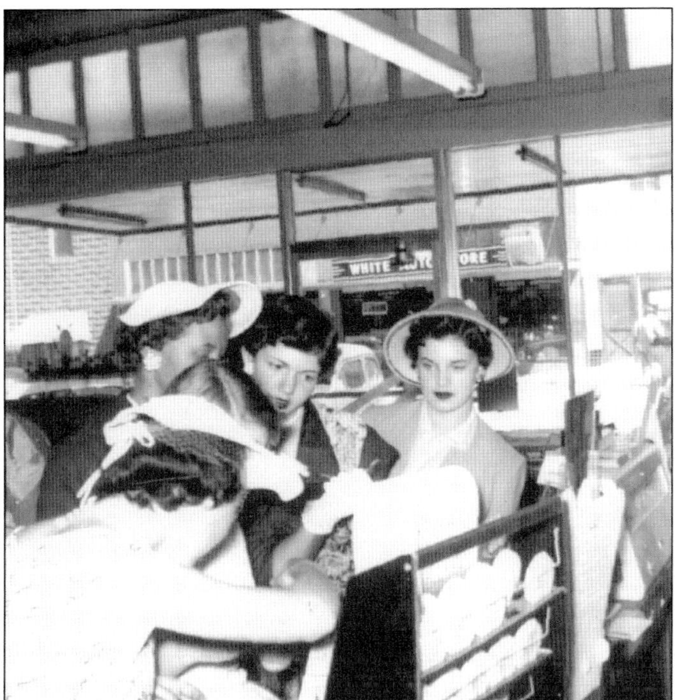

Lester's was also a favorite meeting place on Sundays after church. Pictured here from left to right are Amy Kaker, Linda Turner, Betty Reaves, Roberta Mann Nimmo, and Joanne Shanks Beneke. (Courtesy Joanne Shanks Beneke.)

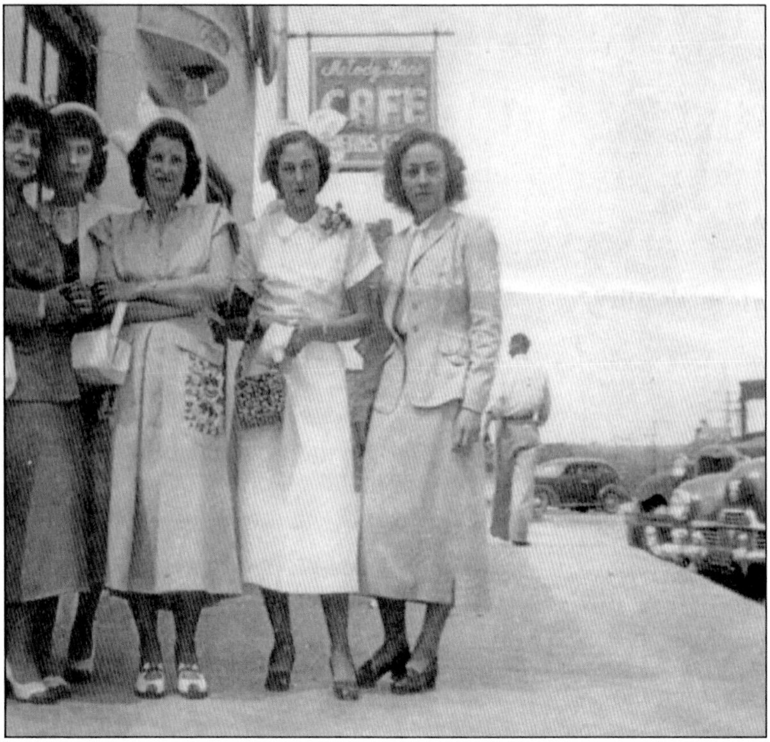

The Melody Cafe was located where the Bridgeport Index is currently located. Pictured here in 1950 are, from left to right, Betty Carlton, Helen Morrison, Dorothy Pierce, Trula Jo Jones, and Nelda Raven.

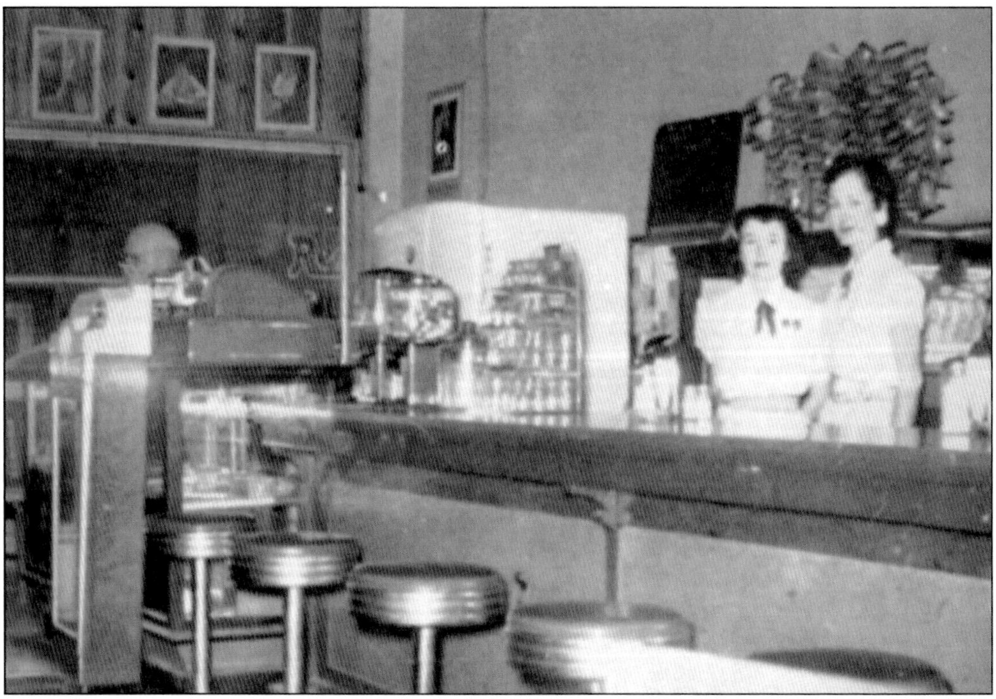

Located next to the Arcadia Theatre at 1019 Halsell Street, the Minute Coffee shop was a favorite breakfast and lunch establishment. In 1958, the cafe was a total loss as a result of a fire.

Bridgeport proudly announced the opening of its new hospital.

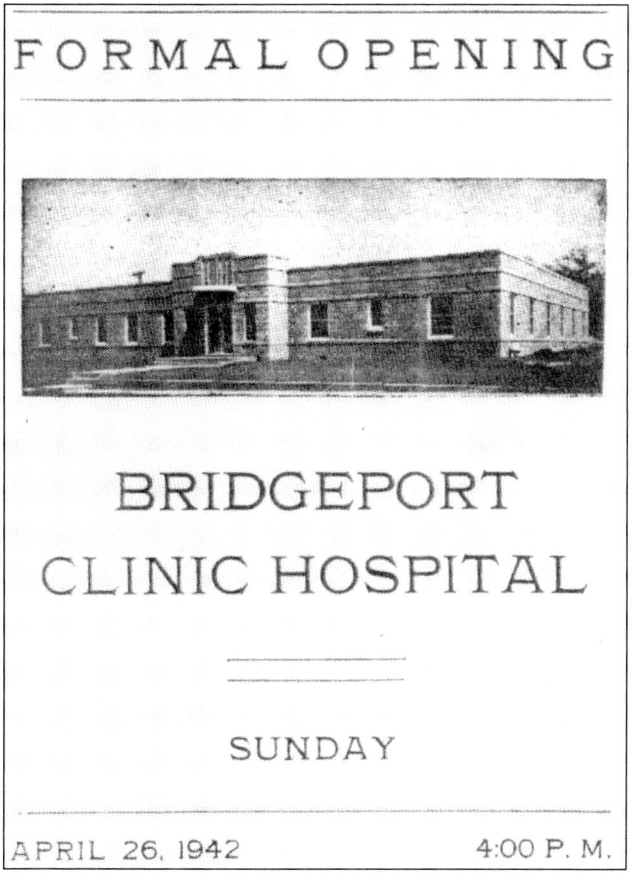
FORMAL OPENING

BRIDGEPORT
CLINIC HOSPITAL

SUNDAY

APRIL 26, 1942 4:00 P. M.

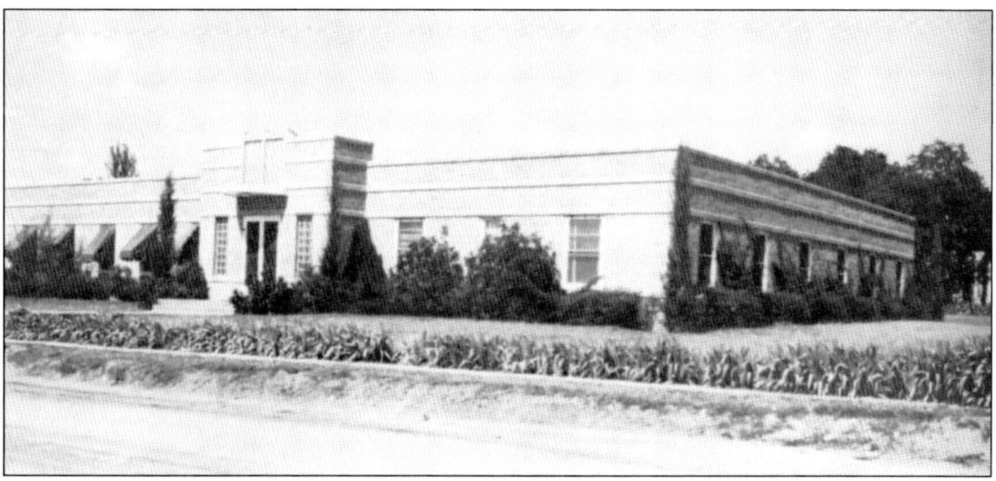

The hospital was located on the northeast corner of Halsell and Thirteenth Streets where the post office is today.

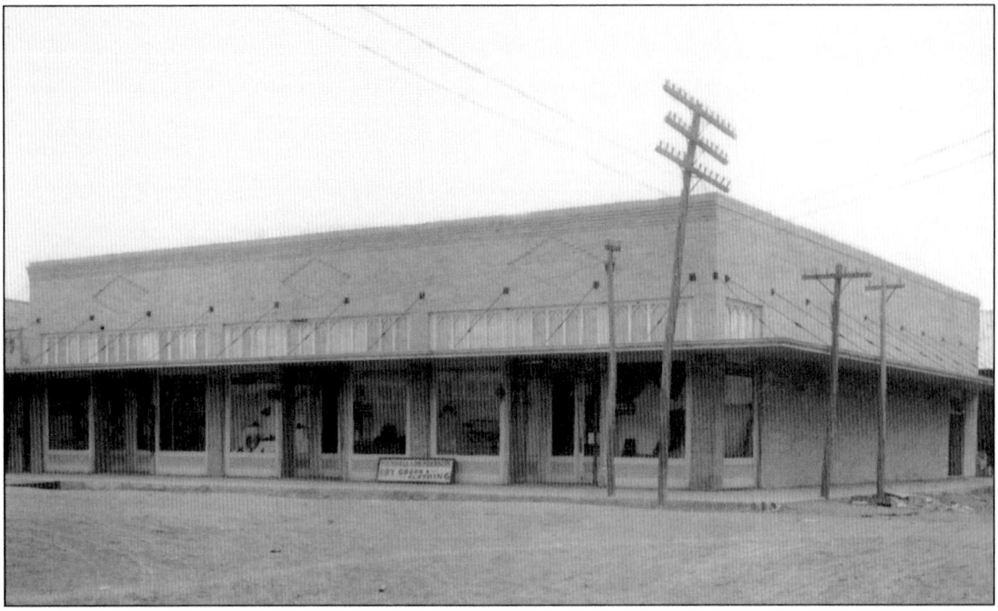

The Kendall and Henderson dry goods and clothing store occupied the new building at the corner of Halsell and Tenth Streets, west of the First National Bank building. The Kaker Brothers Grocery store occupies the corner space.

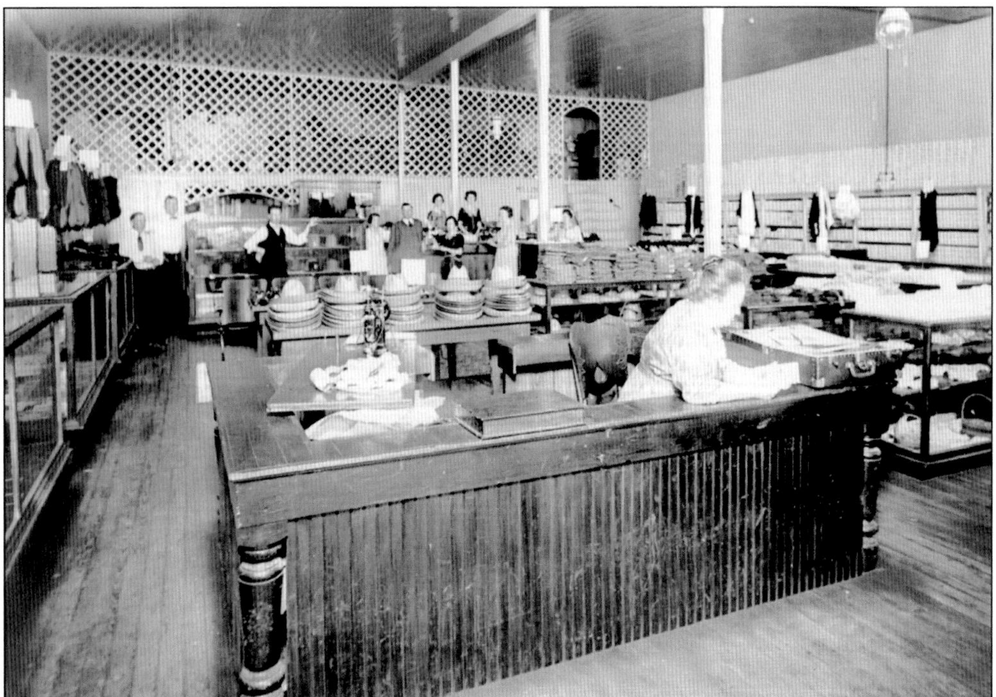

This 1920s photograph shows the inside of the Kendall and Henderson dry goods and clothing store. (Courtesy Leroy Taylor.)

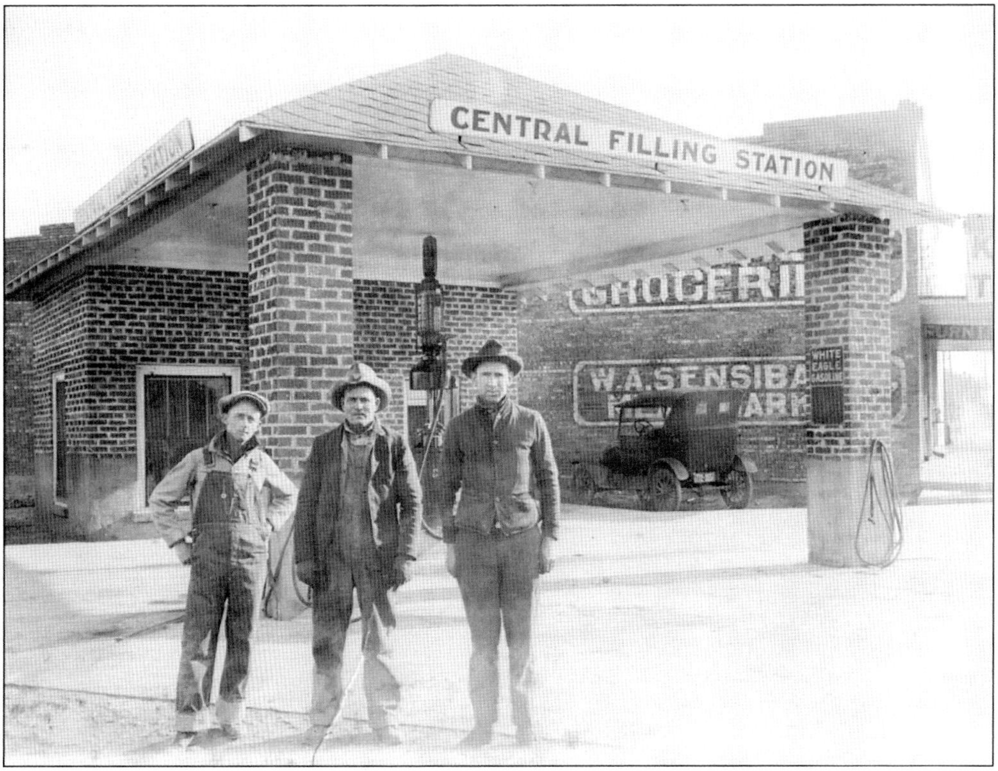

The Central Filling Station was located at 1101–1103 Halsell Street. The only man in this 1927 photograph that can be identified is George McCleary (center). McCleary later opened another gasoline station in the 600 block of Halsell Street.

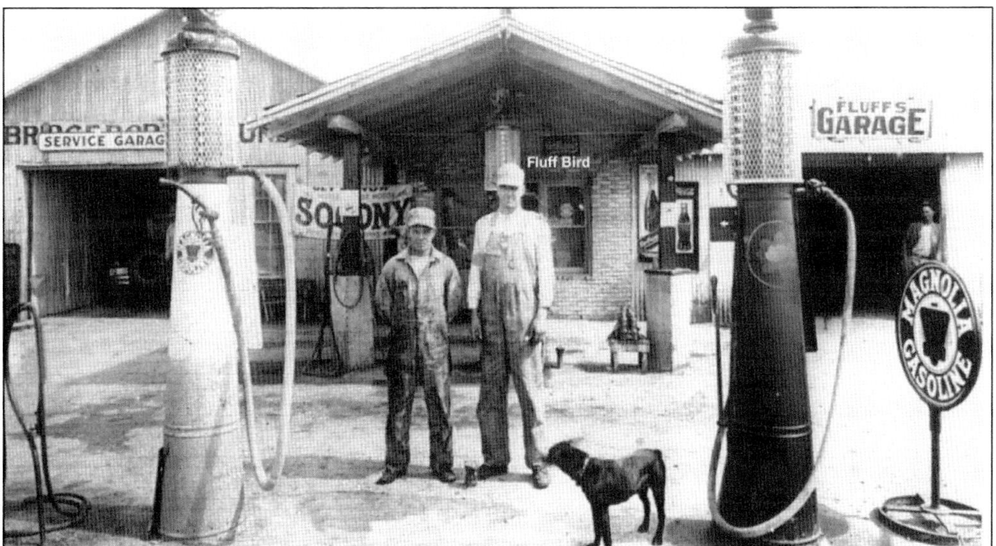

Service stations have been in town as long as there have been automobiles. Owner Fluff Bird (right) stands ready to help motorists with any automobile needs.

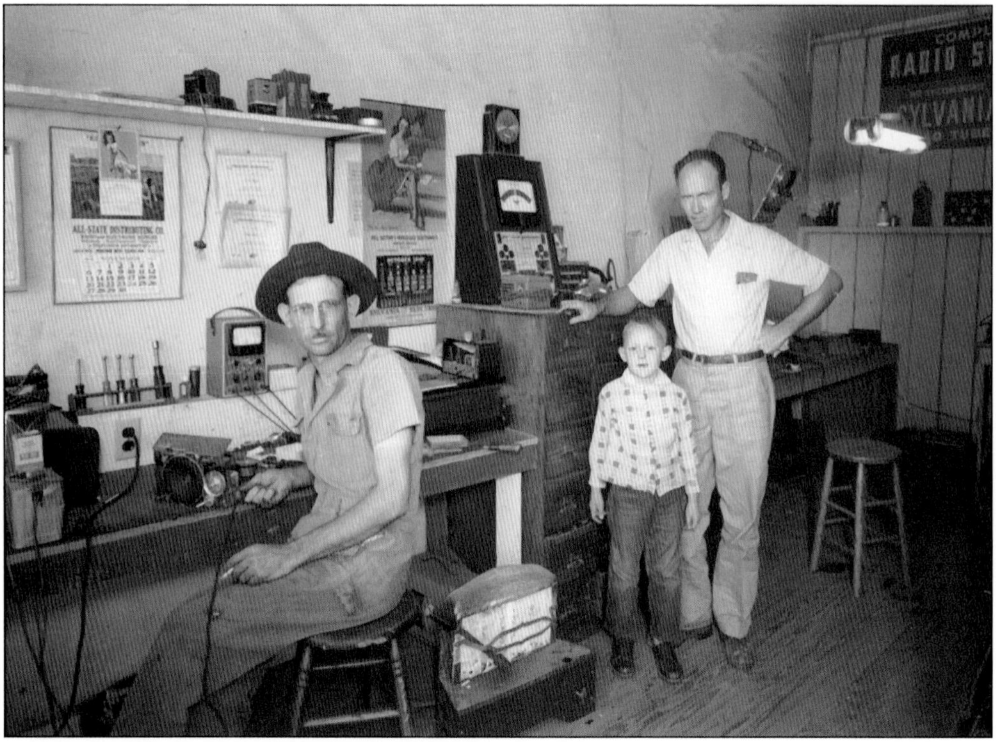

In this 1948 photograph, William Tackel (left) and Valdon Pyeatt, with son Don Pyeatt, are seen repairing radios. This was in the radio era before television.

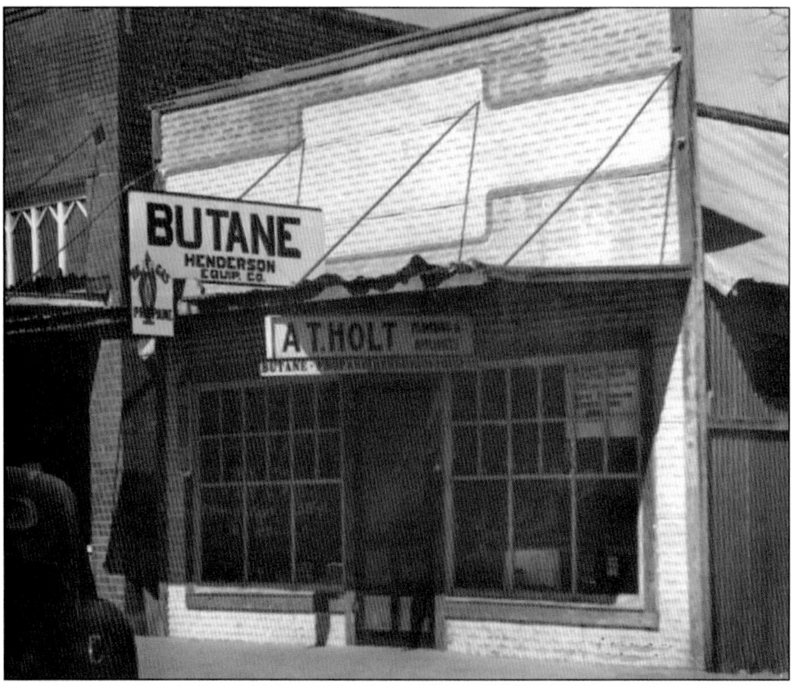

The Holt Plumbing store was later located in the same building that the Pyeatt Radio Shop occupied.

This is a picture of Ernest Jones, and his wife, Willie, in their hardware store.

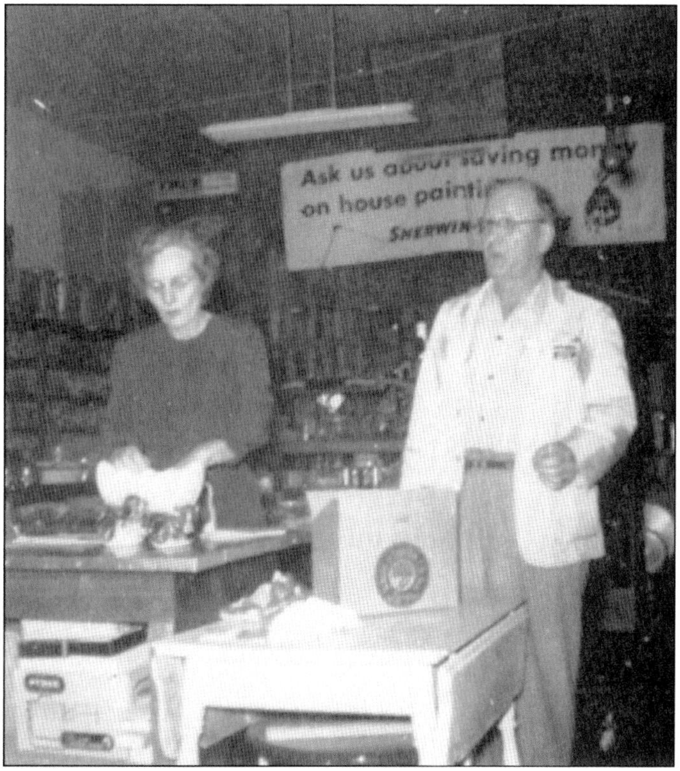

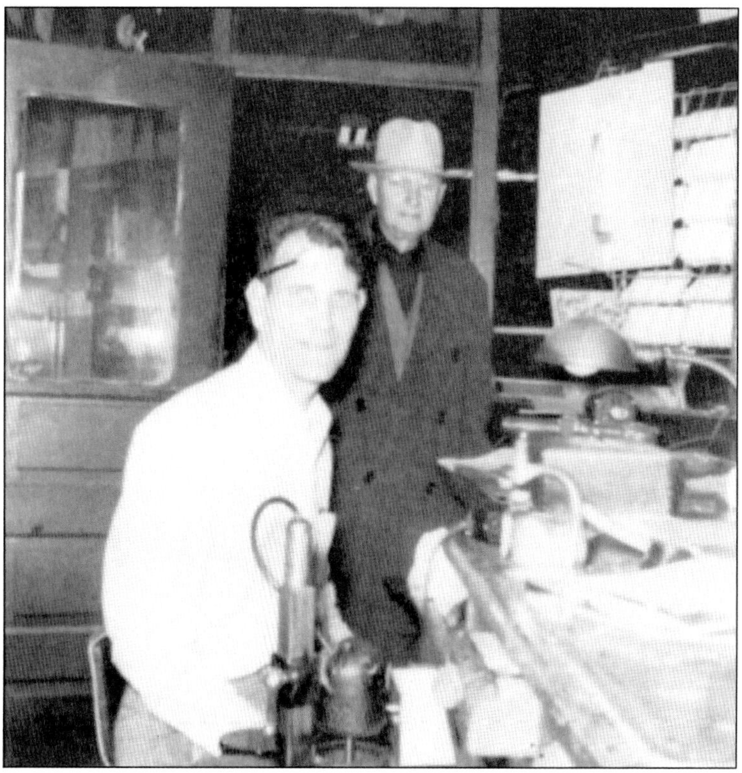

Ross Montford (front) was a jeweler who had a small repair shop in Lester's Drug Store. He was a third-generation Montford whose grandfather farmed south of the old town of Bridgeport. Many railroad employees brought their watches to Montford to certify their accuracy.

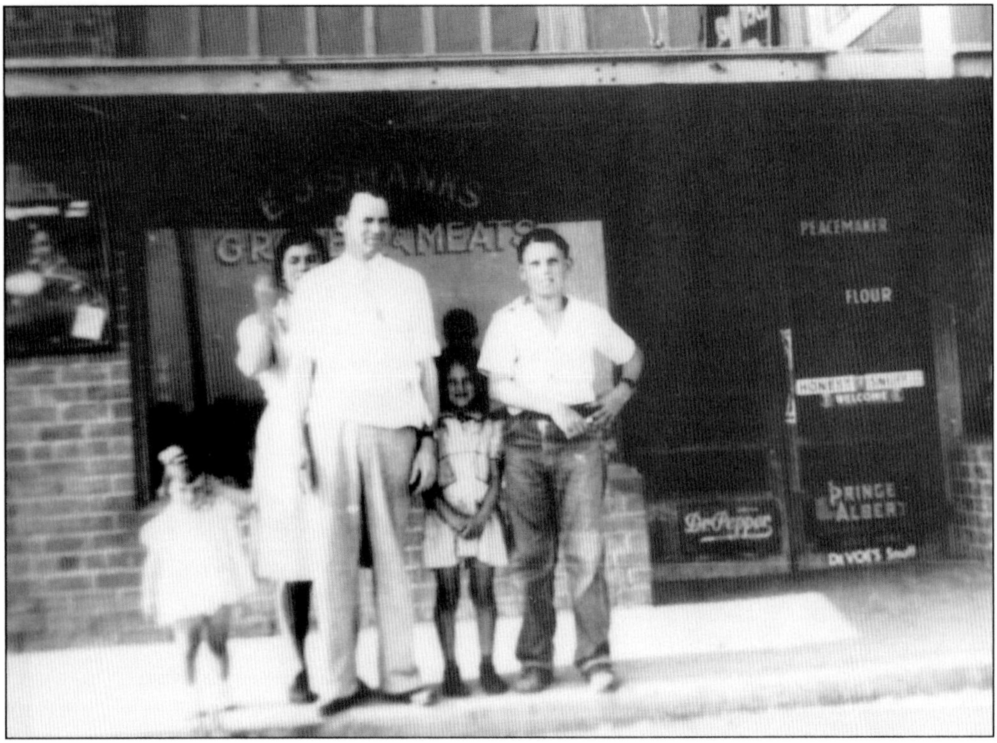

Through the years, many small, family-owned grocery and convenience stores could be found in Bridgeport. In this 1943 photograph, the Shanks family stands in front of their store, Shanks Grocery. The family members are, from left to right, Jackie Shanks Davis, Dema Shanks, E. J. Shanks, Joanne Shanks Beneke, and Gene Shanks. (Courtesy Joanne Shanks Beneke.)

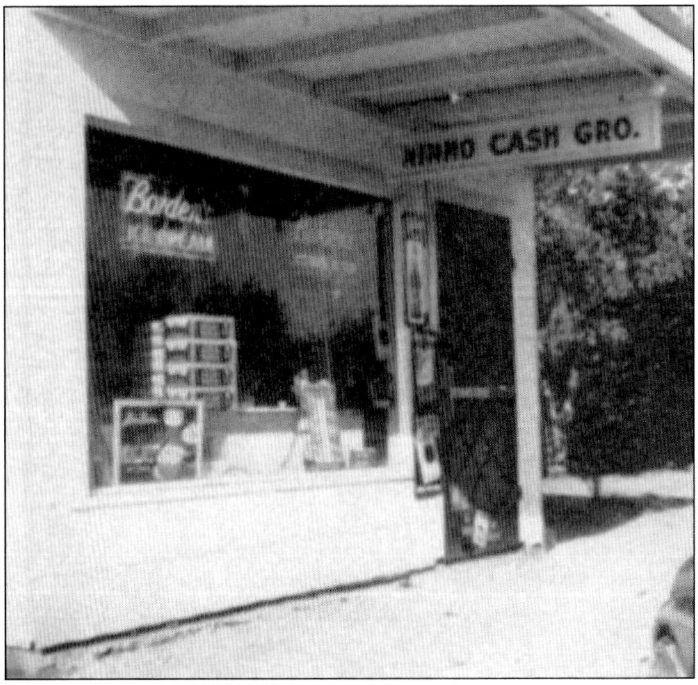

The family-owned and -operated Nimmo Grocery store was located on Halsell Street next to the Star Garage.

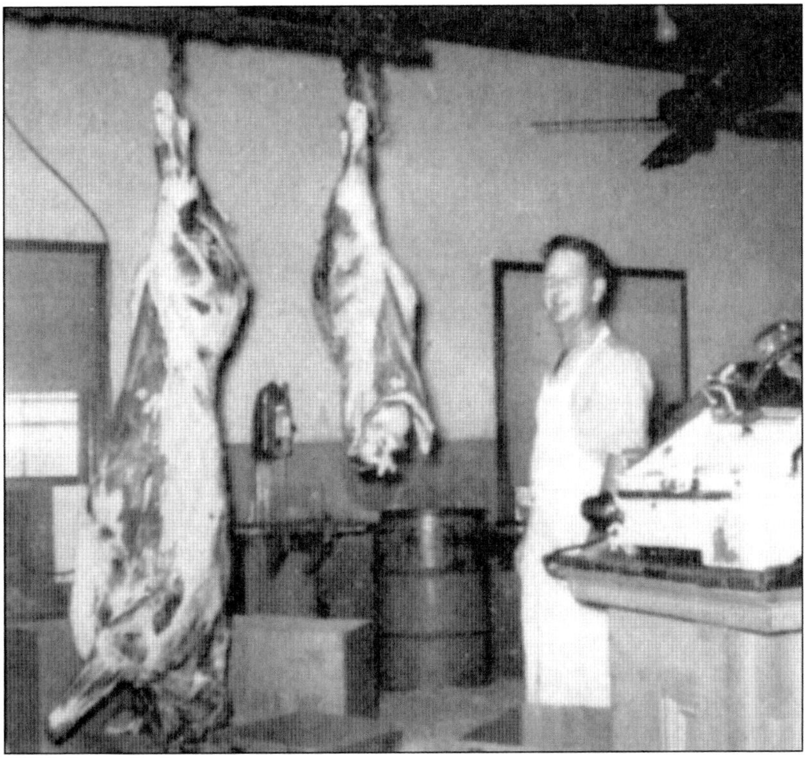

Earl Fagg owned the Zero Food Locker located on Stevens Street. Local residents could rent a drawer in a walk-in freezer and store their meat there until needed. Fagg also served as a butcher and prepared cuts of meat daily.

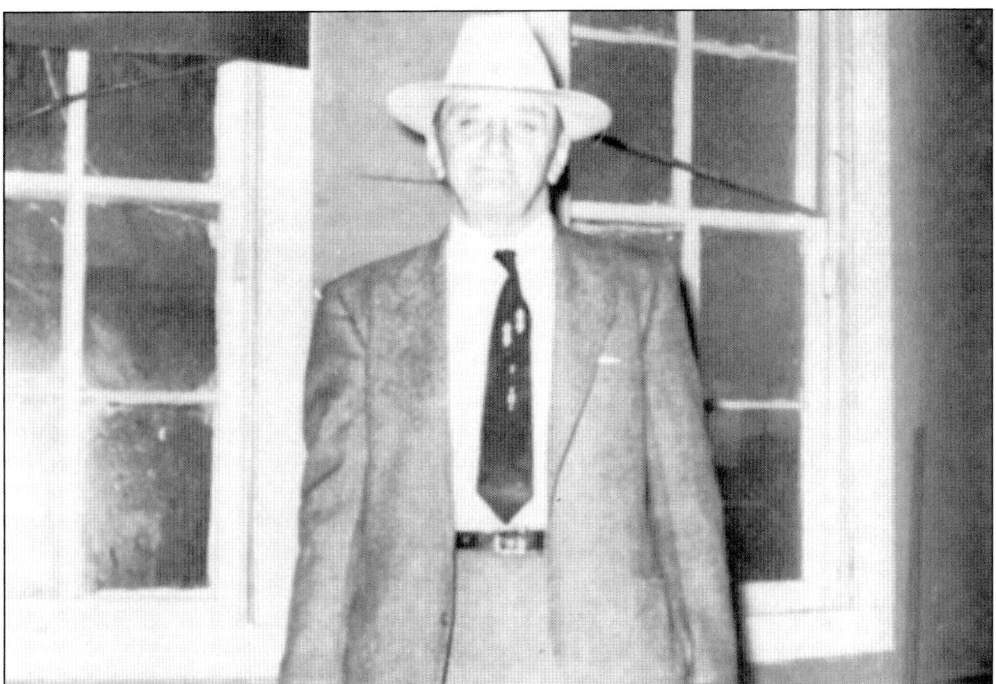

Tom Clark owned the Bridgeport Ice House on Halsell Street, where blocks of ice were delivered to customers throughout town.

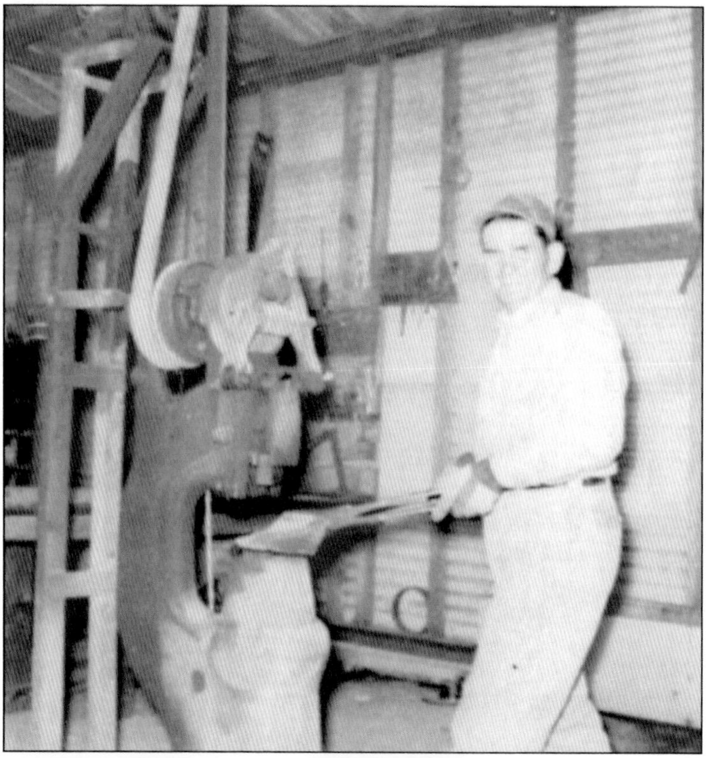

Obed Groves was a blacksmith and is seen here in this 1940s photograph working on a piece of equipment.

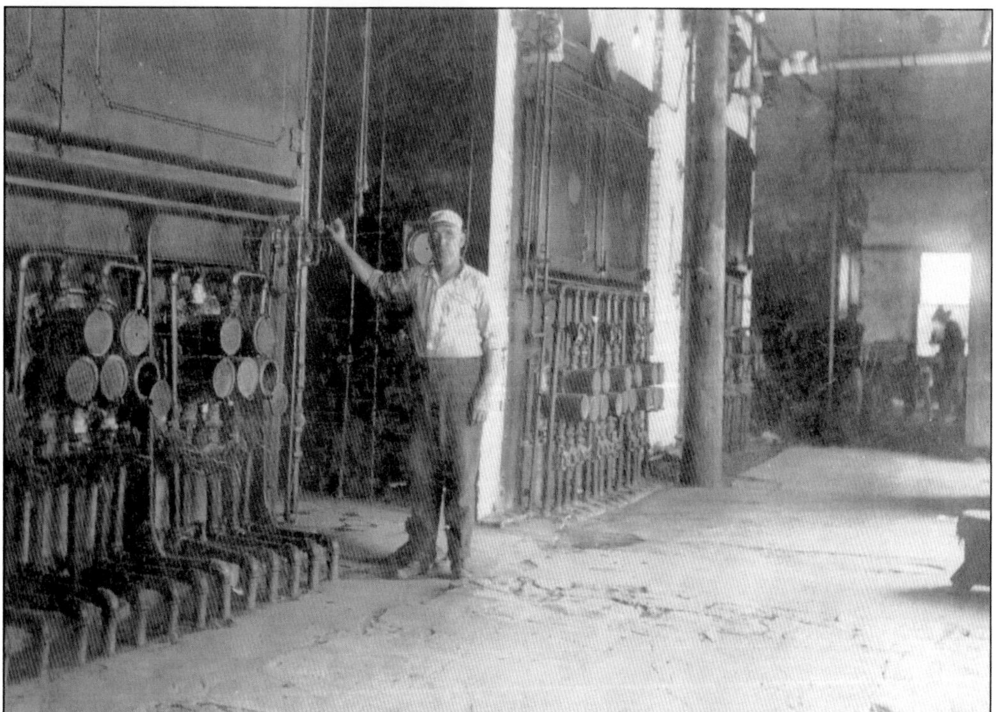

The Magnolia Oil Company maintained a pump station on the west side of town. An employee is pictured monitoring the valves and gauges. (Courtesy Ann Kaker.)

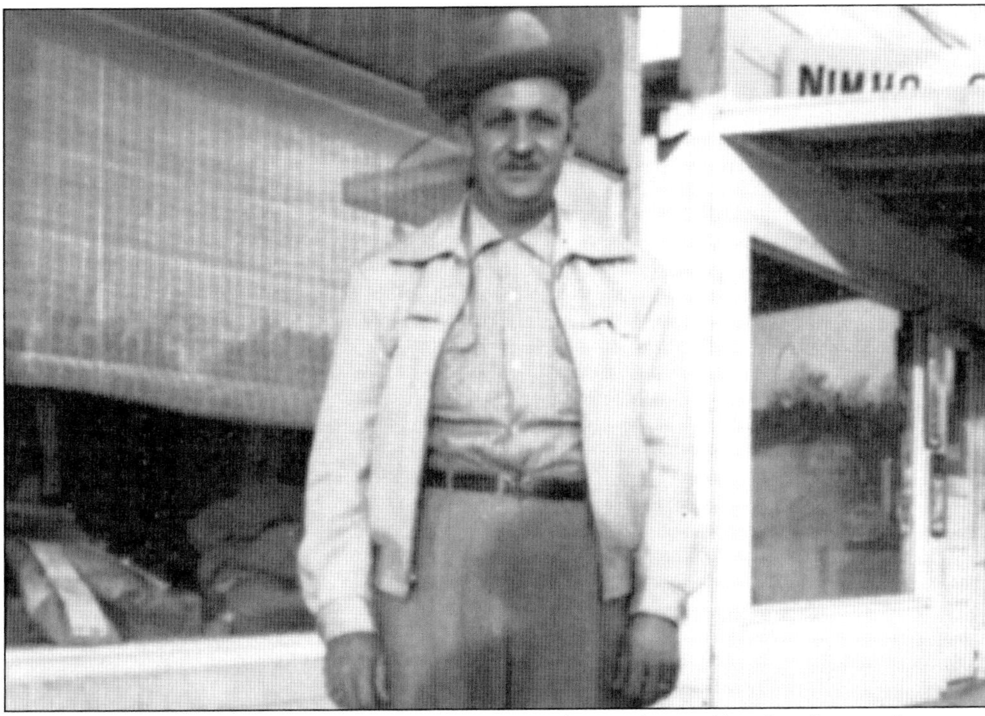

In this 1950s photograph, owner John Minton is standing in front of his dry-cleaning business.

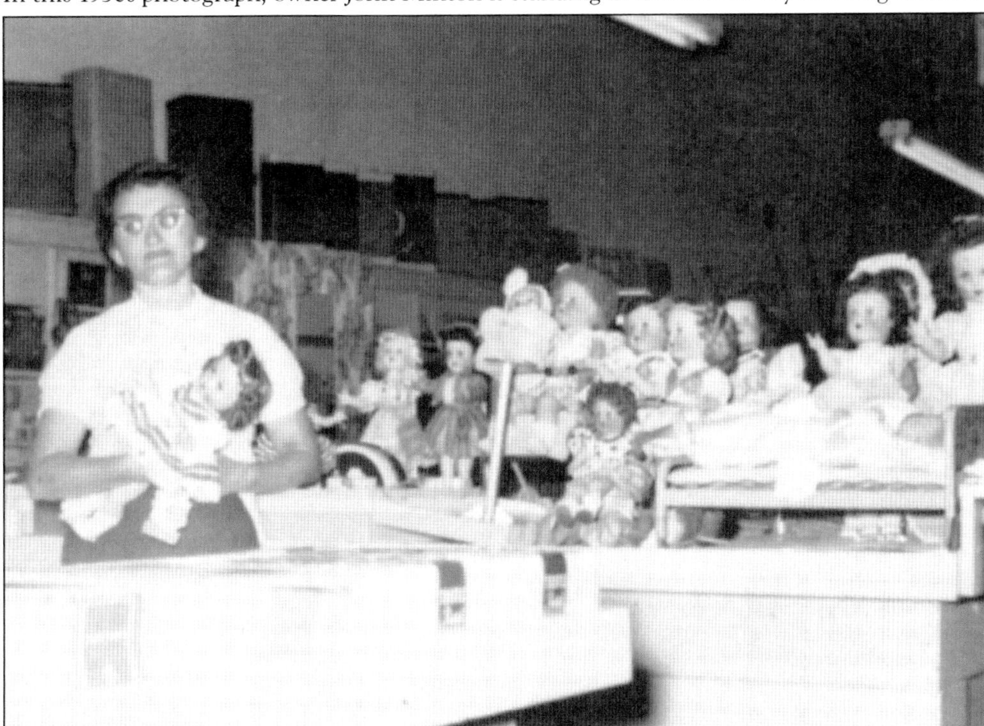

Mayor George Harwood owned Harwood's Variety store, which provided a wide selection of items to choose from.

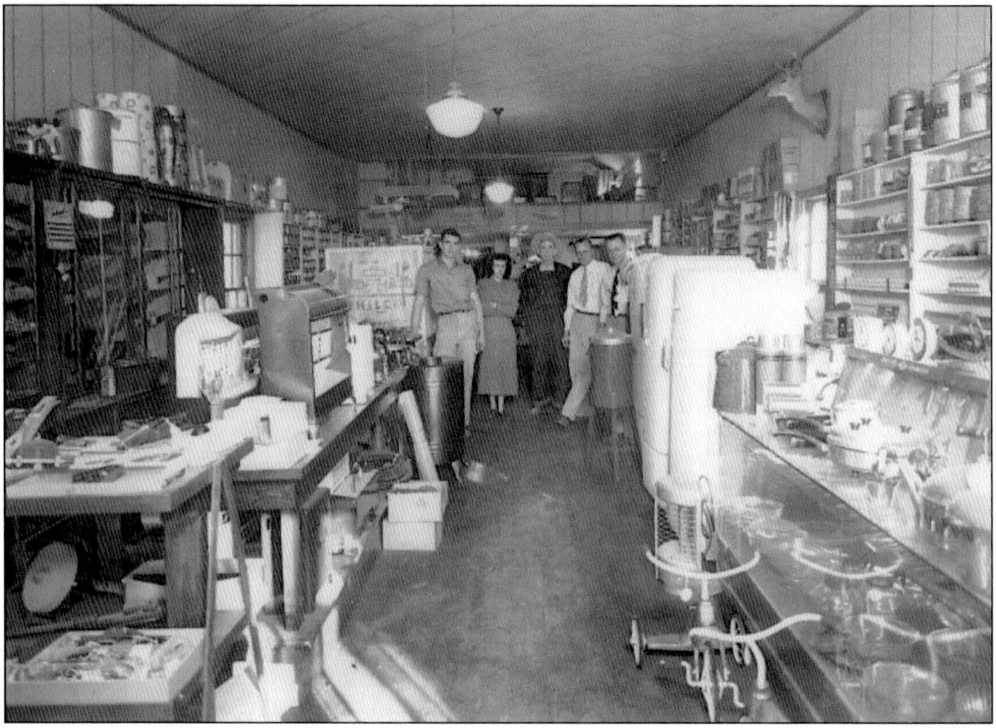

The Gary Nees Lumber Yard was a source of building materials and hardware items. In this 1949 photograph, employees assist a customer. From left to right are John Tackel, Thelma Raven Sprecher, an unidentified customer, Clifford Elliot, and manager Dale Eales.

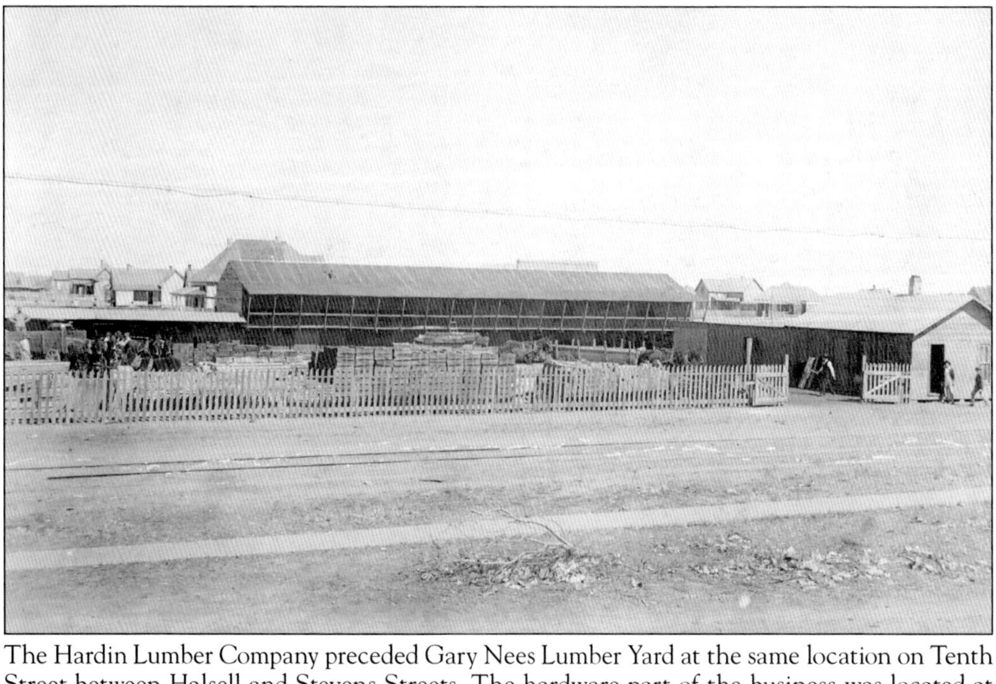

The Hardin Lumber Company preceded Gary Nees Lumber Yard at the same location on Tenth Street between Halsell and Stevens Streets. The hardware part of the business was located at 1003 Halsell Street.

This is a photograph of the favorite ice cream and tamale vendor of Bridgeport. Only known as Cracker Jack, he delighted children and adults all over town with his tasty treats and hearty banter. He first started with a horse and buggy in the late 1920s selling a dozen hot tamales for 10¢ and ice cream cones for 5¢. Cracker Jack later used a wheelbarrow to carry his goodies.

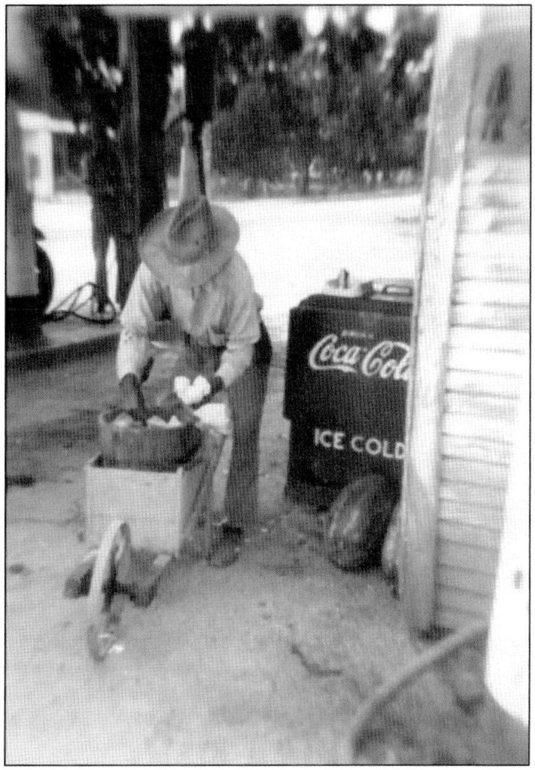

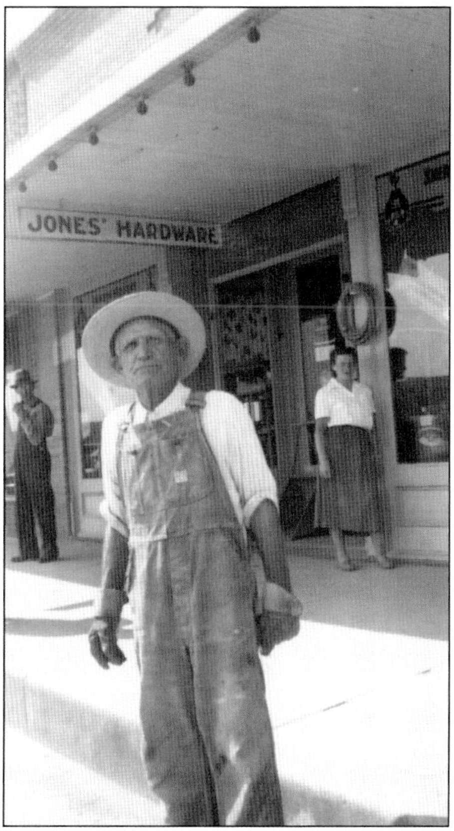

Night watchman and part-time handyman, Tom Anderson is standing in front of Jones' Hardware in this early-1950s photograph. Nevesta Jones is standing next to the front door.

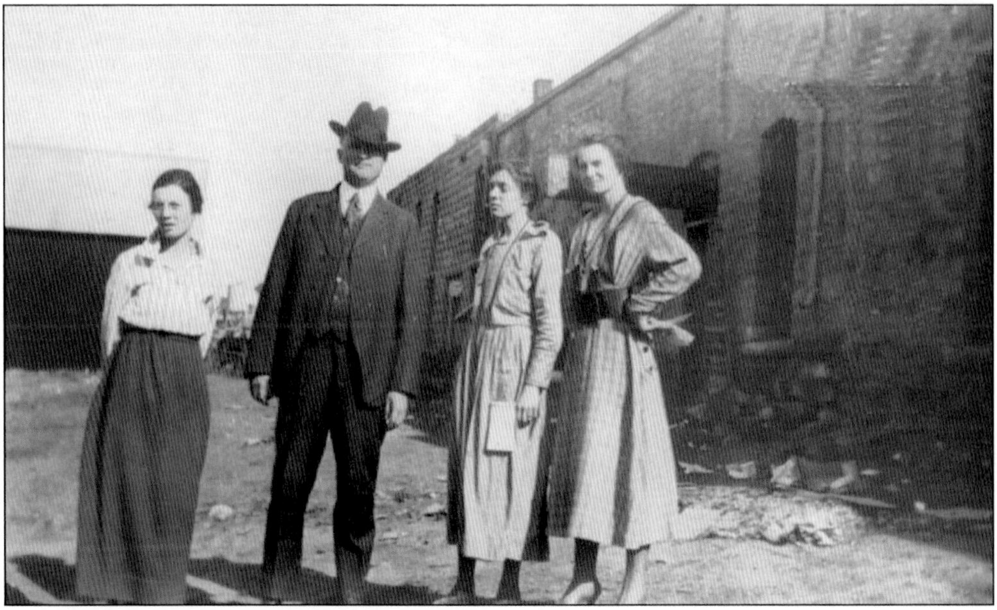

Seen here in a 1920s photograph is Mack Mask, who owned a dry goods store for many years at 1017–1019 Halsell Street. His trademark advertisement ended with "let's go to Mack's Shoe Store, the place to save a dollar."

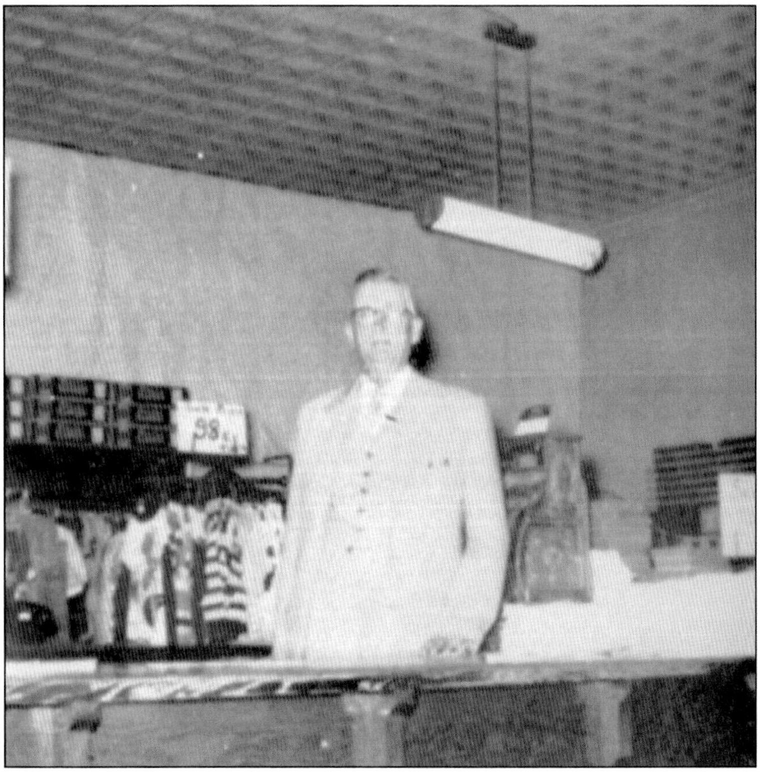

In this photograph, Mack Mask is standing next to the cash register in the middle of the store. Mask finally went out of business in 1970 and died the same year.

The White's Auto store was another hardware store located on Halsell Street in the 1950s.

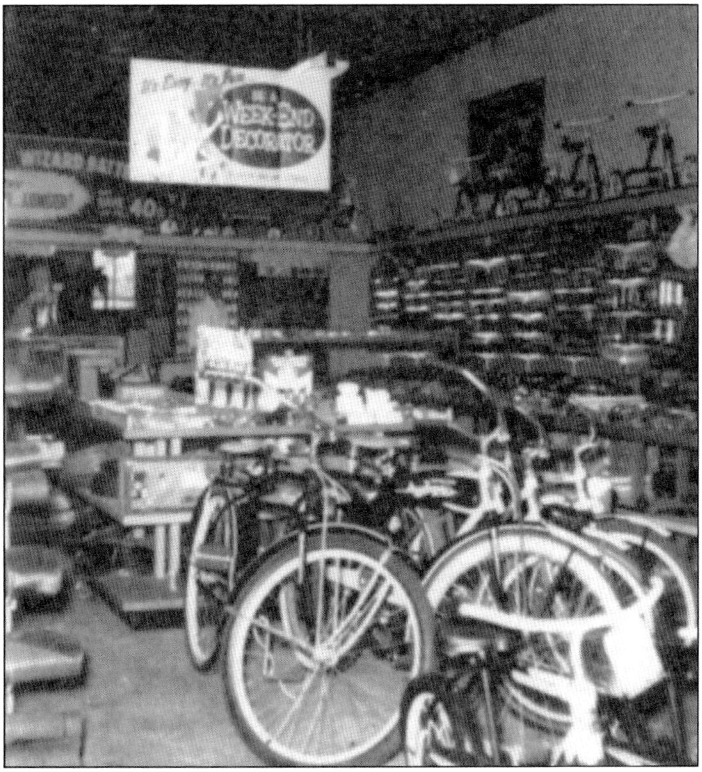

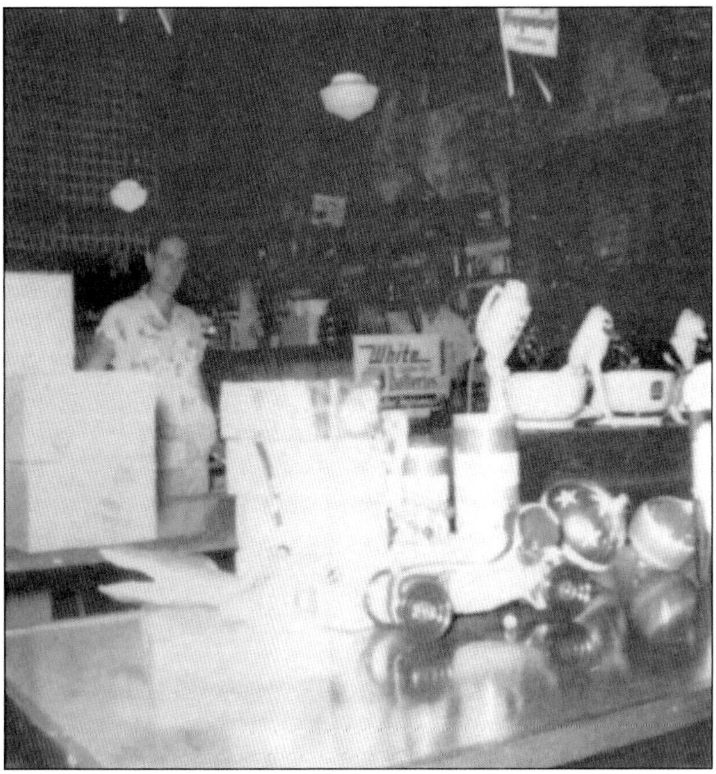

In this early-1950s photograph, Bill Paschall (front) helps his father, Elmer Paschall, who owned the business.

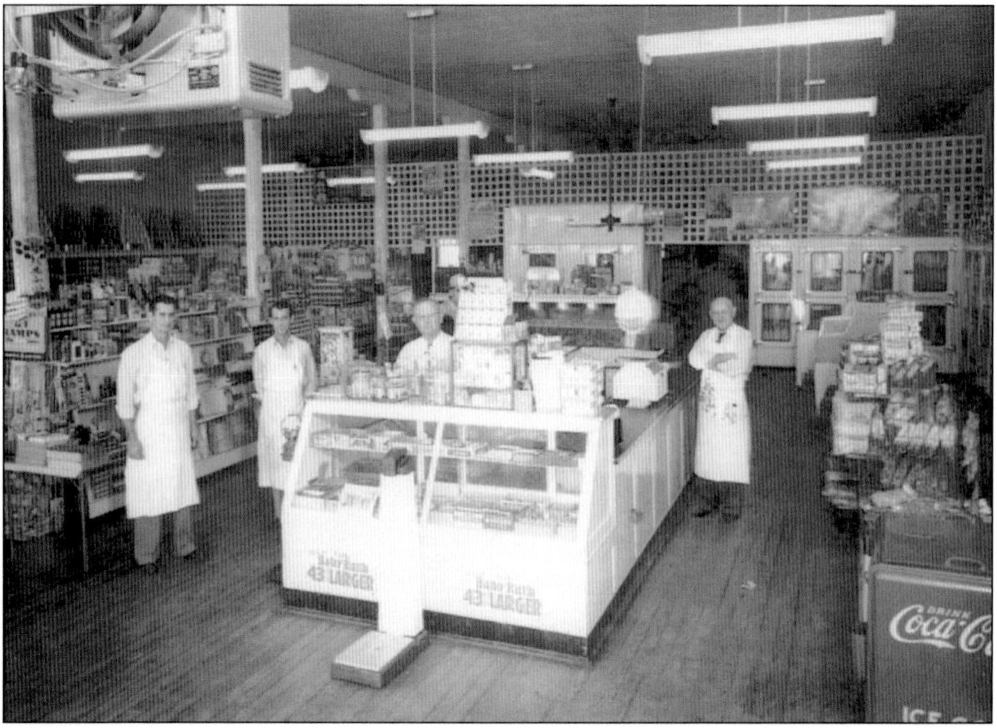

Kakers' Grocery store was located downtown at Tenth and Halsell Streets. Employees pictured here in the 1950s are, from left to right, A. D. Tackel, ? Hudson, Clarence Kaker, and Les Boase. The store burned down in 1960.

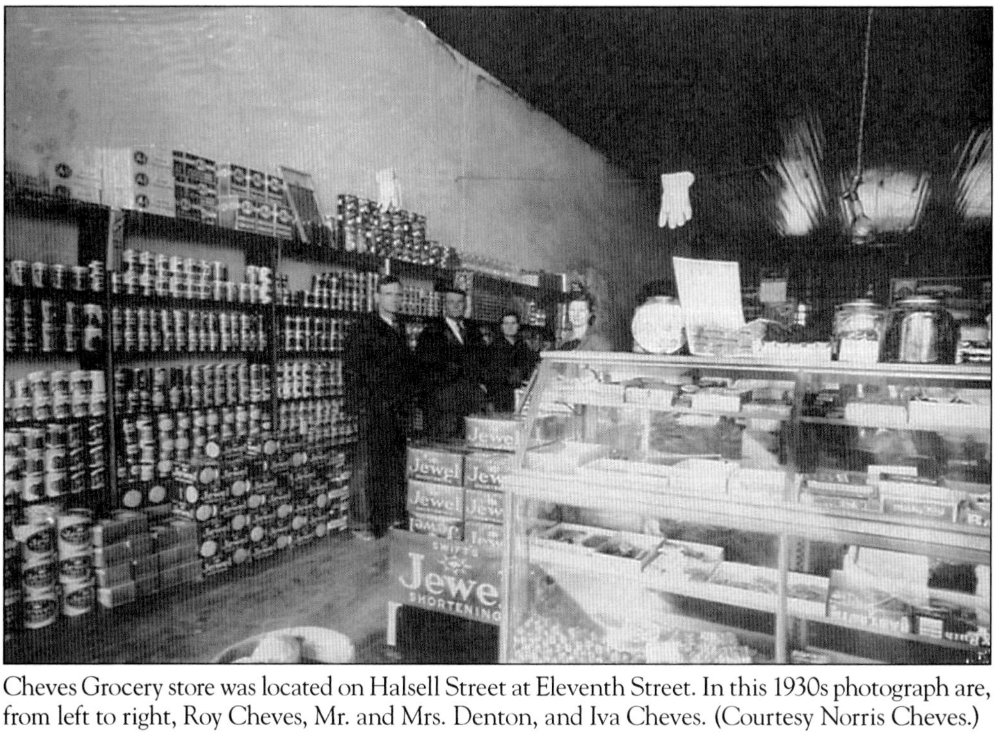

Cheves Grocery store was located on Halsell Street at Eleventh Street. In this 1930s photograph are, from left to right, Roy Cheves, Mr. and Mrs. Denton, and Iva Cheves. (Courtesy Norris Cheves.)

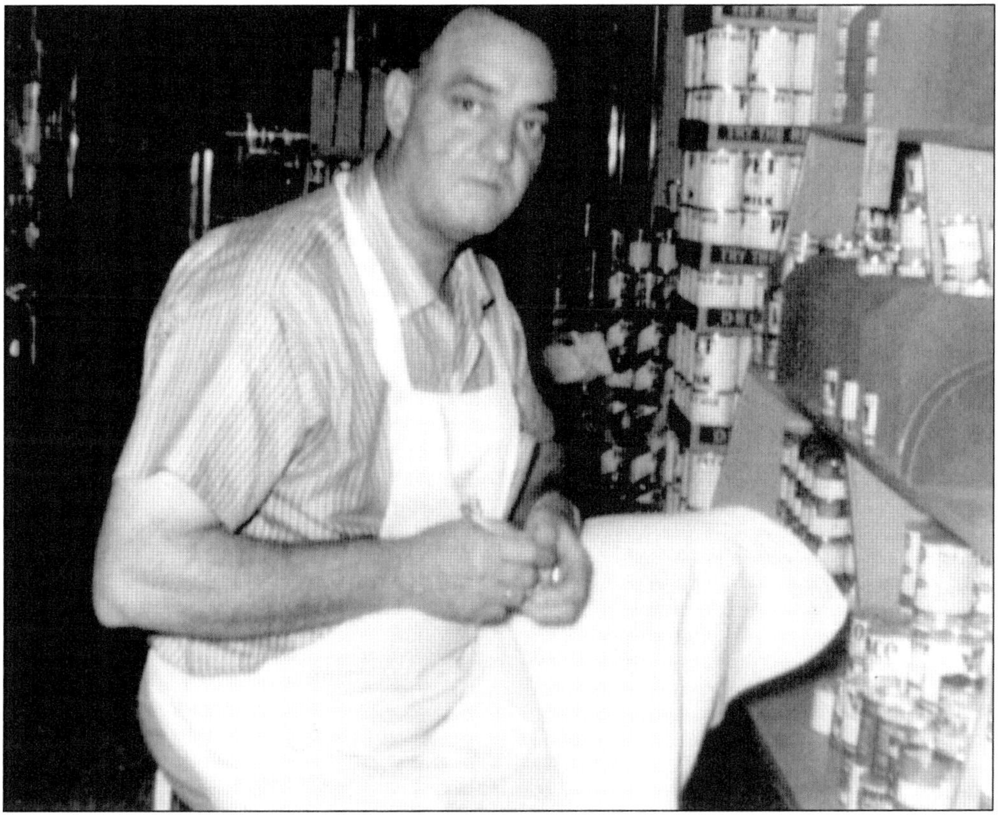

Checking the prices of canned goods is Otis Meek, owner of Spot Cash Grocery. The store was located at 1020 Halsell Street from 1942 to 1964 when a new building was constructed one block east.

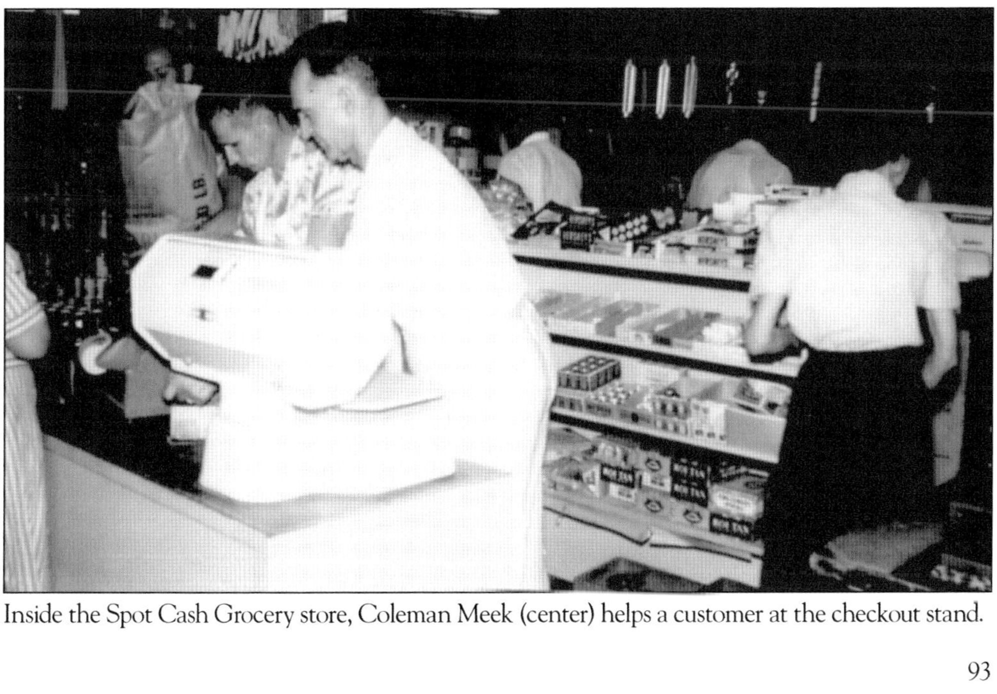

Inside the Spot Cash Grocery store, Coleman Meek (center) helps a customer at the checkout stand.

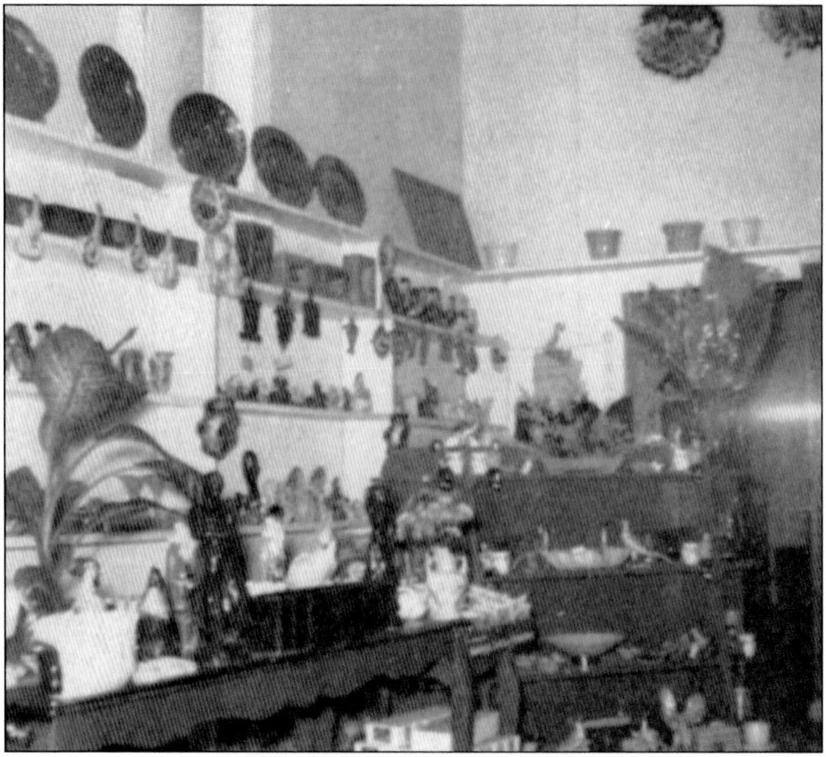

Sarah Jane's flower and gift store has been in business at the same location on Halsell Street for over 50 years.

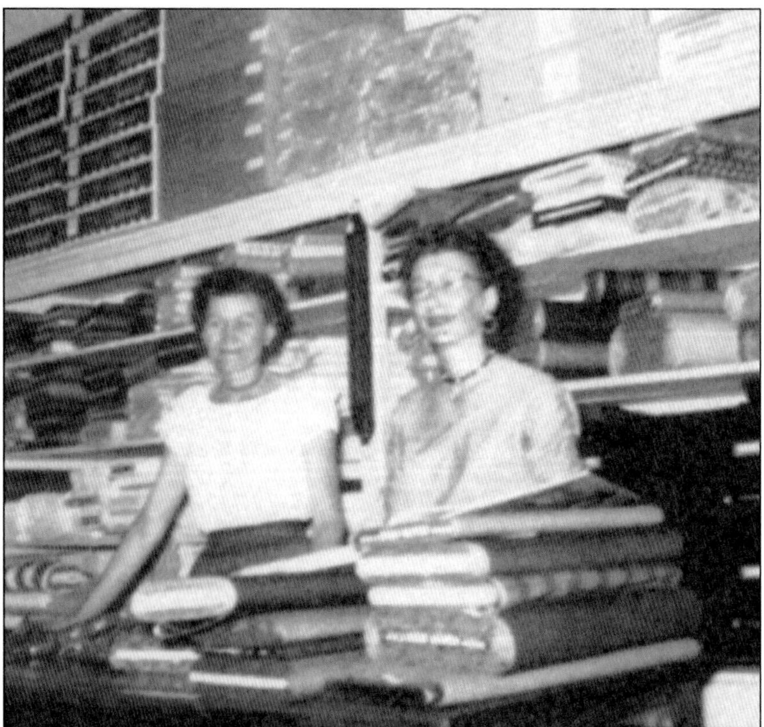

Billie Green's Dry Goods always had a good selection of fabrics. Pictured here are two employees, with Merle Bolding on the right.

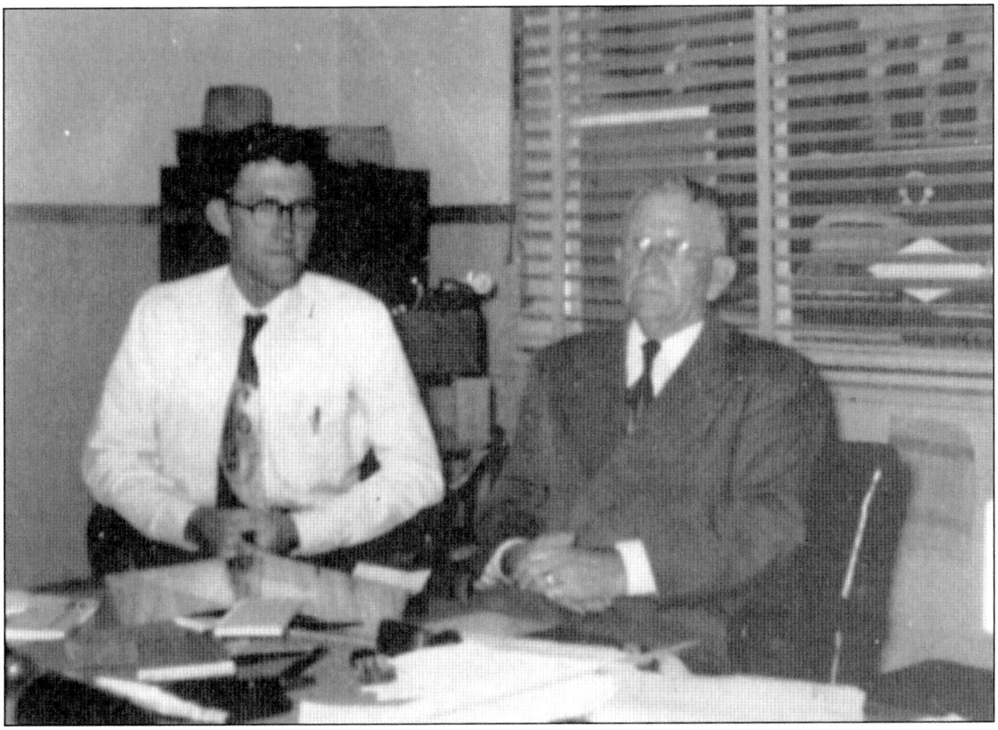

Wilson Ray (left) and Vic Baldridge were officers at the First National Bank for many years. The bank was chartered in 1907.

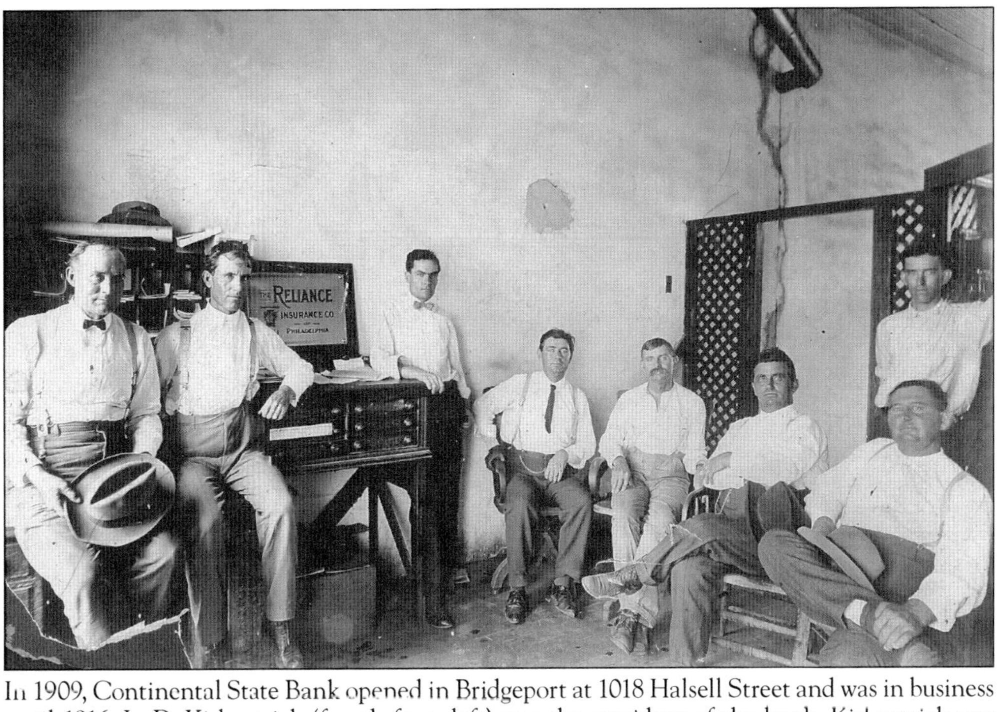

In 1909, Continental State Bank opened in Bridgeport at 1018 Halsell Street and was in business until 1916. L. D. Kirkpatrick (fourth from left) was the president of the bank. Kirkpatrick was later elected mayor of Bridgeport. (Courtesy David Maxine.)

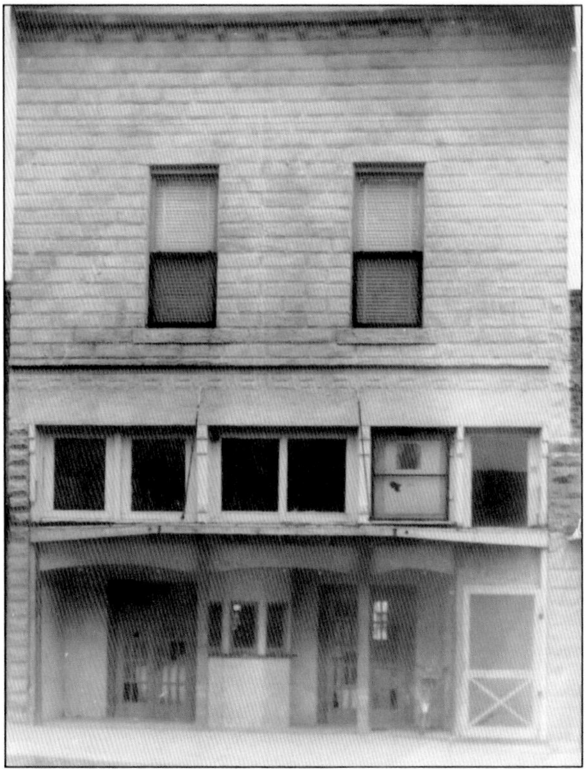

This building located at 1008 Halsell Street has had many tenants over the years. The ground floor has functioned as a movie theatre, and numerous retail businesses have operated there. The upstairs has been an apartment house and a hotel.

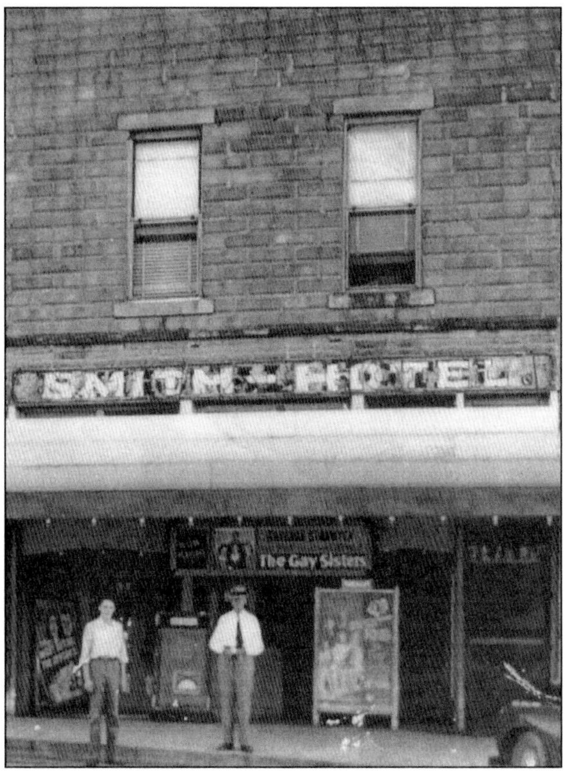

Bill Paschall (left) operated the projector at the National Theatre during high school and earned $15 a week.

In 1946, John Curley built the Arcadia Theatre across the street from the old National Theatre at 1007 Halsell Street. The last movie shown was *Spencer's Mountain* in 1963. The Bridgeport Fine Arts Association began a renovation of the building in the late 1990s, and the structure has now been restored and is used for many different events.

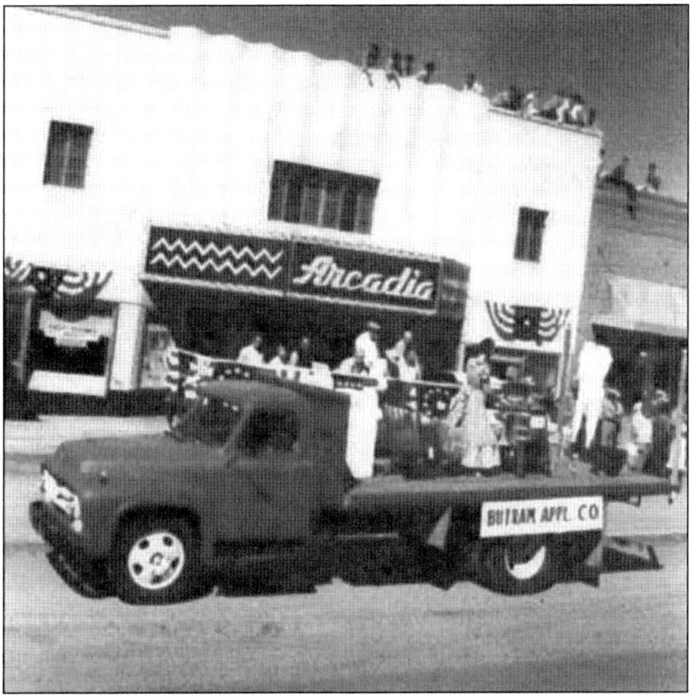

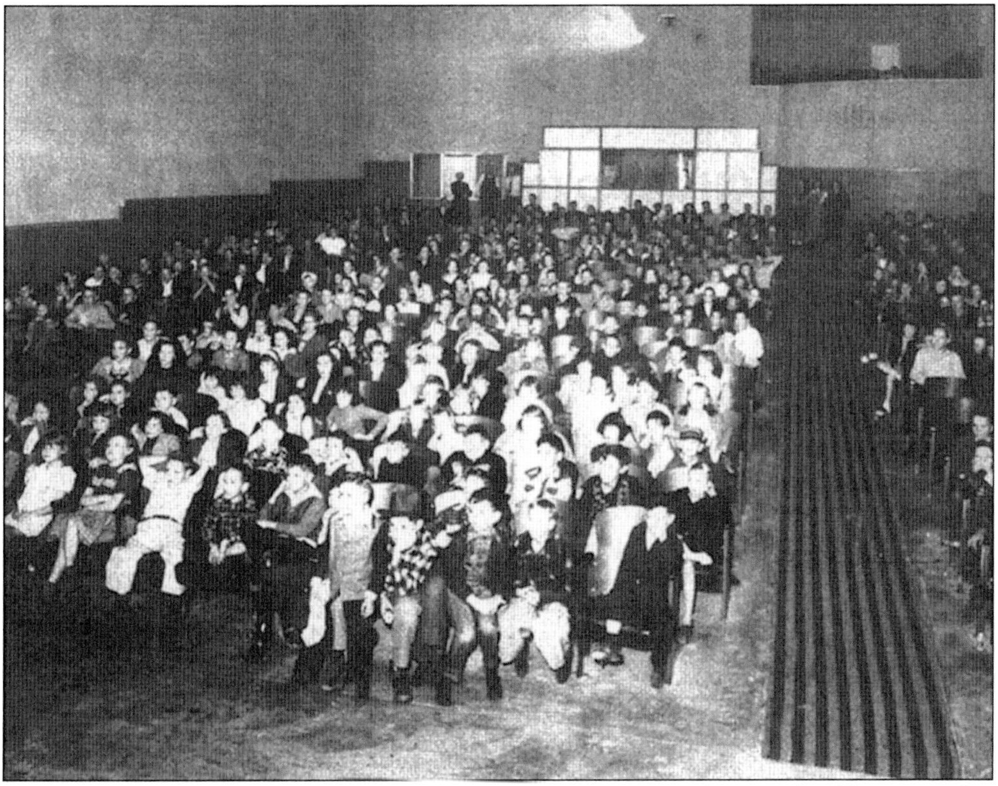

Grade school students have gathered for an awards ceremony at the Arcadia Theatre in this early-1950s photograph.

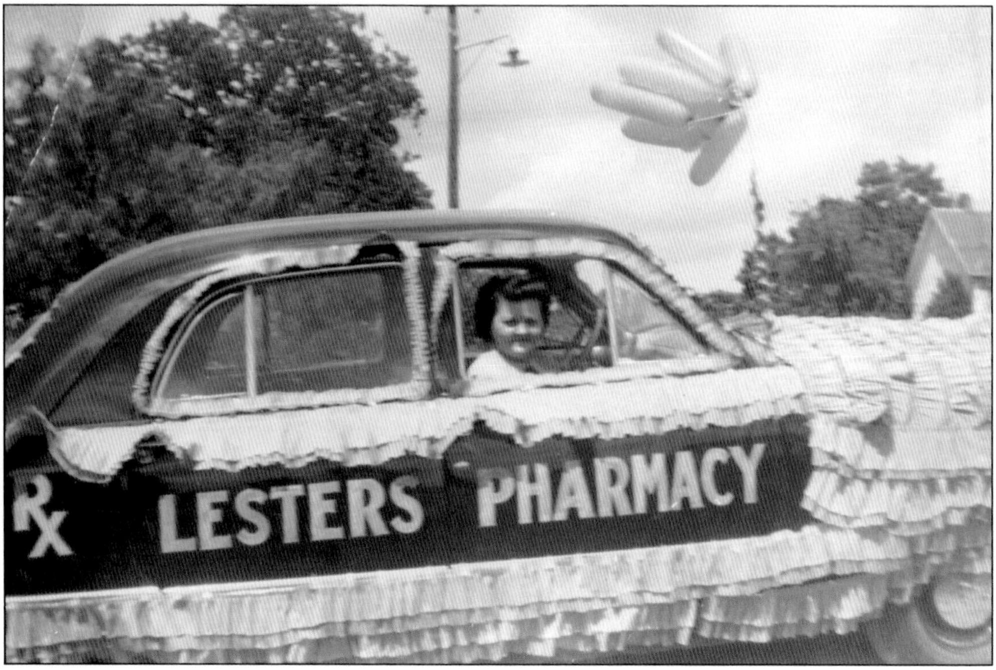

Local businesses and organizations decorated cars for a parade celebrating the Fourth of July county fair. Pictured here in 1950 is Fay Lester.

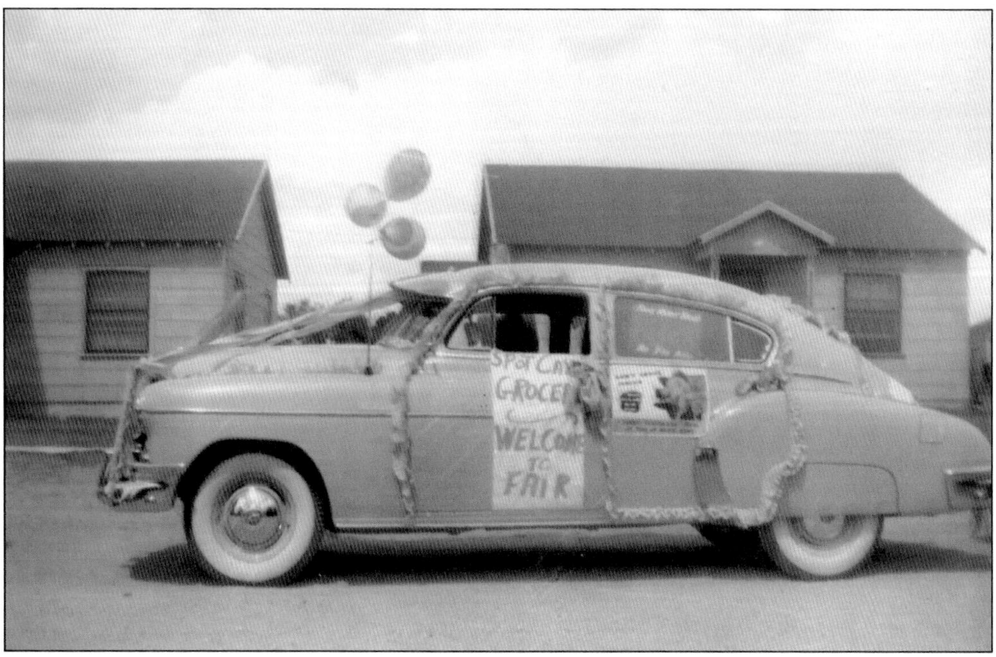

Prizes were awarded to the best-decorated vehicle in the parade.

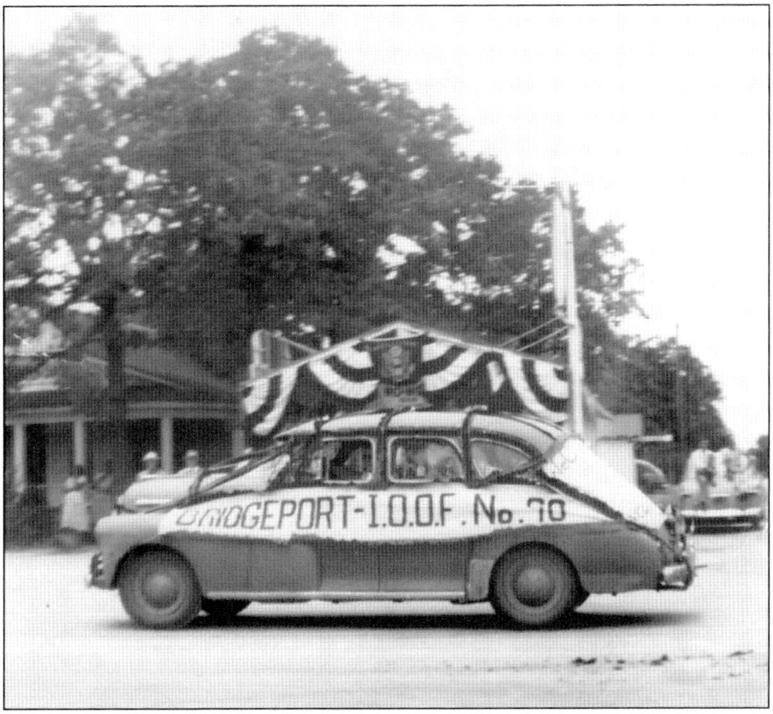

Vehicles in the parade traveled west on Halsell Street, through downtown, and finished at the city park.

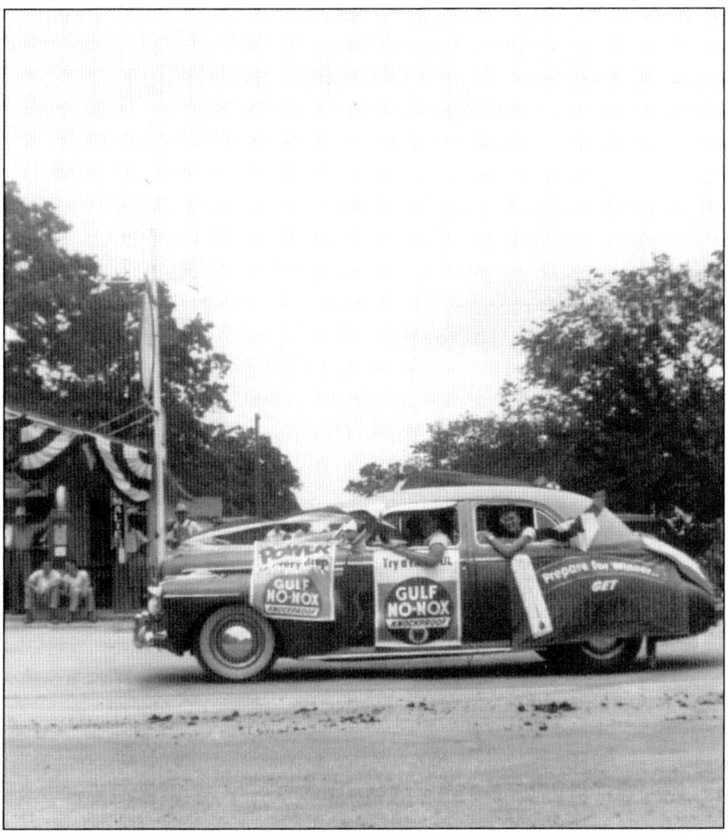

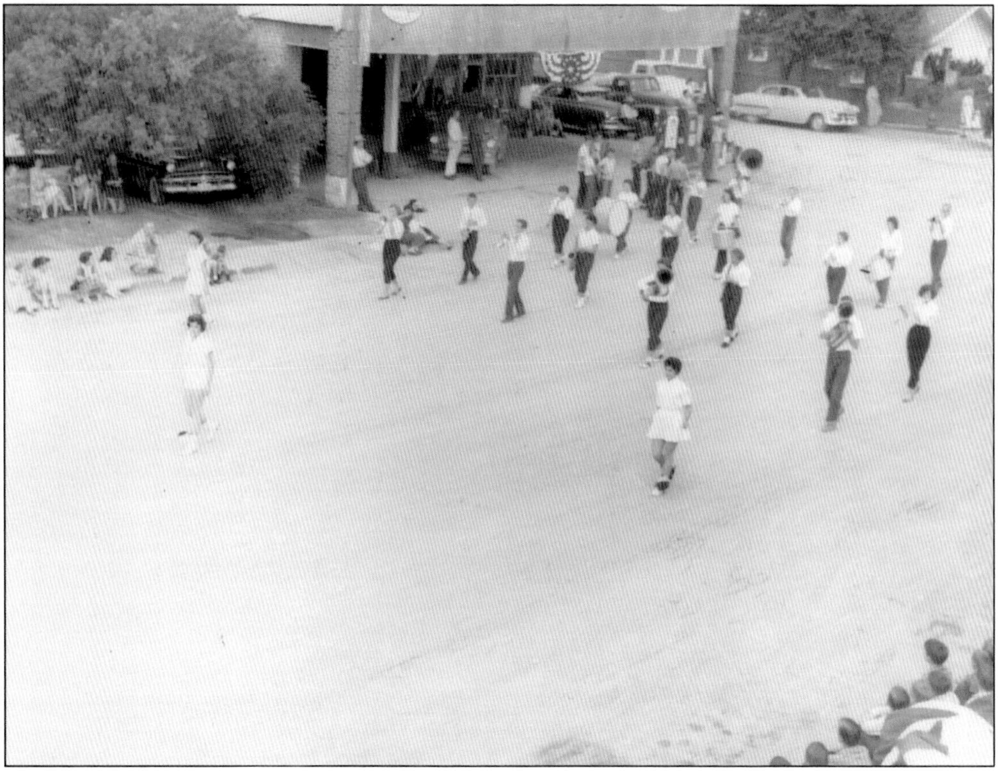

In this 1950s photograph, the high school band marches past the Star Garage at Twelfth and Halsell Streets in another parade.

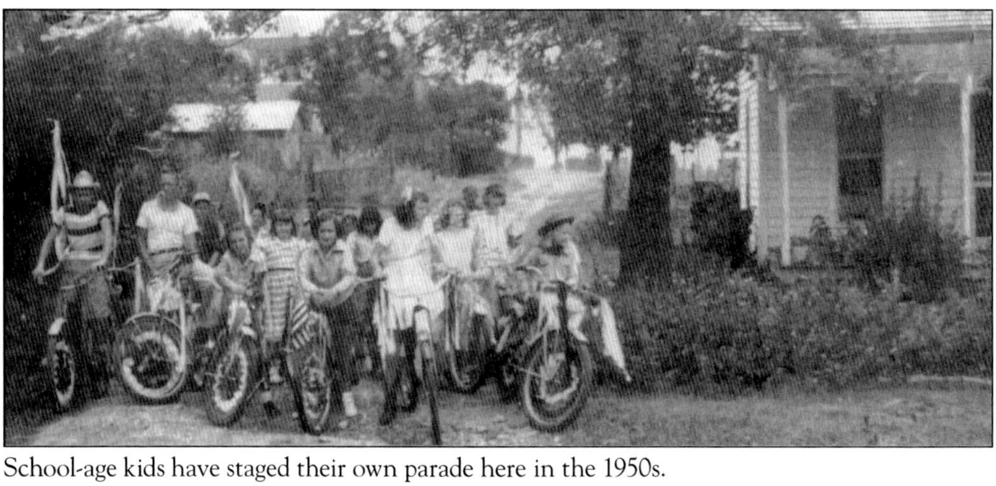

School-age kids have staged their own parade here in the 1950s.

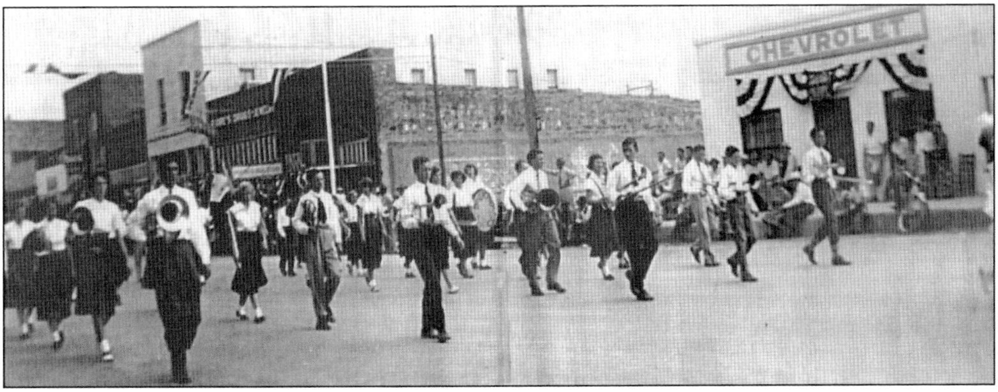

As can be seen in both of these images, parades downtown were always well attended. The Bridgeport High School marching band is the focus in both of these photographs.

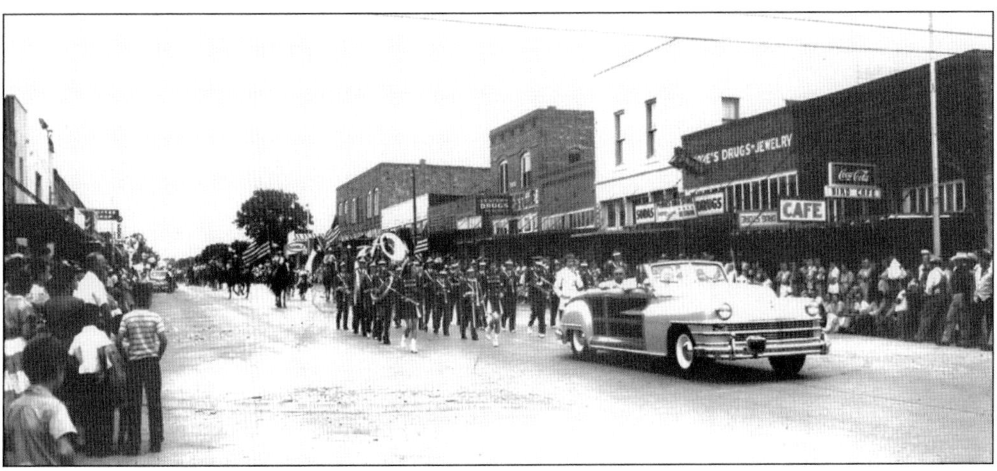

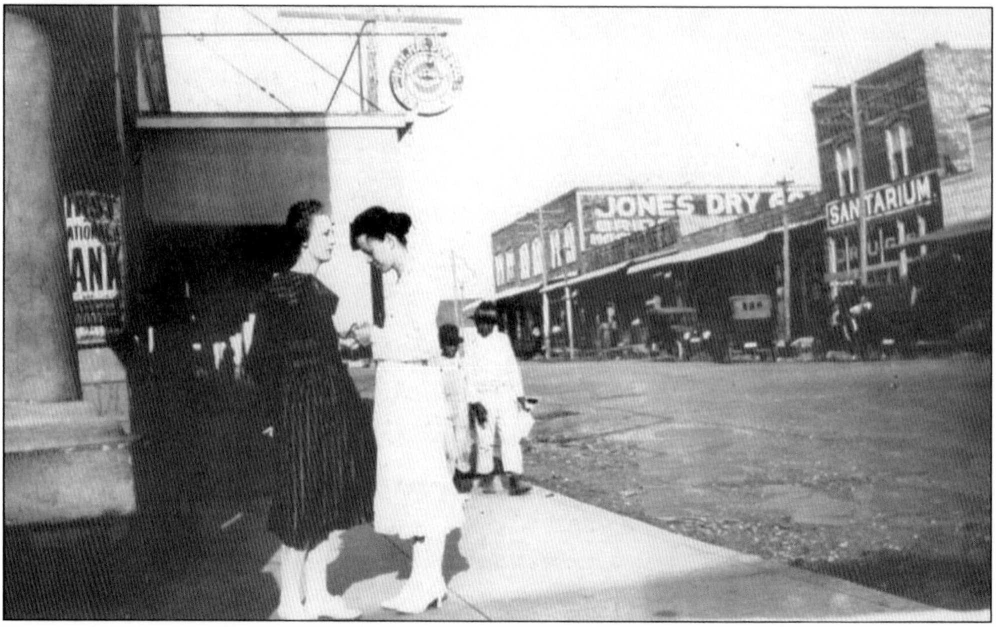

Doctors Thomas Buckner and son Kassie Buckner originally owned the building at 1007 Halsell Street. It was used as a sanitarium with family living quarters in the back of the upstairs until it was sold to the Masonic Lodge No. 587 in 1925.

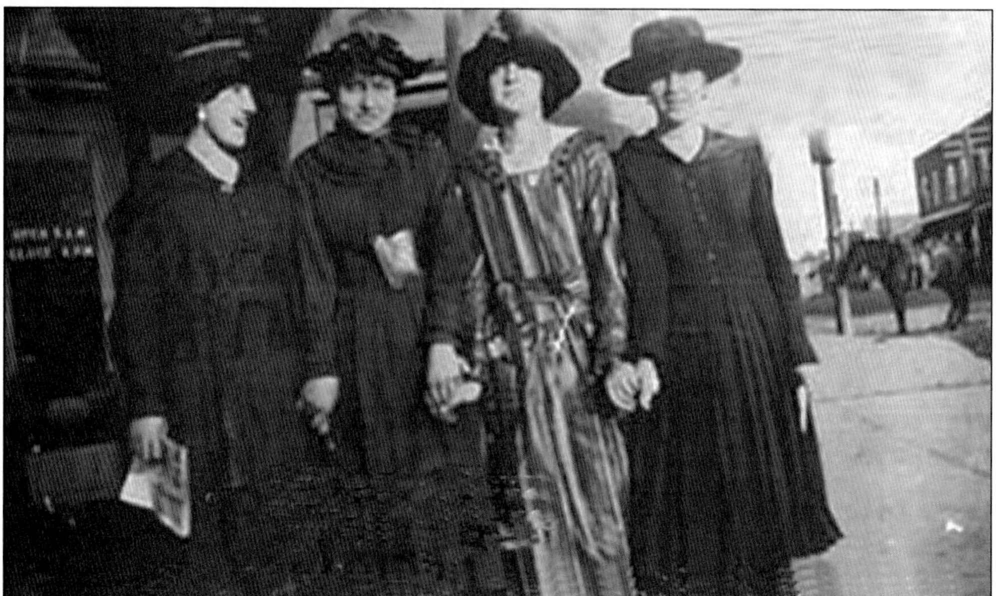

The sidewalk in front of the First National Bank building was a busy place. Seen here in the 1920s are, from left to right, Maude Brock, unidentified, Ola Ford, and Verda Blackwell.

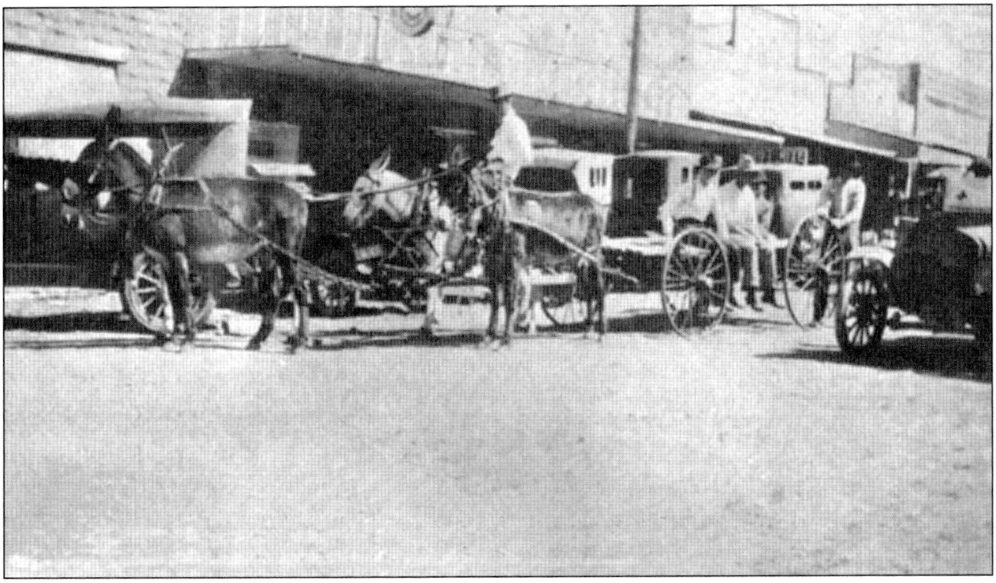

The buildings pictured here in 1920 are, from left to right, the First National Bank, Hardin Lumber, W. A. Brown Grocery store, and Just Rite Cleaners. The men riding on the wagon are, from left to right, Albert Minor, Charlie Minor, Ferd Sensibaugh, and Clifford Alexander.

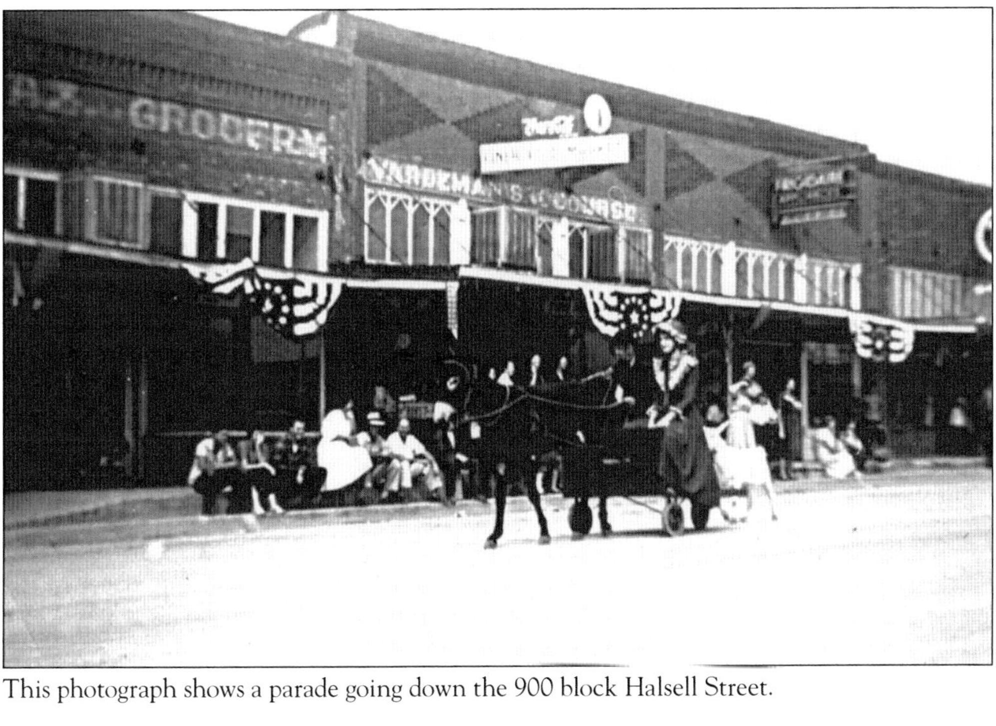

This photograph shows a parade going down the 900 block Halsell Street.

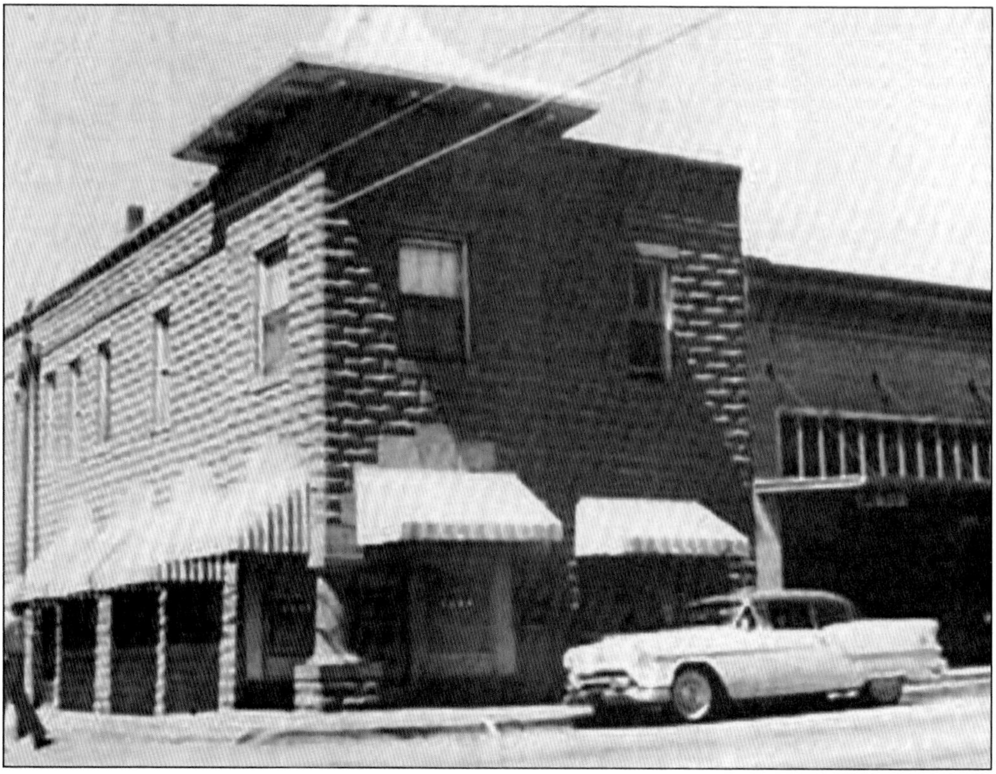

A landmark building in downtown is the First National Bank building, which was constructed in 1908. The second floor housed doctors, lawyers, the telephone company switchboard, and a beauty shop.

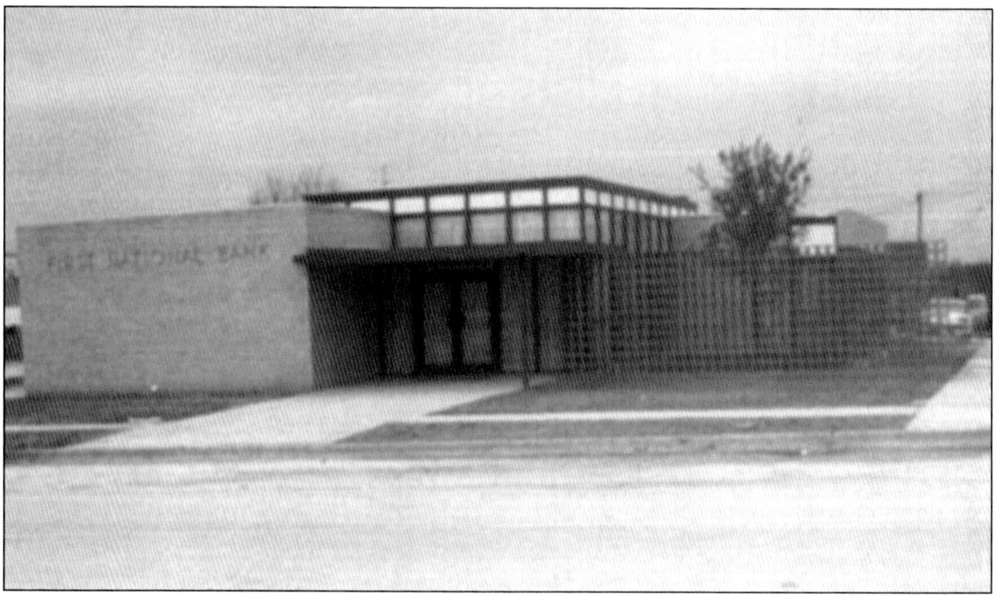

The First National Bank moved in 1959 to its new building located at Stevens and Tenth Streets.

There was always something going on in town to draw a crowd. In the park, a circus performer dives into a net.

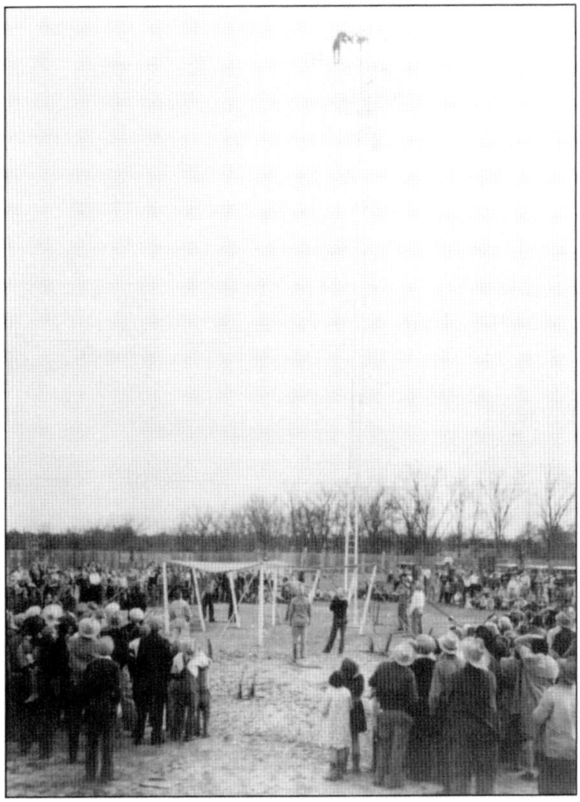

At the height of the Roaring Twenties, a car being given away in 1925 attracted hundreds of people on Halsell Street. (Courtesy Dr. D. C. Sipes.)

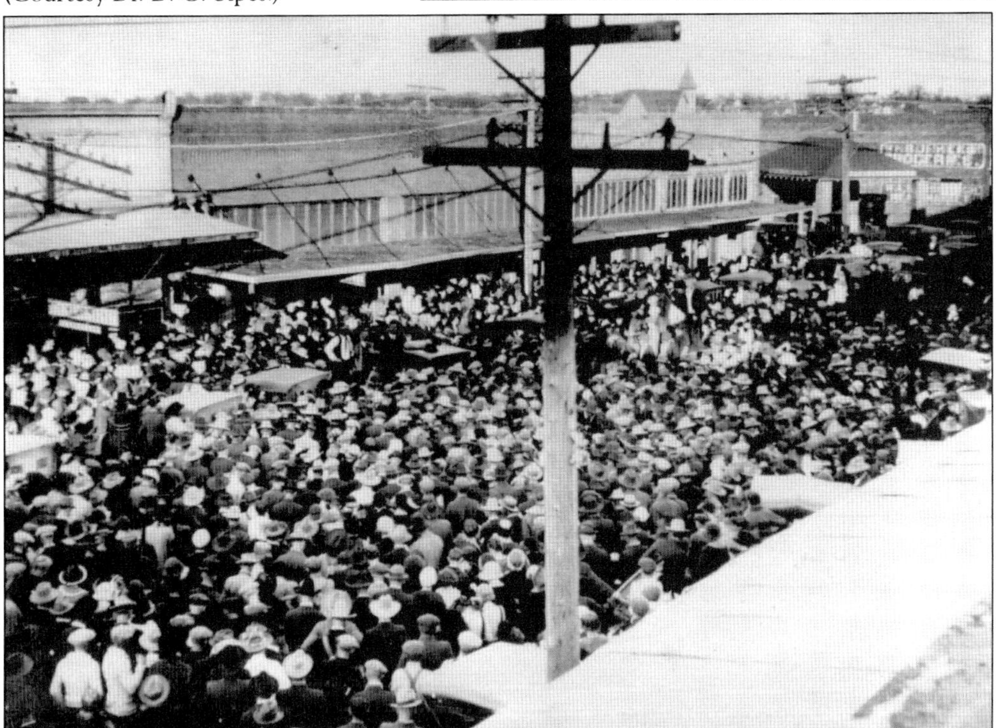

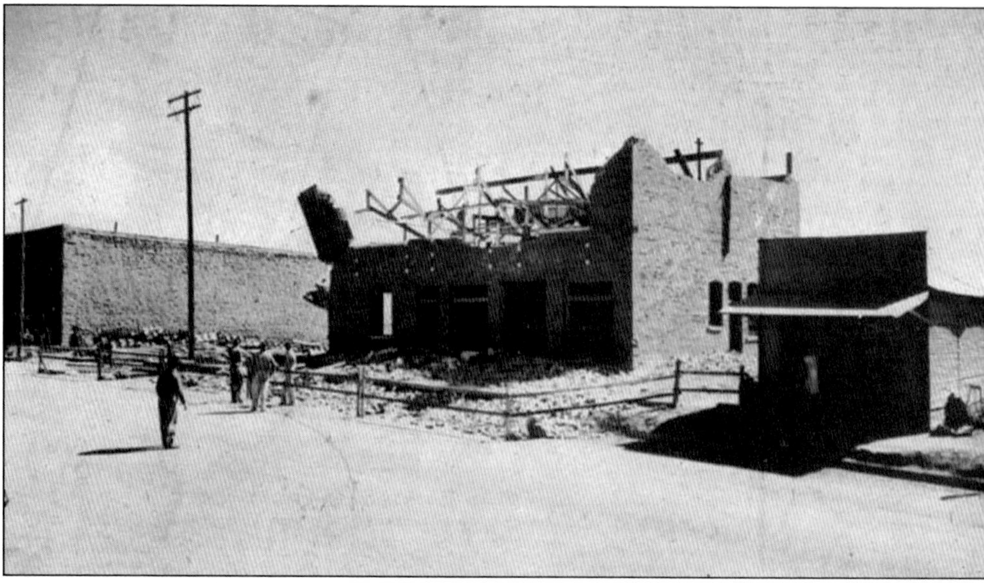

In 1930, the old city hall was torn down at 812 Halsell Street.

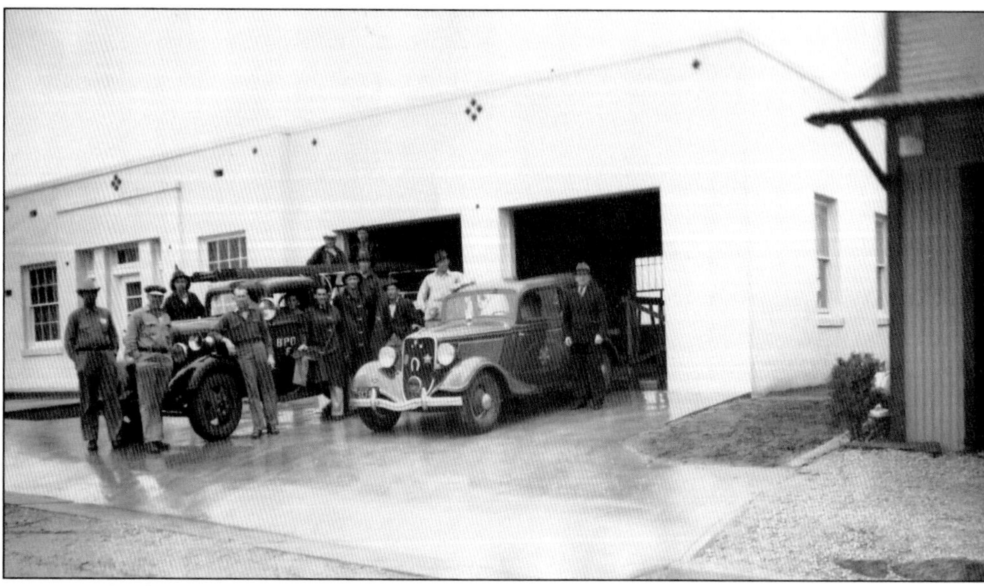

A group of volunteer firefighters show off their new station and city hall, which were completed in 1931. (Courtesy Gilbert and Sue Williams Shawn.)

The 1956 presidential election did not ignore Bridgeport. An Adlai Stevenson campaign bus stopped in town searching for some votes.

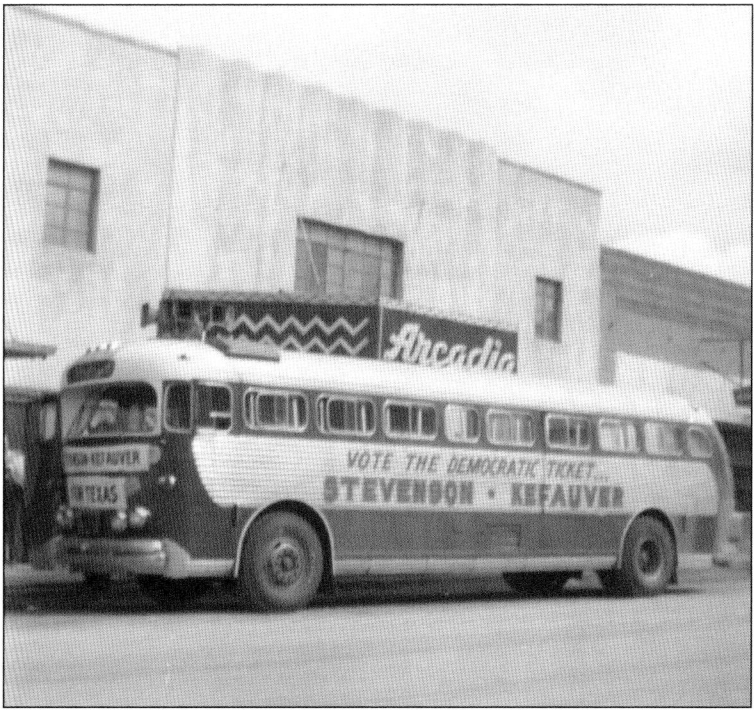

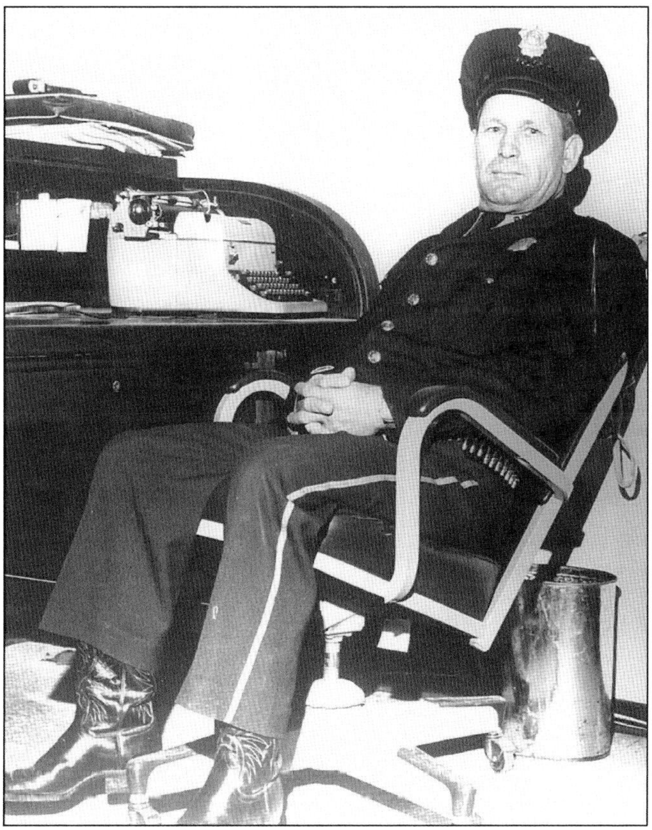

Popular longtime police chief Walter Dale takes a break from his many activities.

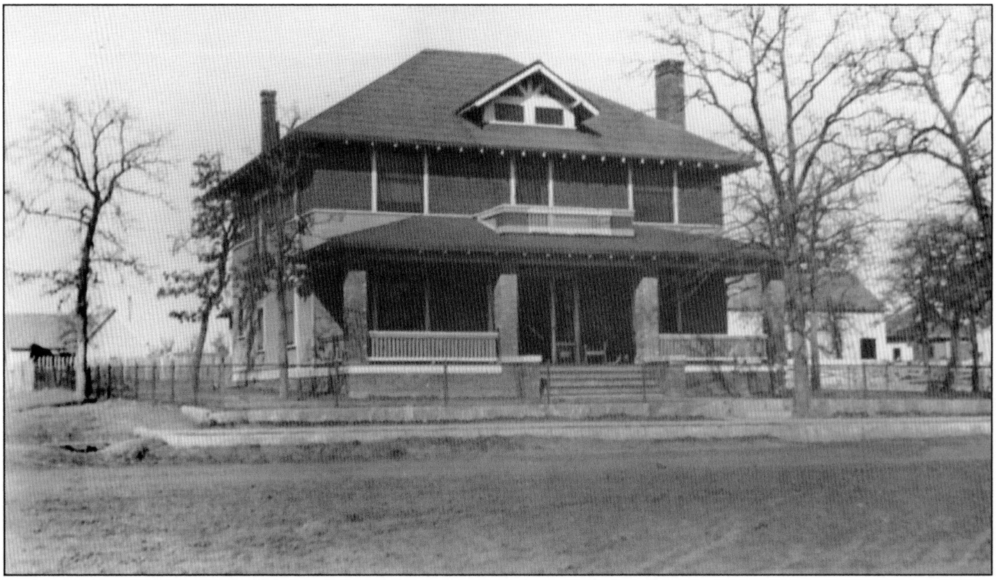

There were many stylish homes built in the early days of Bridgeport. This home, constructed in 1912, belonged to Dr. P. C. Funk and was located on Halsell and Fourteenth Streets. The structure is now home to Jones' Family Funeral Home.

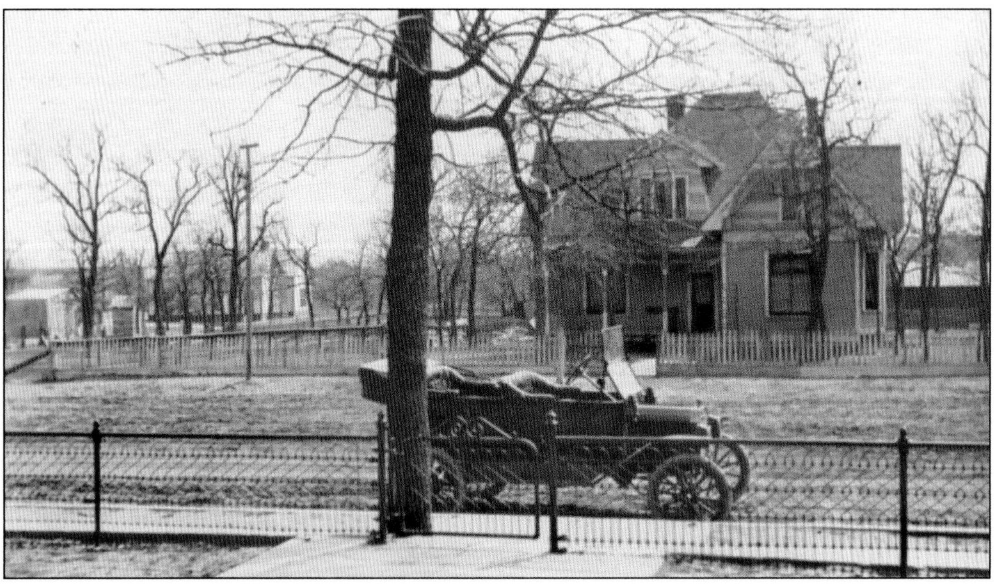

The home of Ernest Jones was located across the street from the Funk home. This home still graces Halsell Street.

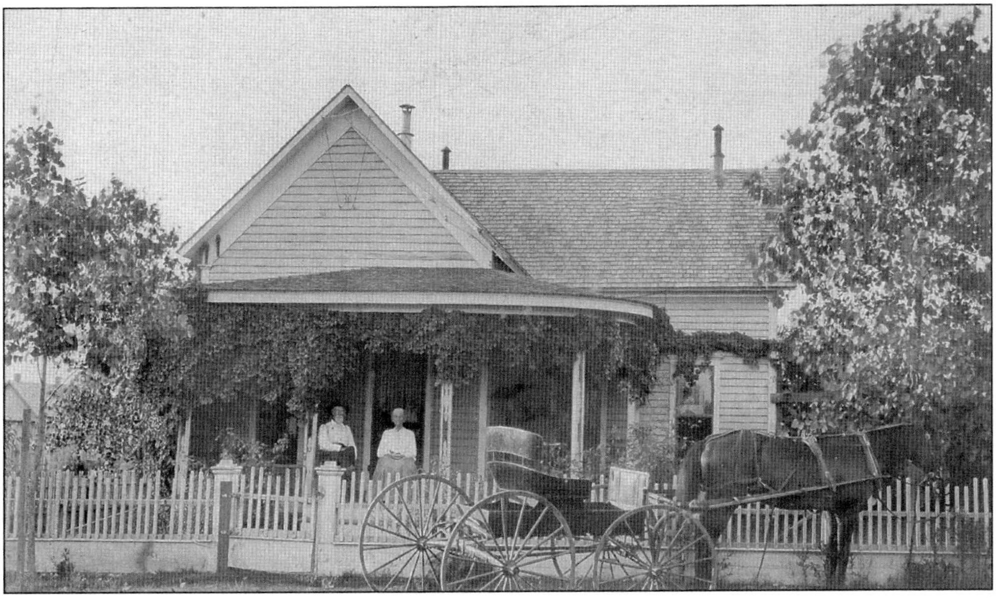

L. D. Kirkpatrick and his wife sit on their front porch. Kirkpatrick was president of the First National Bank for many years and also the first mayor of Bridgeport. (Courtesy David Maxine.)

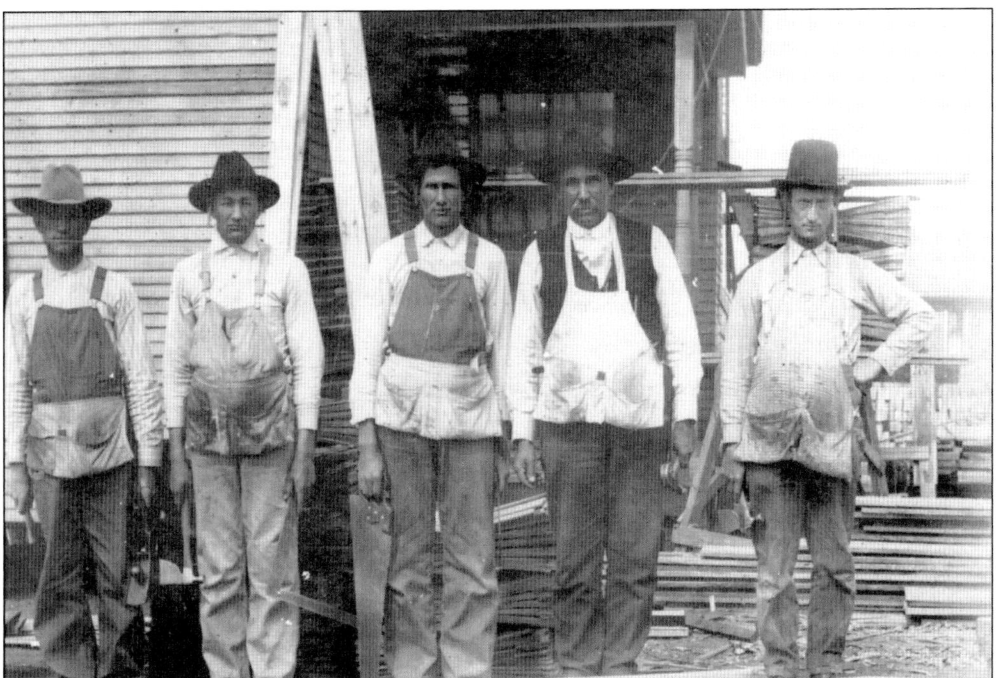

Some of the carpenters who built many of the homes throughout Bridgeport are, from left to right, Jesse Power, Everett Elliott, Jess Elliott, Claud Elliott, and Tom Black.

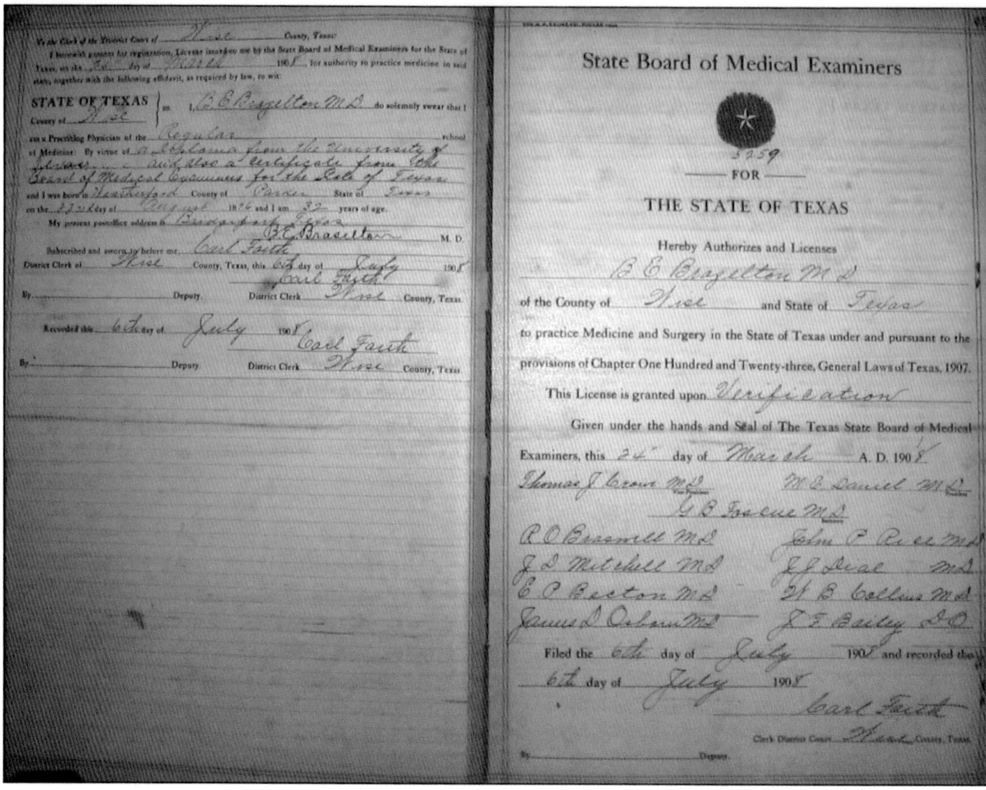

To the Clerk of the District Court of Wise County, Texas:

I herewith present for registration, License issued to me by the State Board of Medical Examiners for the State of Texas, on the 24 day of March 1908, for authority to practice medicine in said state, together with the following affidavit, as required by law, to wit:

STATE OF TEXAS, County of Wise } ss. I, B E Braselton M D do solemnly swear that I am a Practicing Physician of the Regular school of Medicine: By virtue of a Diploma from the University of Texas and also a certificate from the Board of Medical Examiners for the State of Texas and I was born in Weatherford County of Parker State of Texas on the 22nd day of August 1876 and I am 32 years of age.

My present postoffice address is Bridgeport Texas

B E Braselton M. D.

Subscribed and sworn to before me, Carl Faith District Clerk of Wise County, Texas, this 6th day of July 1908

Carl Faith

By .... Deputy. District Clerk Wise County, Texas

Recorded this 6th day of July 1908 Carl Faith

By .... Deputy. District Clerk Wise County, Texas

State Board of Medical Examiners

3259

FOR

THE STATE OF TEXAS

Hereby Authorizes and Licenses

B E Braselton M D

of the County of Wise and State of Texas

to practice Medicine and Surgery in the State of Texas under and pursuant to the provisions of Chapter One Hundred and Twenty-three, General Laws of Texas, 1907.

This License is granted upon Verification

Given under the hands and Seal of The Texas State Board of Medical Examiners, this 24 day of March A. D. 1908

Thomas J Crowe MD, M E Daniel MD, G B Foscue MD, R O Braswell MD, John P Rice MD, J D Mitchell MD, J J Dial MD, E C Becton MD, W B Collins MD, James D Osborn MD, J E Bailey DO

Filed the 6th day of July 1908 and recorded the 6th day of July 1908

Carl Faith

Clerk District Court Wise County, Texas.

By .... Deputy.

Born in 1876 and a graduate of the University of Texas, B. E. Braselton received his license to practice medicine in Wise County in 1908.

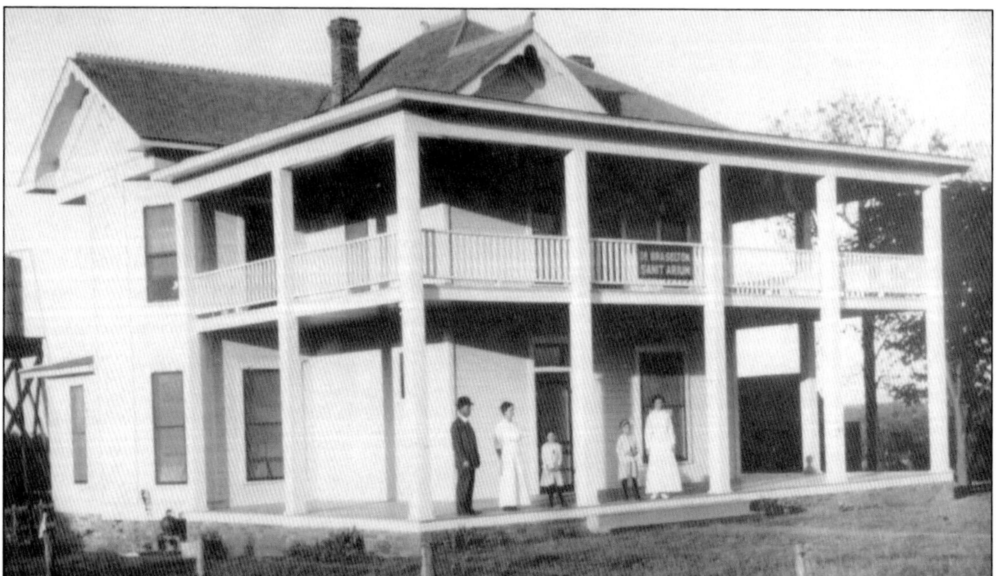

Dr. Braselton built his sanitarium in 1912 east of town in an attempt to improve conditions for his patients. Dr. Braselton is standing on the porch with his wife, daughters Cue (left) and Fae, and nurse ? Stewart. (Courtesy Dr. D. C. Sipes.)

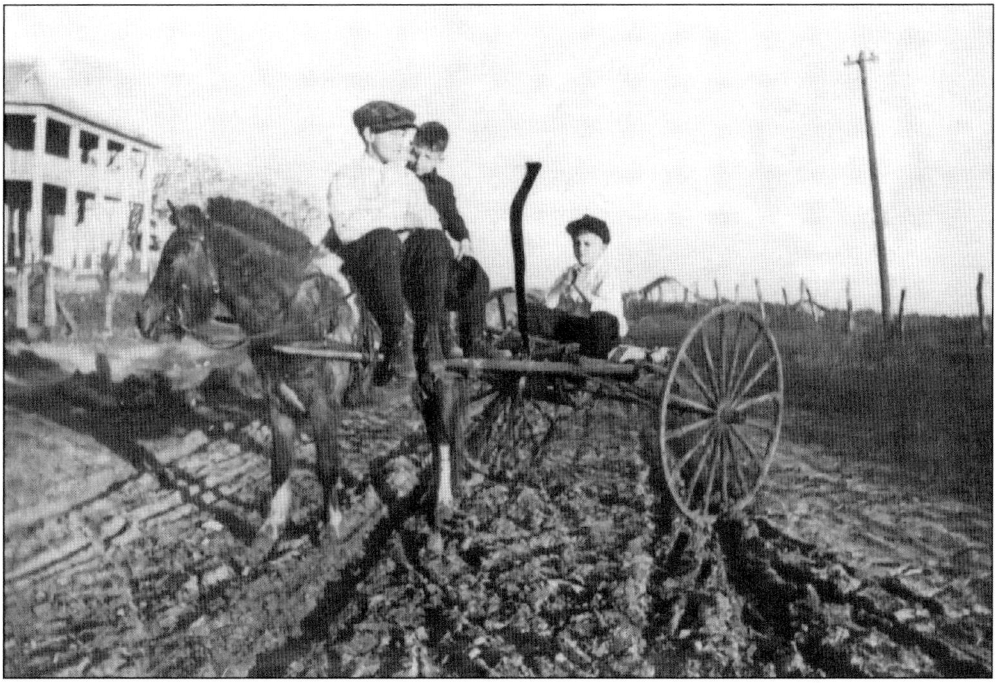

Pictured here in 1912, local boys are riding a buggy in front of the Braselton Sanitarium. Originally in the country, the sanitarium is now a private residence surrounded by residential neighborhoods.

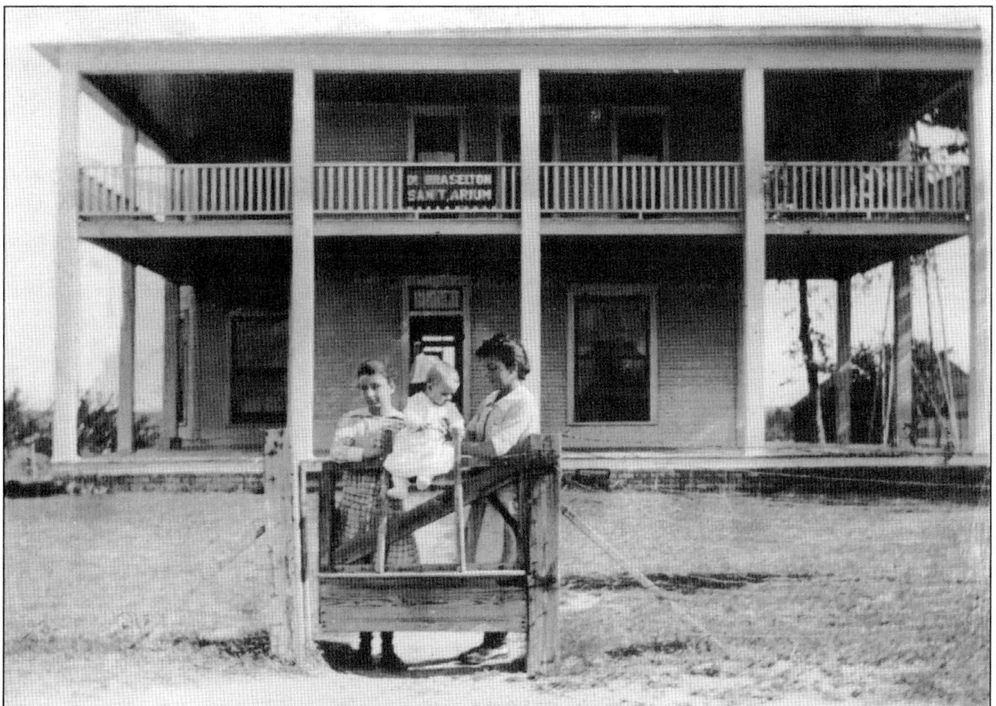

The family lived downstairs and there was a six-bed hospital upstairs. Dr. Braselton treated mostly tuberculosis patients.

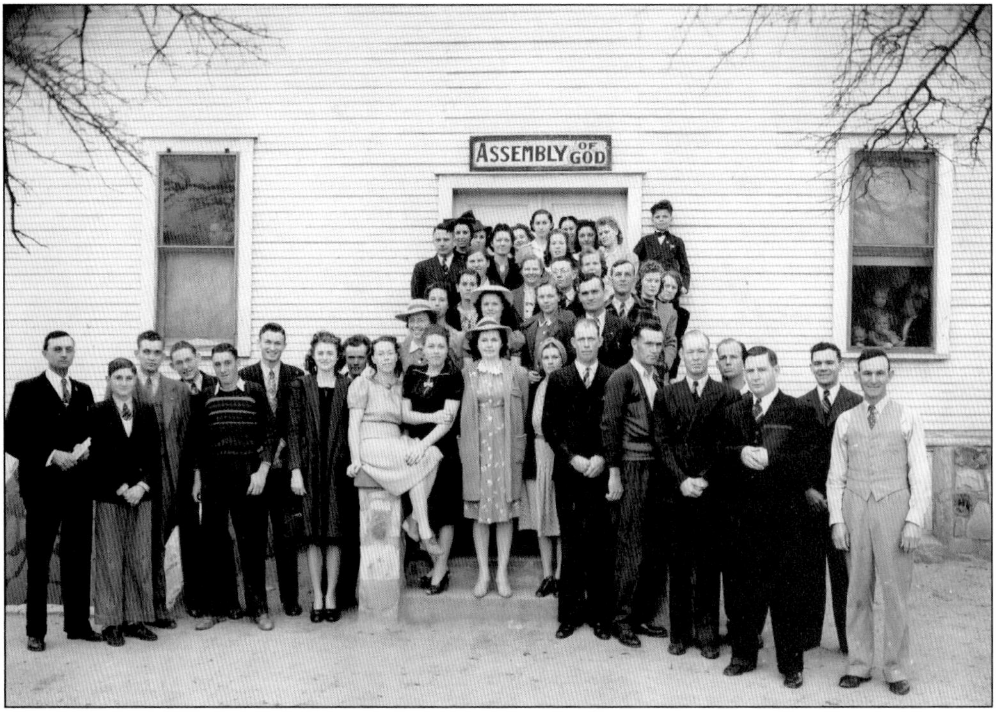

The members of the Assembly of God Church are gathered outside the church, which is located on the west side of Bridgeport.

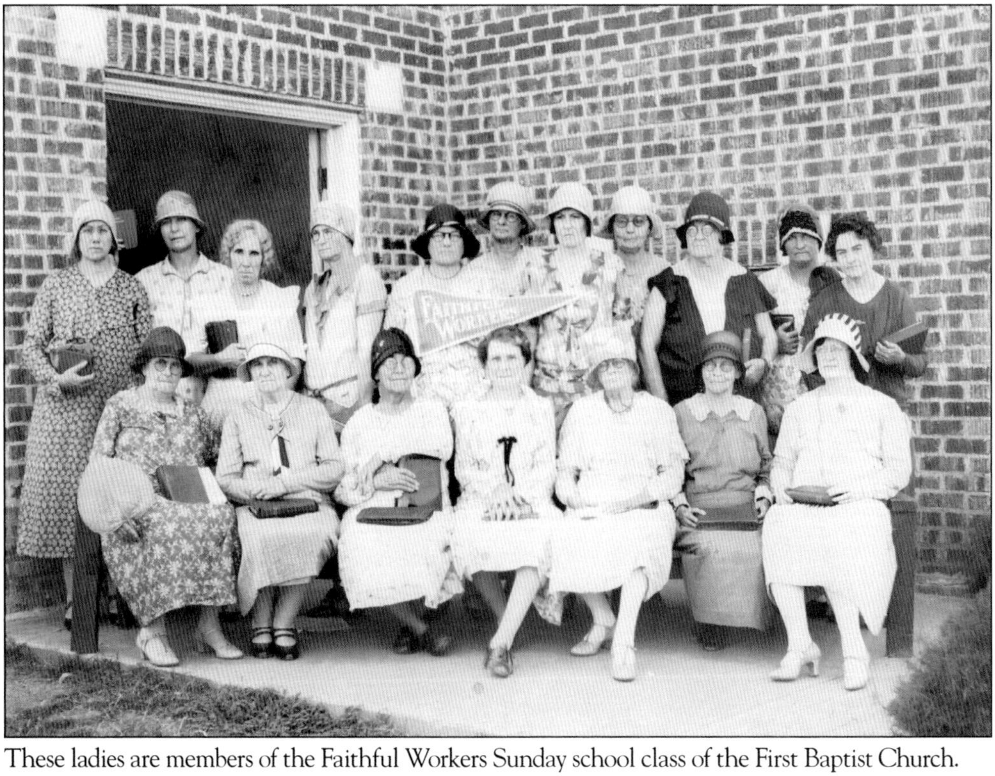

These ladies are members of the Faithful Workers Sunday school class of the First Baptist Church.

This 1942 youth group is from the First United Methodist Church.

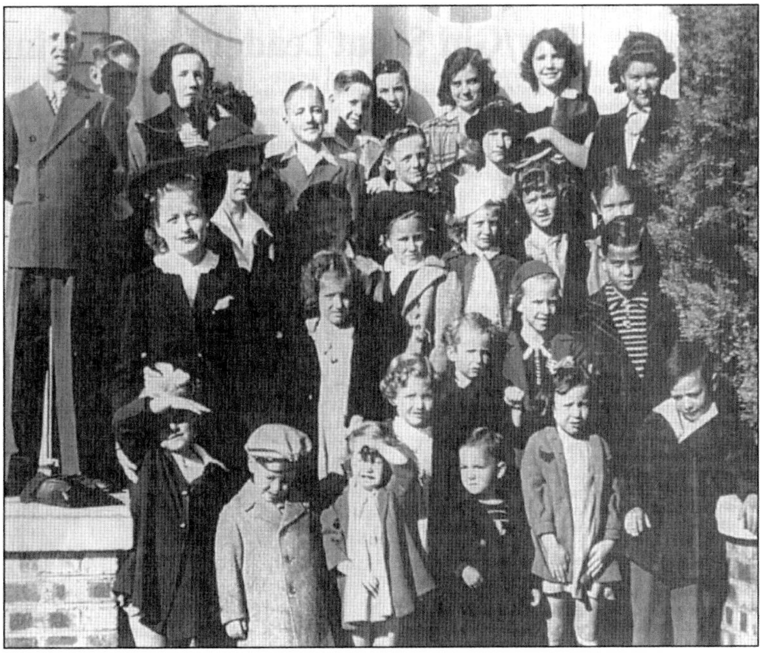

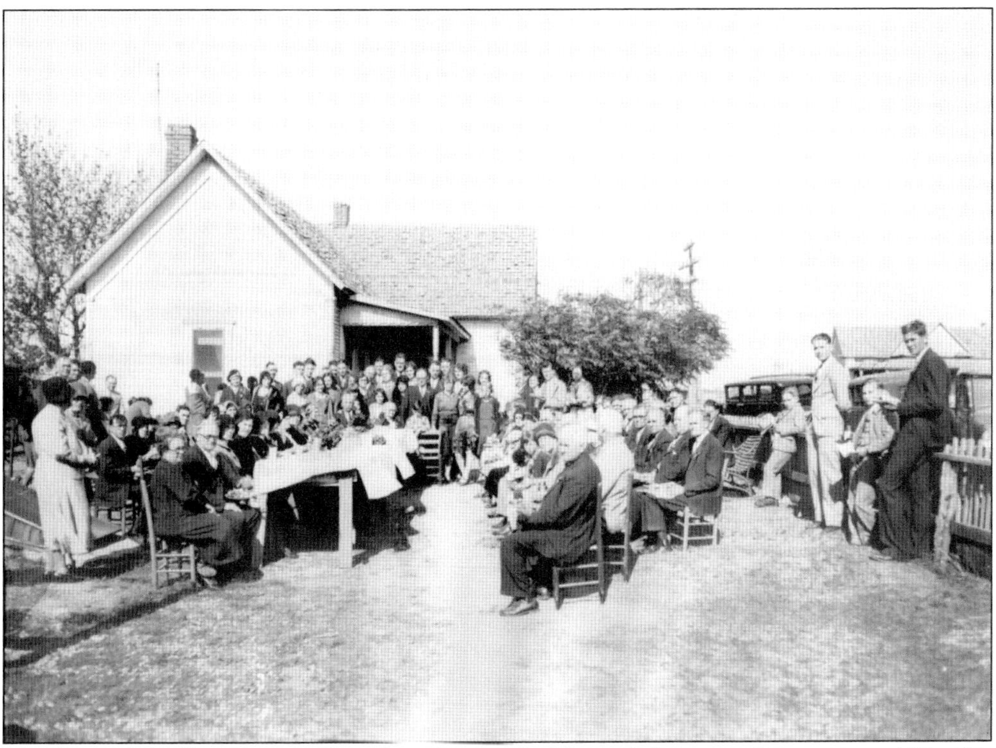

Members of the First Baptist Church gather at the Nesmith home at Carpenter and Twelfth Streets for a Sunday afternoon meal.

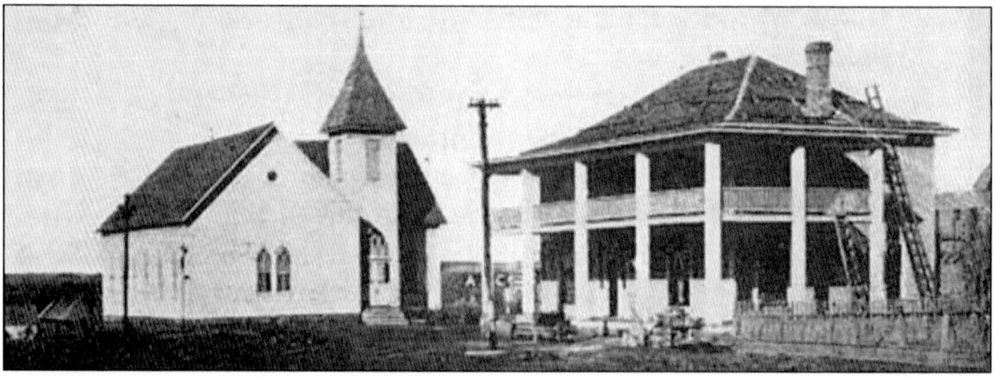

The newly built First United Methodist Church and parsonage are located at Cates and Eleventh Streets.

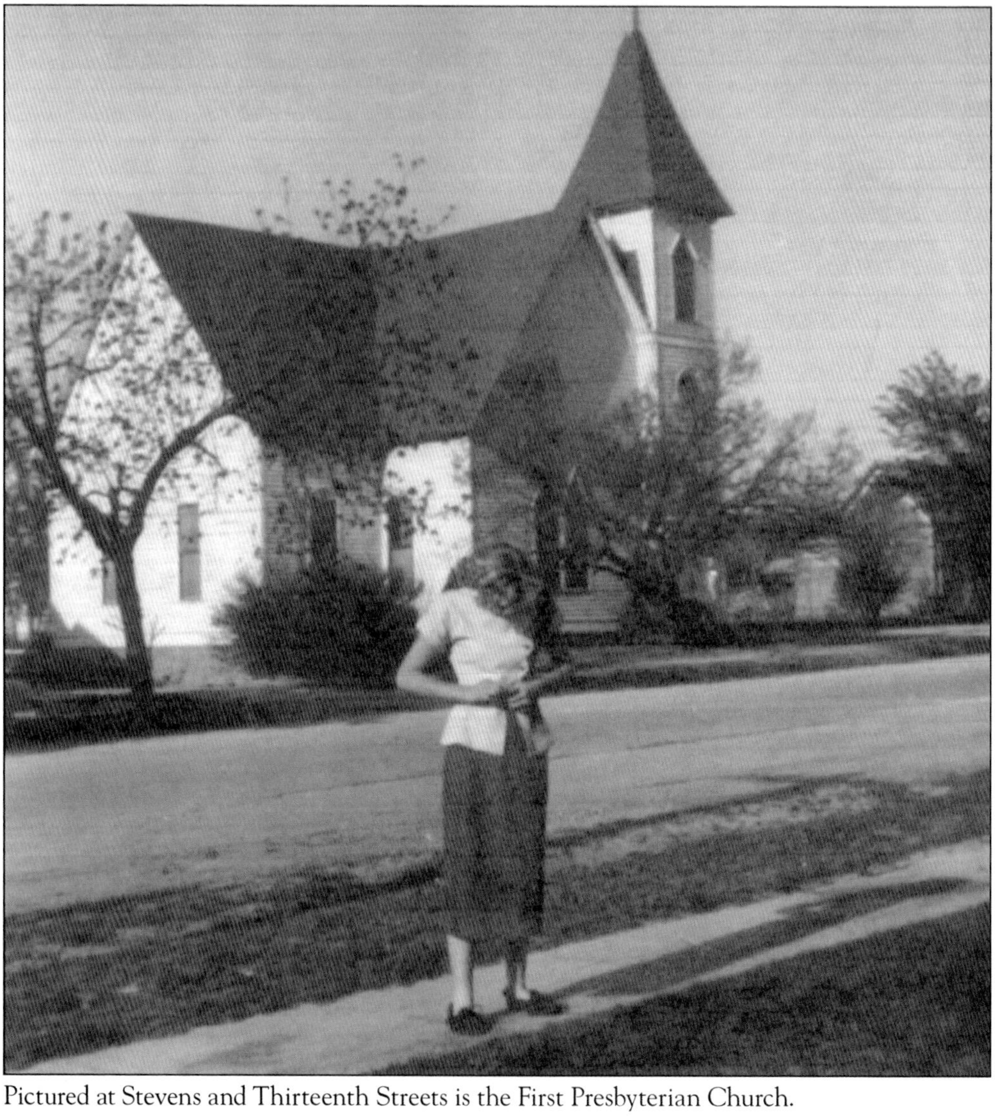

Pictured at Stevens and Thirteenth Streets is the First Presbyterian Church.

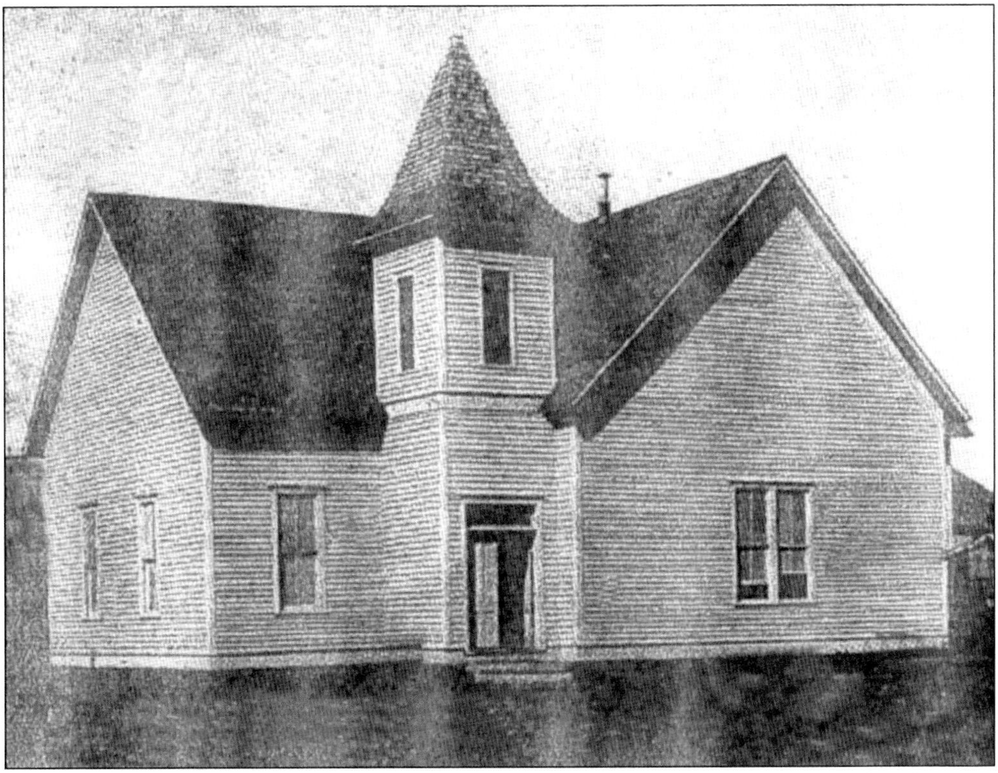

The First Baptist Church was located at 1201 Cates Street. Organized in 1882, this building was erected in 1895.

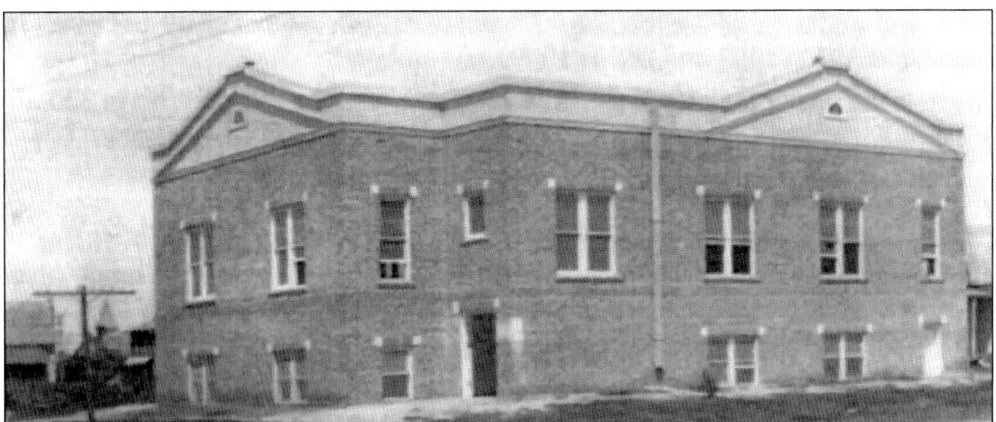

The original wooden church building was replaced with this brick building in 1925.

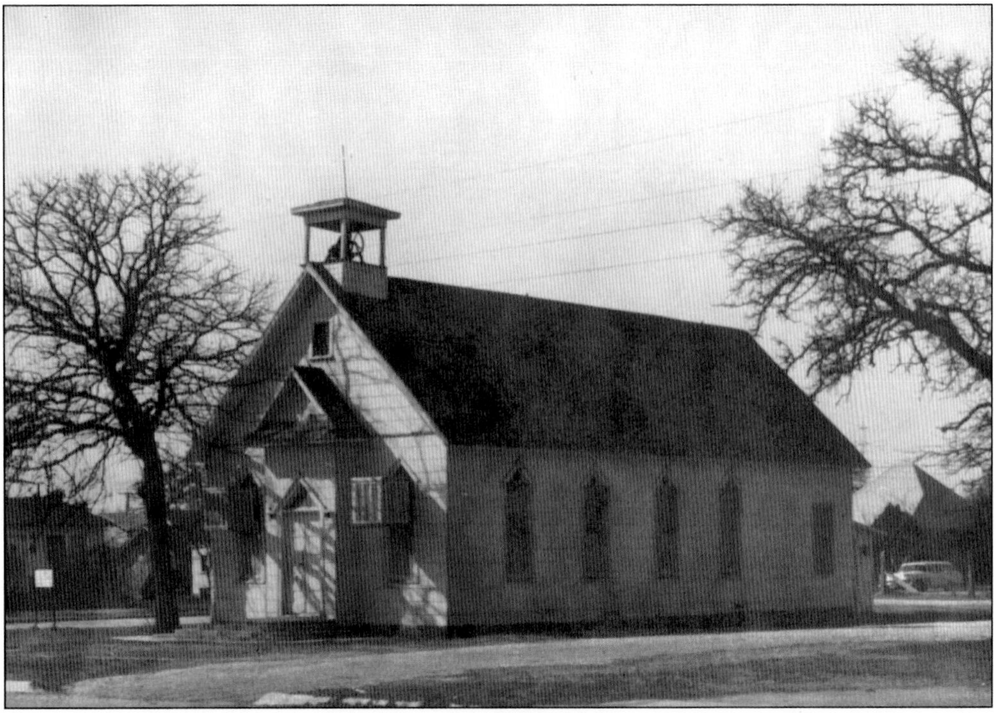

St. John's Catholic Church has been active in Bridgeport since the 19th century. Built in 1908, the church was remodeled several times. In 1968, the church relocated to 1801 Irwin Street.

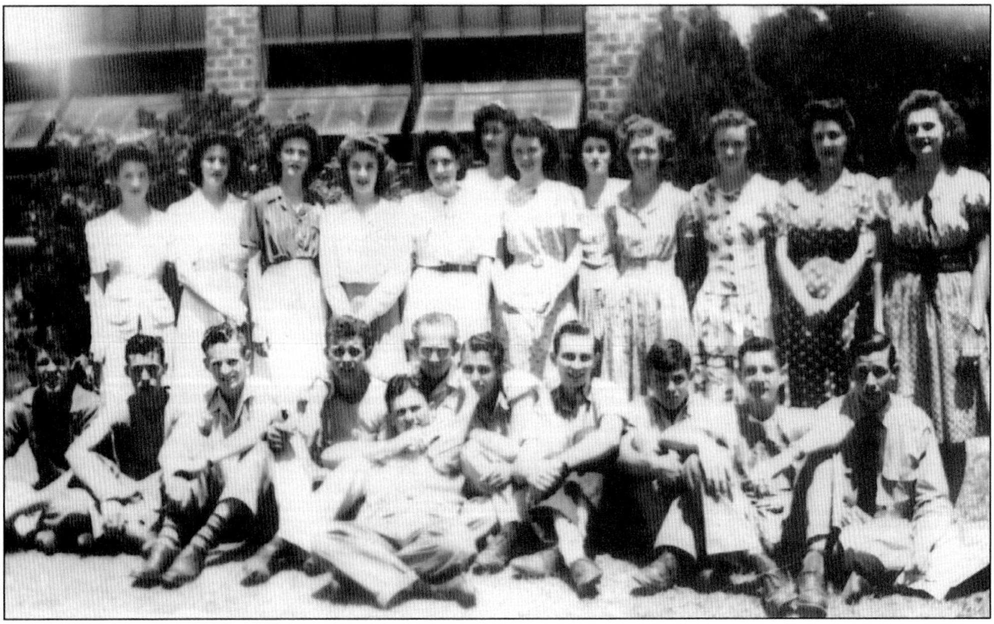

Pictured here is the senior class of 1943. From left to right they are (first row) Harry Clay, J. C. Moody, Billy Floyd McClung, Emit Beason, D. L. Locke, Harley Holt, Buster Stone King, Billy Joe Brown, Manuel Kasner, Norris Cheves, and W. A. Mason; (second row) Dorothy Lamons, Ima Jean Lester, Pansey Lou Atkinson, Trula Jo House, Mary Jo Macafee, Faye Winn, Golda Charles, Zelda Davis, Betty Jane Thompson, Bernice Womack, Norma Ruth Hartsell, and Nell White.

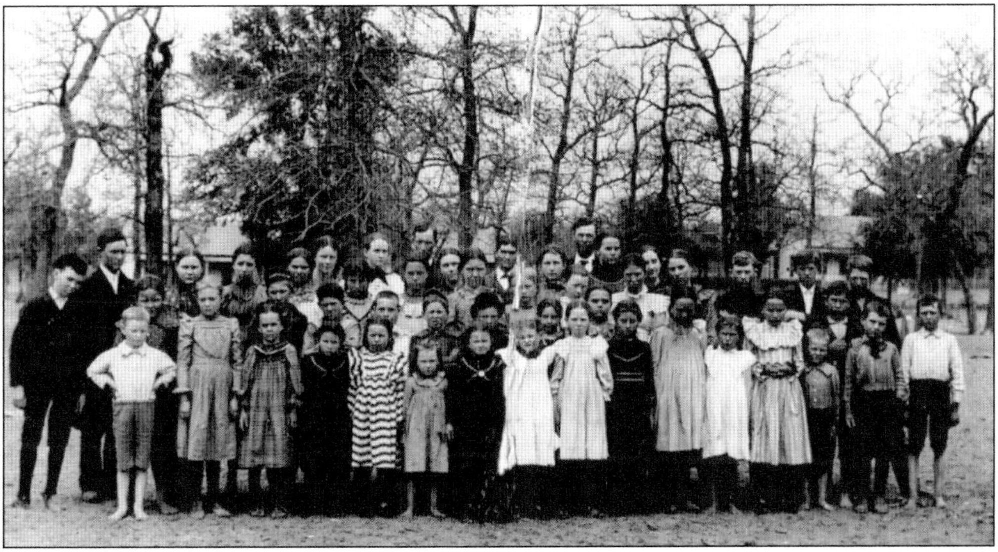

Students, who are believed to be from the Bridgeport school, are gathered for a picture in 1898.

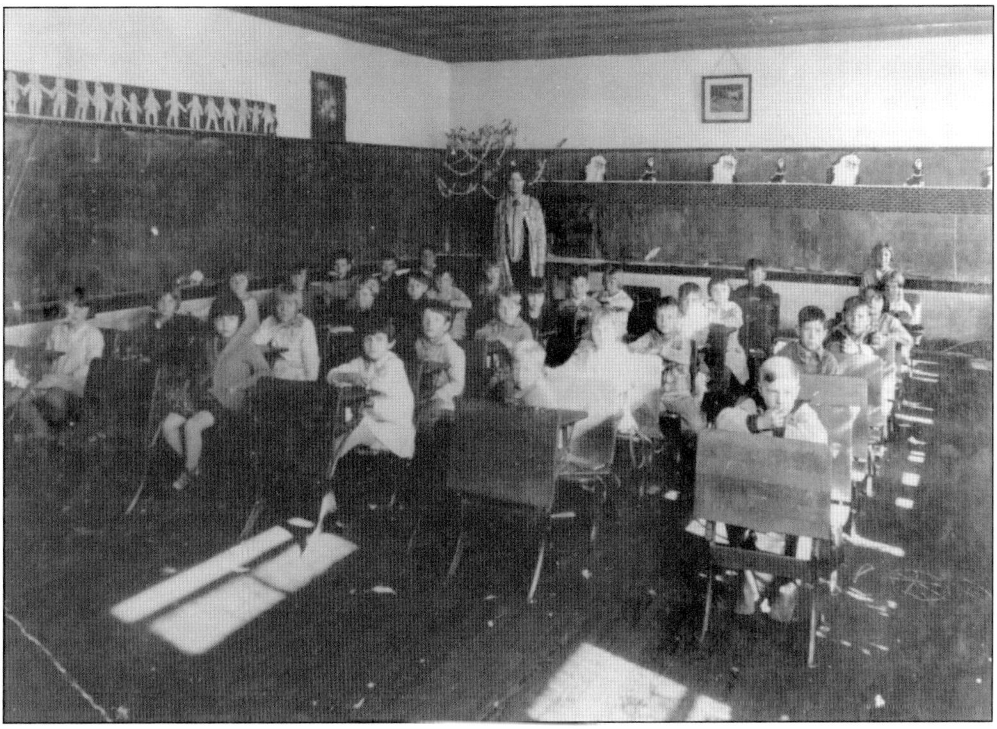

Grade school students anxiously await instructions from their teacher in 1928.

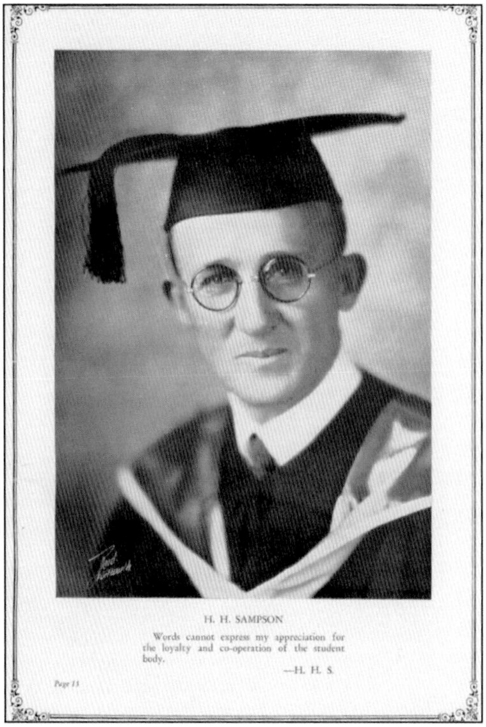

H. H. Sampson, or professor Sampson as he was often referred to, came to Bridgeport in 1920 as the superintendent. His influence over the students was outstanding, as Sampson was involved in all aspects of a student's education. He started the first football team and continued in his position for over a decade.

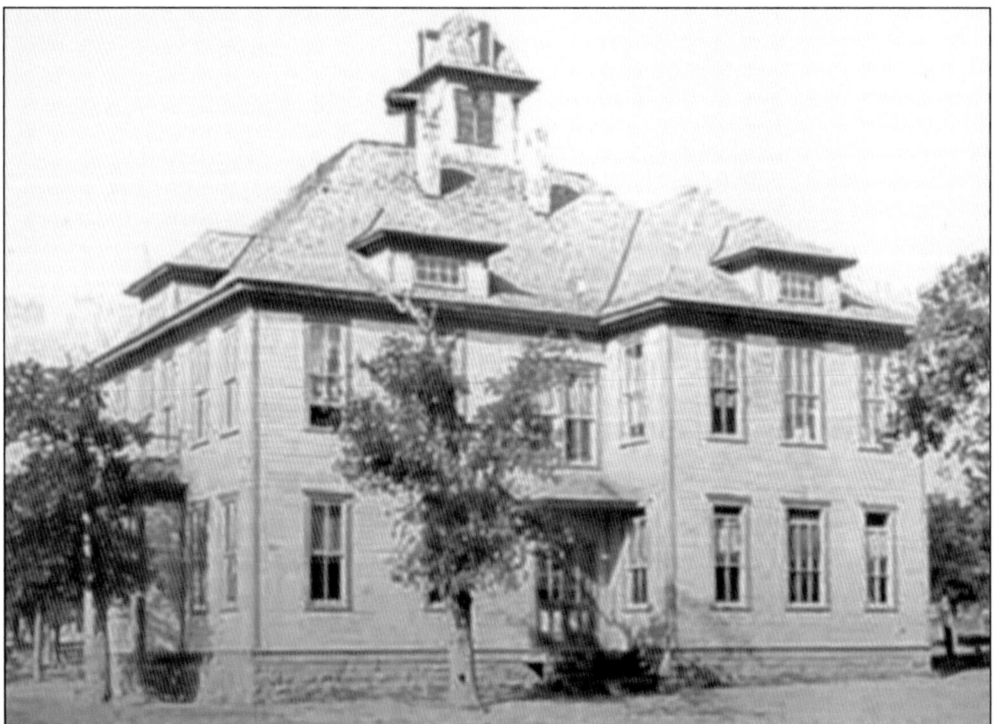

The main schoolhouse for Bridgeport was built in 1902 on Carpenter Street and later replaced with a brick structure built by the WPA in 1929.

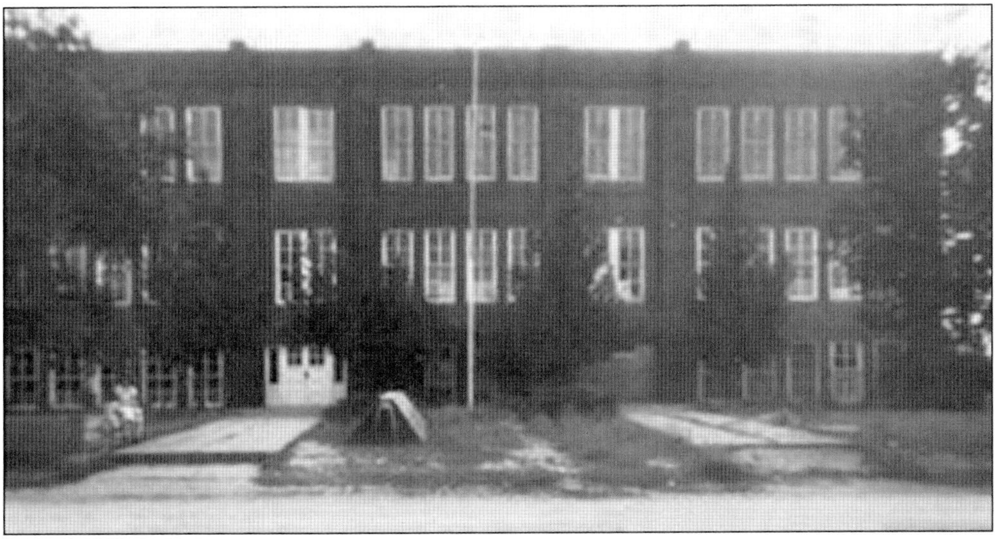

These 1930s photographs show the front entrance to the elementary school (above) located on Cates Street and the high school located on Carpenter Street (below).

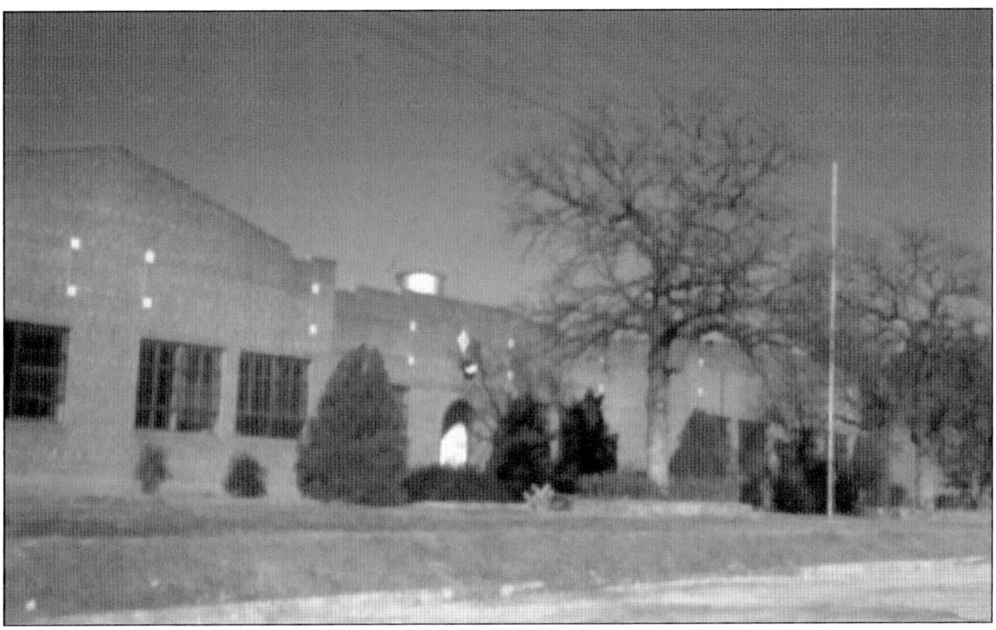

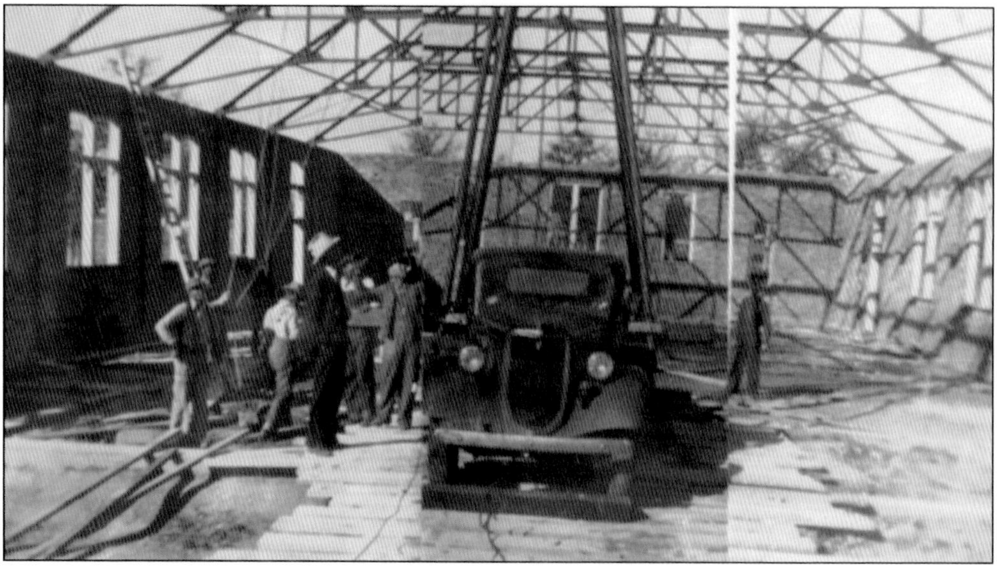

The gymnasium was added to the high school in 1937.

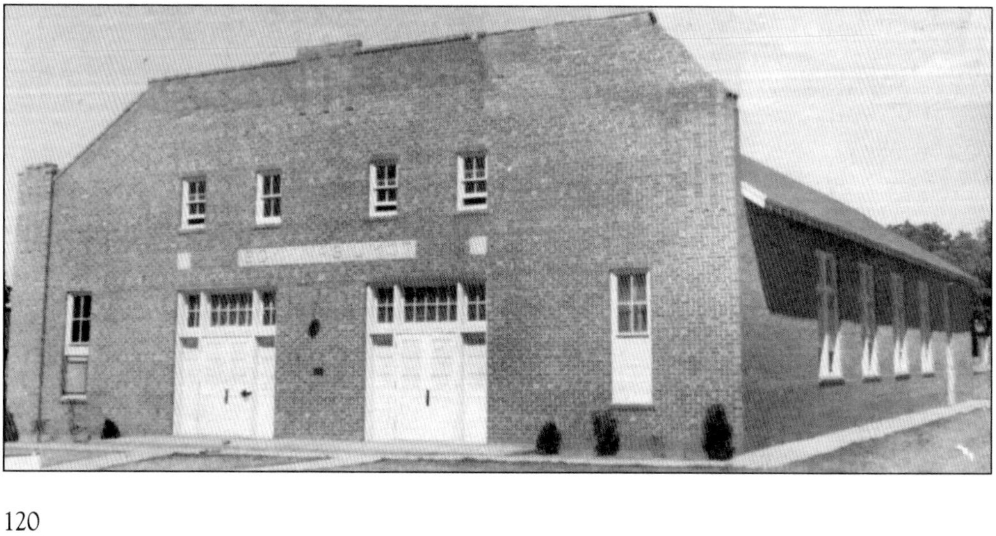

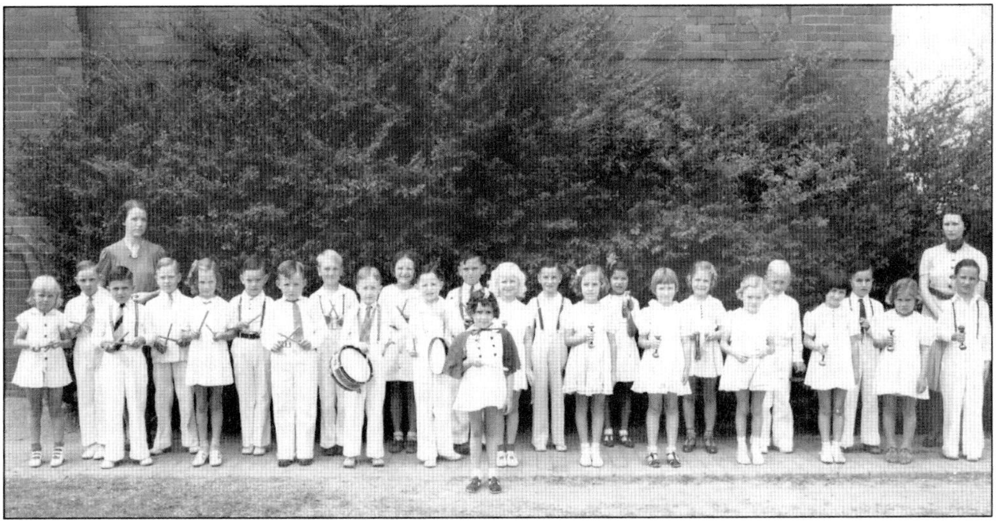

The 1938 first-grade rhythm band is seen in front of the elementary school. The teachers seen here are Mrs. Mauldin (left) and Mrs. Morris.

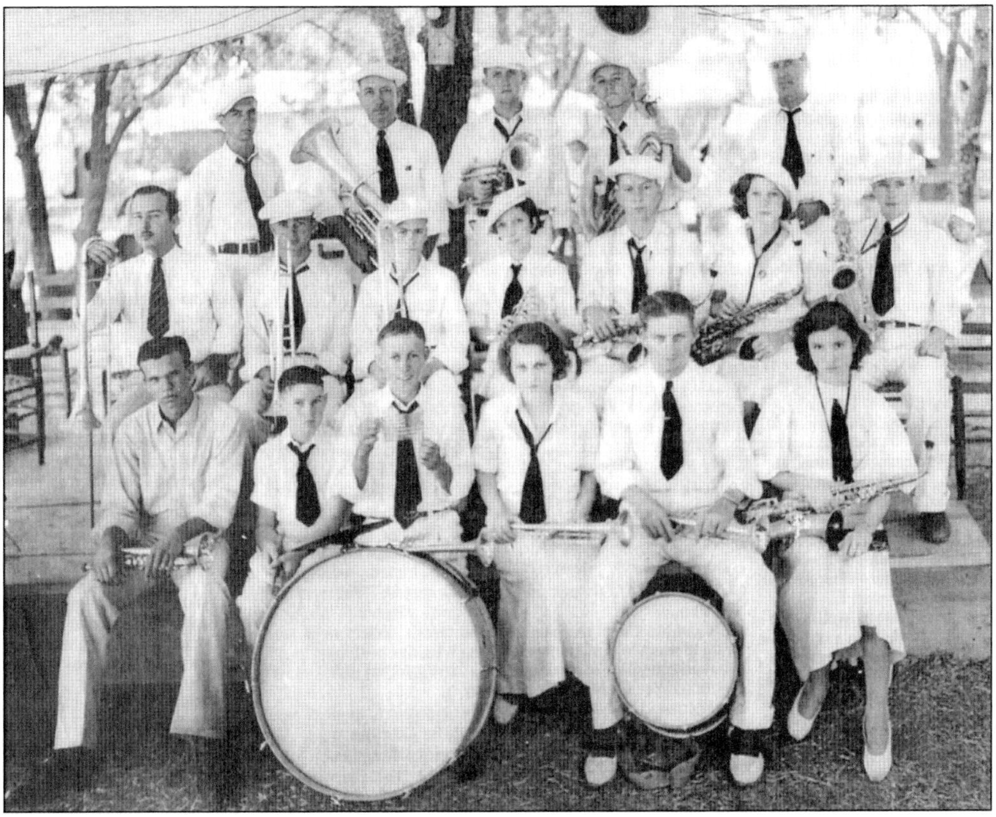

The town band performed in the park on July 4, 1933. The members pictured here are, from left to right, (first row) Norman Shipley, Drew House, James House, Alva Dean McClung, Wayne Locke, and Ruth Ford; (second row) Ted Smith, Harold Locke, "Rat" Barnett, Marjorie Jennings, Robert Simpson, Vista Mae House, and Stephen Curley; (third row) Pollard Jeter, Mr. House, Wilson Ray, Elmo McClung, and Mr. Jennings. (Courtesy Steve Curley.)

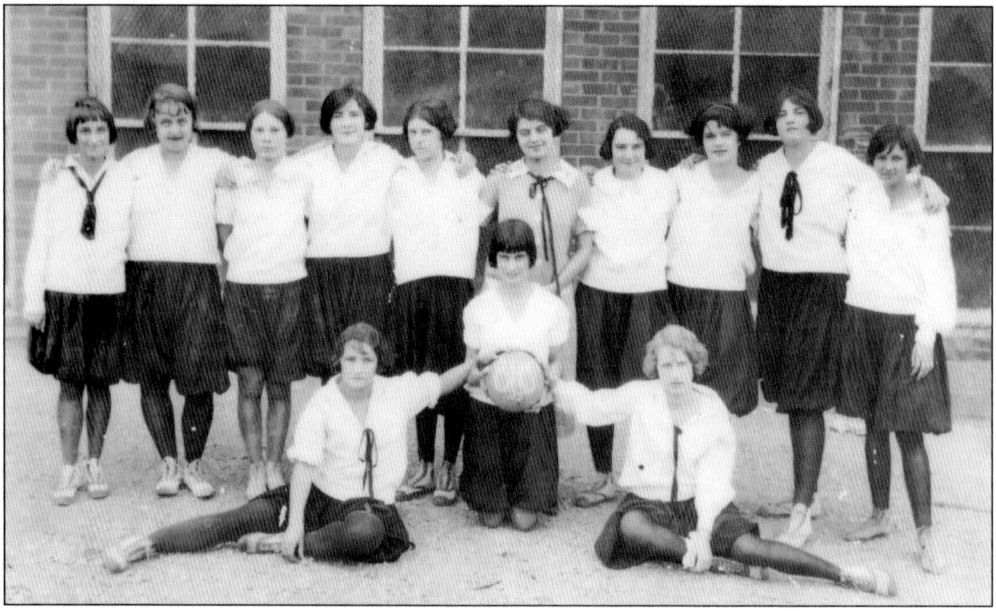

One of Bridgeport's first girls volleyball team is seen here in a 1925 team photograph. The members are, from left to right, (first row) Virginia Renshaw, Sheila ?, and Geraldine Greer; (standing, second row) Opal ?, Sadie Ross, unidentified, Glady Hammock, Zelda Metzinger, coach Burgess, Ruth Culwell, Marygetta Moody, Rena Counts, and Vera Elliott.

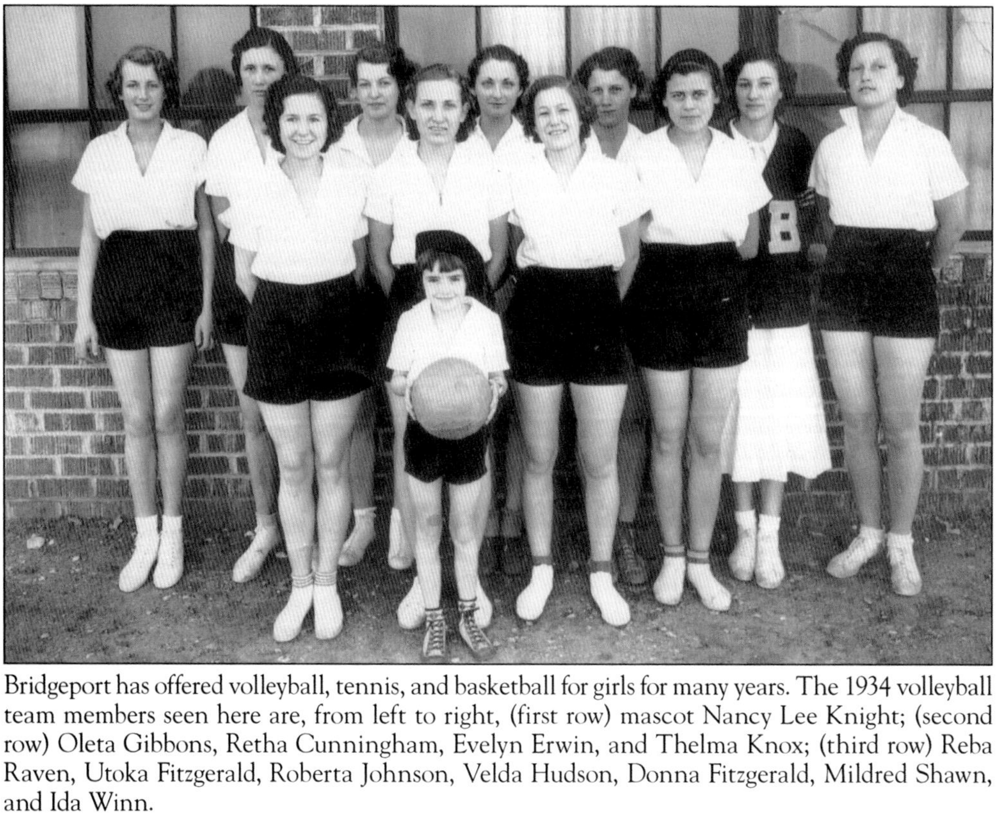

Bridgeport has offered volleyball, tennis, and basketball for girls for many years. The 1934 volleyball team members seen here are, from left to right, (first row) mascot Nancy Lee Knight; (second row) Oleta Gibbons, Retha Cunningham, Evelyn Erwin, and Thelma Knox; (third row) Reba Raven, Utoka Fitzgerald, Roberta Johnson, Velda Hudson, Donna Fitzgerald, Mildred Shawn, and Ida Winn.

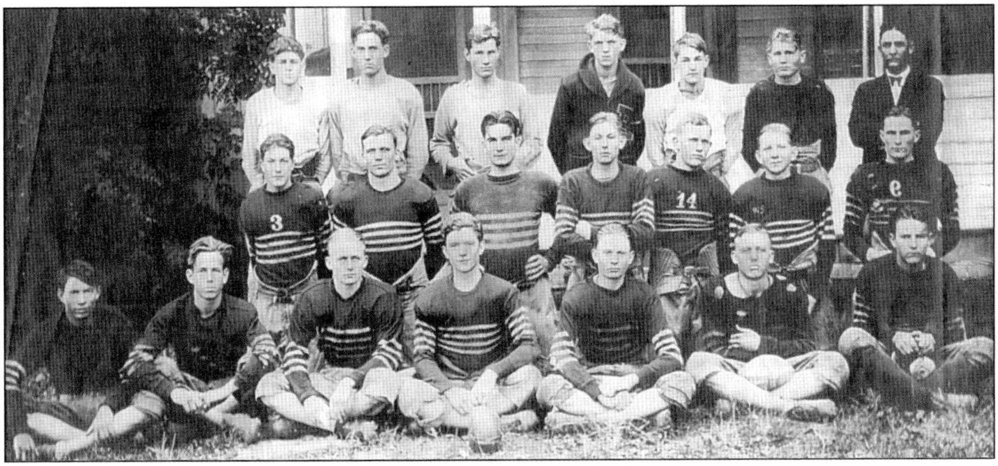

This is the 1928 football team. Pictured from left to right are (first row) unidentified, Q. L. Bradford, ? Vanhoose, C. Y. Rone, Roger Ray, Buster Green, and R. J. Ross; (second row) John Medley, W. J. Mann, Bill Coulburn, J. D. Anderson, Velton Elder, Joe Bingham, and unidentified; (third row) Leon Hawkins, Dallas Rish, ? Carter, ? Elder, Charles Cadwell, ? Ramsey, and coach T. H. Jenkins.

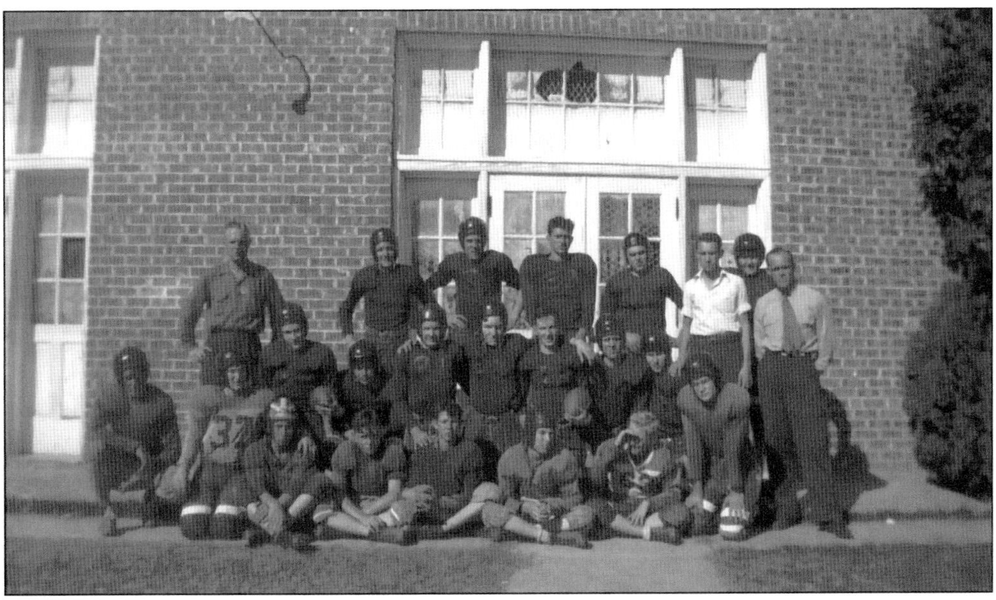

The 1945 football team members are, from left to right, (first row) John D. Tackel, Durad Green, Bill Winn, Ronald Cheves, Jimmy Newton, Buford Hobbs, and George Price; (second row) June Shannon, Amos Boring, Paul Garrett, Bobby Elder, Don White, Roy Lee Davidson, Wilbur Colkendofer, and Ted Albriton; (third row, standing) coach J. D. King, Carlos Mann, Windy Giles, James Price, Gene Shanks, Royce Raven, Carl Ray Jones, and coach Massey.

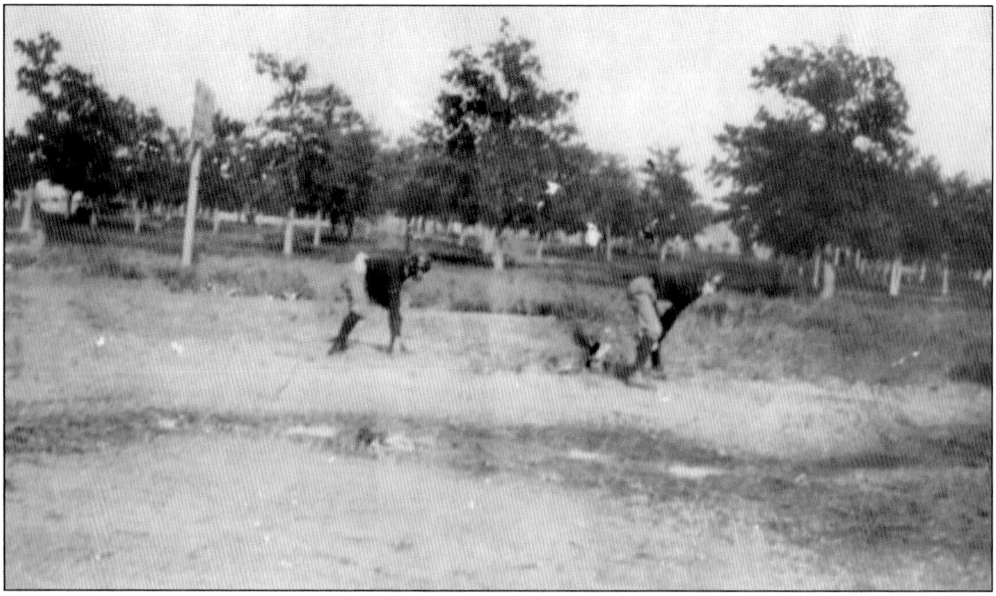

The practice field for the football team has come a long way from the beginning of the program.

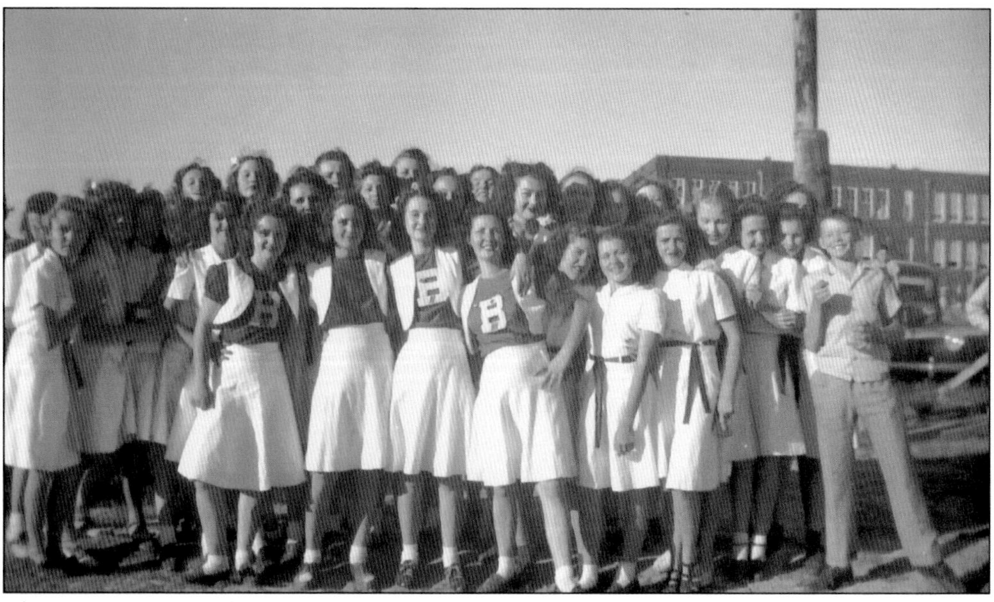

The 1946 pep squad always could be counted on to cheer on the Bulls.

Members of the 1940 basketball team posing here are, from left to right, (first row) Billy Reid, Woodrow Mattie Mann, Maurice Waters, Tom Byrnes, and Edward Barnett; (second row) Cecil Stary, Bill Royston, Winifred Garrett, Lawrence Whatley, and Frank Bordner; (third row) Edward Row, Alvie Newton, coach Byrd, Glen Johnson, J. E. Christy, and Curtis Thompson.

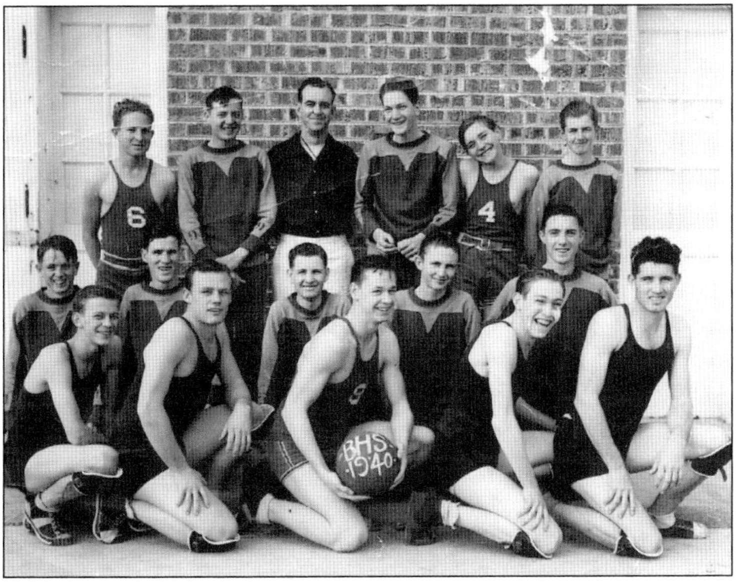

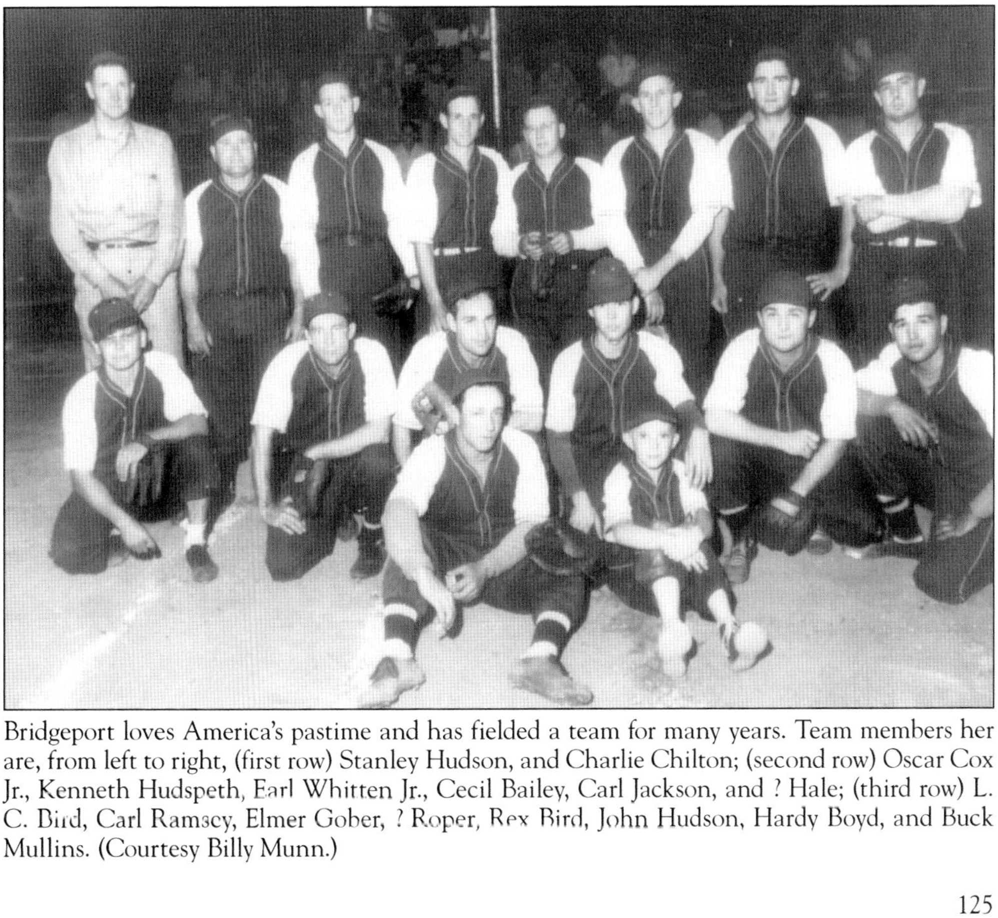

Bridgeport loves America's pastime and has fielded a team for many years. Team members her are, from left to right, (first row) Stanley Hudson, and Charlie Chilton; (second row) Oscar Cox Jr., Kenneth Hudspeth, Earl Whitten Jr., Cecil Bailey, Carl Jackson, and ? Hale; (third row) L. C. Bird, Carl Ramsey, Elmer Gober, ? Roper, Rex Bird, John Hudson, Hardy Boyd, and Buck Mullins. (Courtesy Billy Munn.)

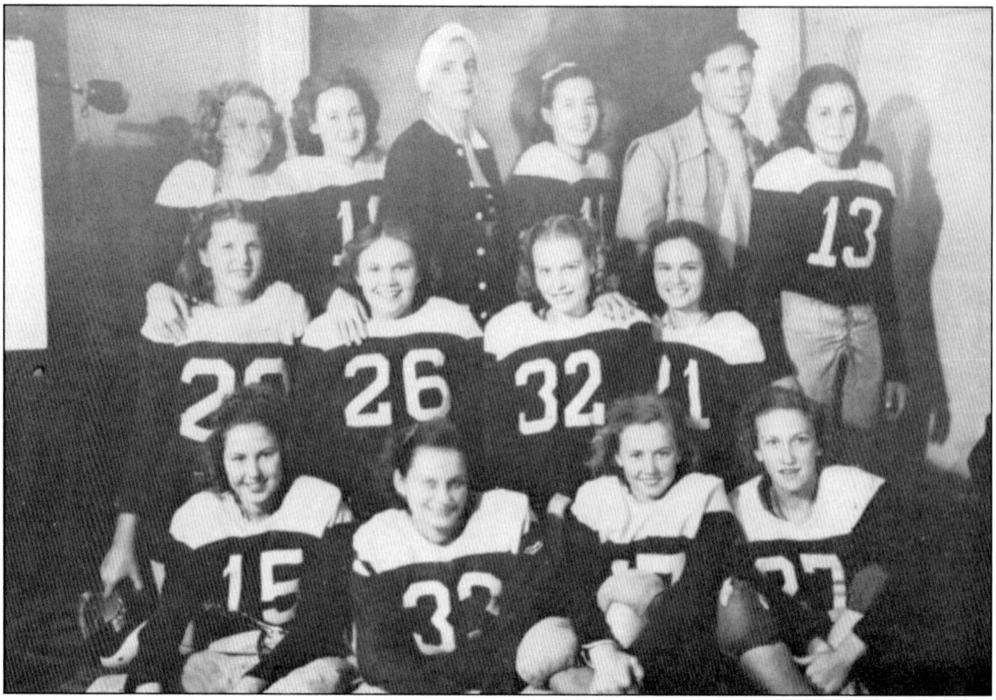

In 1947, football was not just for boys. In a special powder puff game, the seniors challenged the junior girls. The senior girls pictured here are, from left to right, (first row) Reynolds, Hvezdos, Martin, and Hartsell; (second row) Dethloff, Eales, Nabors, and Parker; (third row) Culwell, White, Mann, Bailey, Hudspeth, and Admire.

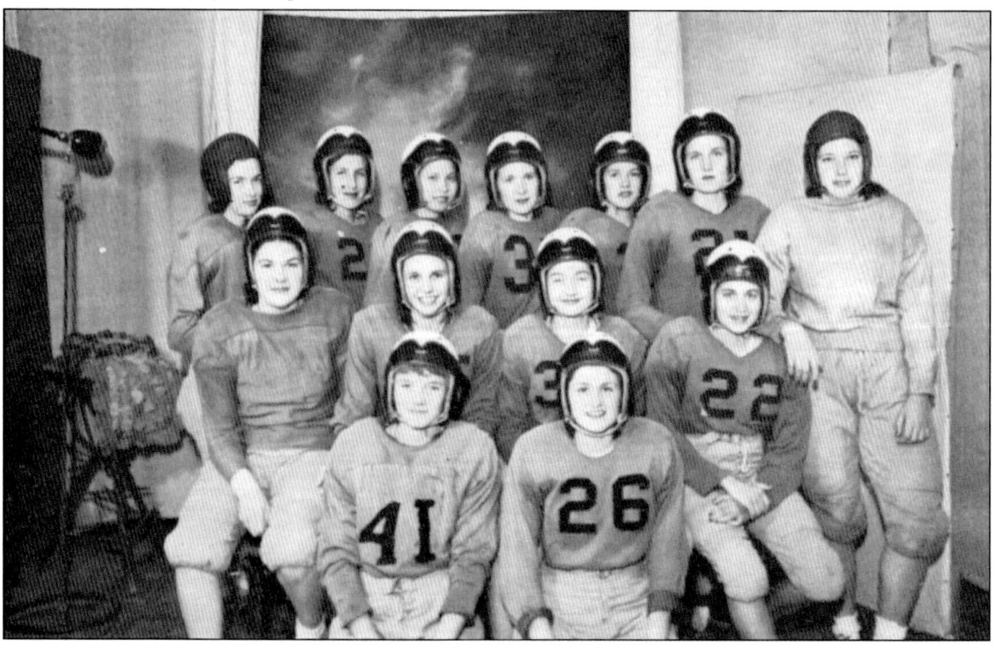

The junior girls who have bravely donned helmets and pads are, from left to right, (first row) Elder and Culpepper; (second row) Thomas, Bird, Gore, and Cage; (third row) Beeson, Findley, Dethloff, Denton, Crum, Lewis, and Boner.

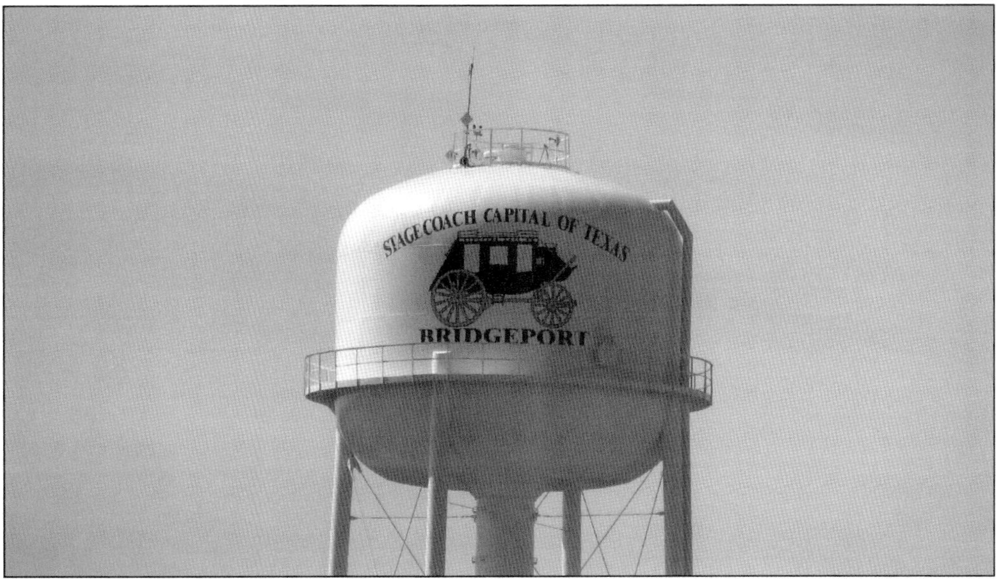

Today visitors traveling to Bridgeport from Decatur are welcomed to the "Stagecoach Capitol of Texas."

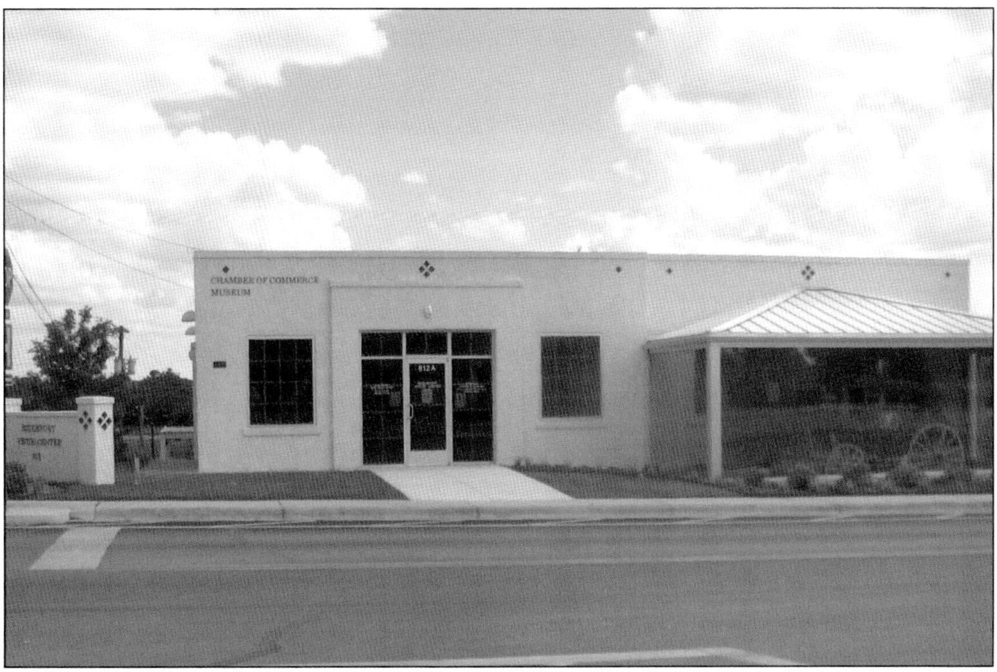

The renovated city facility at 812 Halsell Street now is home to the visitor's center, heritage museum, and authentic Concord stagecoach replica.